# NEW TESTAMENT
# GREEK
## FOR PREACHERS AND TEACHERS
## FIVE AREAS OF APPLICATION

*Neal Windham*

UNIVERSITY
PRESS OF
AMERICA

Lanham • New York • London

Copyright © 1991 by
# University Press of America®, Inc.
4720 Boston Way
Lanham, Maryland 20706

3 Henrietta Street
London WC2E 8LU England

**Library of Congress Cataloging-in-Publication Data**

Windham, Neal.
New Testament Greek for Preachers and Teachers :
five areas of application / Neal Windham.
p.   cm.
Includes bibliographical references and indexes.
1. Greek language, Biblical—Grammar.   2. Bible. N.T.—
Language, style.   3. Bible. N.T. Greek—Study.   I. Title..
PA817.W55   1991
487'.4—dc20   91-18229 CIP

ISBN 0–8191–8325–3 (alk. paper)
ISBN 0–8191–8326–1 (pbk., alk. paper)

 The paper used in this publication meets the minimum requirements of
American National Standard for Information Sciences—Permanence
of Paper for Printed Library Materials, ANSI Z39.48–1984.

To

*Miriam, Luke, and Charis*

my companions in the sojourn

# TABLE OF CONTENTS

# List of Tables

# Preface

Bridging the gap between ancient Greek text and modern Christian audience has never been easy. Somehow, pronouns, participles, and principal parts just don't seem to have much in common with the likes of sin and salvation or judgment and mercy. Much less do they appear to relate to current economic crises and strained international relations. And--need I say it?--they don't preach very well, either.

In this textbook I have attempted to narrow this gap. It is not that *Greek*, as such, addresses the modern problems, but the text of the New Testament *does*, and it has come to us in the form of Koine Greek.

Year after year, ministerial students sign up for Greek with varying expectations. Some seek little more than a passing grade. Others may be aiming at a reasonable comprehension of the basics. Still others look toward complete mastery of the language. Actually, none of these motives, not even the last one, is quite high enough. It is that student who sees in the study of Greek a genuine key to understanding the text whose motivation will carry him or her farthest. This book is written with just such a student in mind.

In this effort, I am indebted both to my own Greek teachers and the authors whose names you regularly see throughout the pages of this book. I have made every effort to introduce you to the several categories of exegesis via the standard terminology these and other authors have chosen and used, in most cases, for many years. As such, this little textbook should serve not only to bridge the gap between Greek and preaching/ teaching, but also to bridge the gap between first year Greek grammars and more advanced tools of exegesis.

The Greek text used throughout the book is the United Bible Societies' *Greek New Testament*, third edition (Corrected), copyright 1983, used by permission. There may be some minor variations on occasion    (a missing particle, conjunction, etc.), but only in the interests of brevity in the examples. English translations are my own, unless otherwise noted. Many thanks to the United Bible Societies for permission to use this text.

Thanks also to the GRAMCORD Institute, Deerfield, Illinois, which has made an intricate New Testament database available to institutions and individuals for detailed research in the Greek text. This database is to syntax what the standard concordance is to word study. It allows researchers to concord simple and complex syntactical constructions, as well as words belonging to a specific semantic field. I have found the software very helpful in turning up examples for various parts of the book. (The package is available at *The GRAMCORD Institute*, 2065 Half Day Road, Deerfield, Illinois 60015.)

I owe a large debt to many others as well. In particular, my students and colleagues at Lincoln Christian College and Seminary have provided constant support, both by way of carefully reading portions of the manuscript and in their general encouragement to see the project through to completion. Special thanks to Tom Tanner and Bob Lowery, both of whom read and commented on the entire manuscript. Thanks also to Bob Hull, who supplied long distance help. As ever, my wife, Miriam, has been very supportive through the entire project, both in proofing the manuscript and providing me with quality writing time. Thanks, Miriam.

Neal Windham
*Lincoln Christian College and Seminary*
February, 1991

## TABLE OF ABBREVIATIONS

| | |
|---|---|
| ABCF | ablative case form |
| ACF | accusative case form |
| ASV | American Standard Version |
| BAGD | Bauer, Arndt, Gingrich, Danker Lexicon |
| *Byz* | majority of Byzantine manuscripts |
| DCF | dative case form |
| e.g. | for example |
| esp. | especially |
| f. | one page following |
| ff. | multiple pages following |
| GCF | genitive case form |
| ICF | instrumental case form |
| i.e. | that is |
| LCF | locative case form |
| LN | Louw/Nida lexicon |
| LXX | Septuagint |
| ms | manuscript |
| mss | manuscripts |
| M-M | Moulton and Milligan's lexicon |
| NASB | New American Standard Bible |
| NA26 | Nestle-Aland 26th edition Greek New Testament |
| NCF | nominative case form |
| NEB | New English Bible |

| | |
|---|---|
| NIDNTT | New International Dictionary of New Testament Theology |
| NIV | New International Version |
| p. | page |
| pp. | pages |
| RSV | Revised Standard Version |
| spec. | specifically |
| TDNT | Theological Dictionary of the New Testament |
| TEV | Today's English Version |
| *txt* | text |
| UBS3 | United Bible Society's Greek New Testament third edition (corrected) |
| VCF | vocative case form |
| vs | version |
| vss | versions |

## CHAPTER 1

## INTRODUCTION

Not too very long ago a new car salesman asked what I did for a living. I pointedly responded, "I teach Greek." Like others whom I have told the same, he looked at me as though I were from another planet and replied, "For heaven's sake." There was a brief pause (as is also customary in these circumstances), and I responded, "Yes, that's it. For *heaven's* sake!" At this he seemed even less apt to know just what direction the conversation should take. So I explained what this fascination with Greek was all about, took a disappointing test drive, and went to the next dealership. I have not seen that dealer again, but I would like to think that he has a better appreciation of people who teach and take Greek. This textbook is written with the understanding that such an endeavor is not a trivial pursuit into things arcane and irrelevant, but at the very heart of ministerial training, a discipline exercised "for heaven's sake."

Of course, this is not the first Greek textbook to appear. In fact, there are many elementary Greek grammars on the market today and just as many or more out of print. Traditional texts such as Machen's[1] continue to be useful in colleges and seminaries while newer texts

[1] J. Gresham Machen, *New Testament Greek for Beginners* (New York: The Macmillan Company, 1962).

like those of Drumwright,[2] Goetchius,[3] and Hewitt[4] are finding an audience as well.   But while these textbooks primarily seek to present the rudiments of Greek for purposes of language learning--a necessary first step-- this book has a different intent.   It introduces begin- ning students to those phases of exegesis where the study of Koine Greek offers its greatest contributions to understanding the message of the New Testament, contri- butions which are generally unobtainable from an English translation.    As such it cannot possibly replace the aforementioned texts but only complement them; it is not a beginning grammar, but a book about exegesis and, to a lesser degree, exposition.

This book is designed for any student who has com- pleted or nearly completed a course in elementary Greek, though it may also be useful as a reference manual for more seasoned students and ministers.   It assumes some (though limited) translation proficiency and at least a casual acquaintance with general hermeneutical princi- ples.

In view of the fact that approaches to the study of Greek have changed considerably in recent years, some attention is given to the needs of students who have not had a traditional course in Biblical Greek.   At one time, Koine Greek was  nearly always taught much as any lan- guage, with emphasis on memorization of forms and vocabu- lary (translation being a primary goal).   Today, however, instructors are sometimes introducing Greek in courses which emphasize acquisition of the alphabet, introduction to the noun and verb systems, rudiments of syntax, and so

[2]Huber J. Drumwright, *An Introduction to New Testament Greek* (Nashville: Broadman, 1980).

[3]Eugene Van Ness Goetchius, *The Language of the New Testament* (New York: Charles Scribner's Sons, 1965).

[4]James Allen Hewett, *New Testament Greek: A Beginning and Intermediate Grammar* (Peabody, Massachusetts: Hen- drickson Publishers, 1986).

forth. The goal is not translation, but familiarity with distinctive features of the language. In the end, students should (it is hoped) be able to read a commentary based on the Greek text, use Greek-based tools of exegesis with measured proficiency, and in general follow discussions based on the Greek text. Although this book is not designed primarily for students whose course work fits this description, such students may also benefit from what follows.

**The Goal of Greek Studies.** Aside from the question of how Greek is being taught (to which we will briefly return), there is the more fundamental question, "Why study Greek in the first place?" Ministries students study Greek because the New Testament was written in this language, and it has long been recognized that a knowledge of the original language of any text is basic to the correct understanding of that text. Study of Greek prepares ministers to read commentaries (often based on the Greek text), evaluate English translations, perform word studies, determine which words belong in the text of the New Testament (or at least see why the editors of the UBS third edition and the Aland 26th edition made the choices they made), and evaluate the exegetical significance of forms, syntax, even discourse--all vital components within the larger spectrum of hermeneutical concerns. Whether you are trying to prepare an accurate Sunday School lesson, express proper theology in the lyrics of a song, or write a solid expository sermon, Biblical Greek is a foundational block without which you may stumble, or even miss the point.

Thus, the target of all Greek studies is to discover what the text actually meant when it first appeared. We wish to present a consistent and accurate witness of Christ to the church and the world, one which is based on a correct understanding of the text (not a translation) of Scripture. To do any less would be an accommodation to the ways of mediocrity.

Please, don't get the wrong idea. Greek is no panacea. There is no magic involved. Simply learning to read the New Testament in Greek does not guarantee that we will know God any better (although I was once informed of a Sunday school teacher who left his class with the distinct impression that they simply could not understand the Biblical teaching on salvation if they did not know Greek!). To the contrary, a deepening appreciation and understanding of Greek, far from making us spiritually arrogant, leaves room only for humility.

Nor does a thorough understanding of Greek guarantee good hermeneutics. "Knowing Greek" is not synonymous with "doing exegesis." Learning Greek is only one part of the total hermeneutical process, albeit the *foundational* part. It must be studied in concert with a solid course in hermeneutics, one which delves into such matters as cultural background, customs, geography, genre, understanding the author's intention, context, and parallel accounts--to mention only some of the issues involved. In the final analysis, a knowledge of Greek may be the necessary key to successfully unpacking any one of these hermeneutical ingredients, and this is pre- cisely why we say that Greek is *foundational*. It is not synonymous with exegesis, but there would be no exegesis without it.

Perhaps we should think of Greek as containing the raw ingredients with which the New Testament authors worked. The elements of this language are rather like eggs yet in the shell and bacon in the package, waiting to become breakfast. What will be done with these ingredients only the cook knows. We may find our eggs fried or scrambled, our bacon diced in the eggs or whole, by itself.

The raw ingredients for the several books which form the New Testament were the vocabulary, forms, and syntax of Koine Greek, not modern English. By the direction of the Holy Spirit, New Testament authors fashioned these ingredients to form God's Book. To be sure, they shaped the ingredients in largely understandable ways--under- standable, that is, to ancient Greek-speaking peoples of the Biblical world. But at many points there remain le- gitimate questions about the meanings of words, phrases, and clauses, questions whose answers will best be found in a careful look at these raw ingredients and how they were blended.

**A Comparison.** On the one hand, it is easy to appreciate the New Testament in its various English renderings. We have grown up with its favored words. Its message seems clear. Commentaries based on the English text and designed to help us understand it abound.

But the raw ingredients of English translations are not the same as those of the Greek New Testament. "Fellowship" is associated with building programs and congregational dinners in the American church of the twentieth century; κοινωνία, on the other hand, is mentioned in contexts of financial giving, acceptance of estranged brothers, and the physical suffering of certain Christians in the church of the first.

"The love of God" is at once understandable, or so it seems, in English translations. But upon closer examination ἀγάπη τοῦ θεοῦ does not always mean one and the same thing, even within a single book. 1 John 4:9 clearly bespeaks God's love for us, while in 5:3 the opposite, our love for God, is just as clearly at issue. (Both use the ambiguous phrase, "love of God," in English translations.) One does not have to know Greek to see this, but Greek syntax studies do provide the right tools for making proper judgments about interpreting such difficult phrases.

Romans 8:35 also speaks of the "love of God." Or is it the "love of Christ"? Perhaps it is the "love of God which is in Christ Jesus." Who's to say? All three readings show up among ancient manuscripts of the New Testament (in Greek, of course), and to some extent among English translations as well. The NASB reads, "love of Christ," but has "love of God" in the margin along with the note, "Some ancient manuscripts read 'God.'" But *which* manuscripts? Does it make a difference? If not, why did the editors of the NASB include this note in the first place? And just as importantly, why did the

editors of other study Bibles leave it out?    More than
that, how are we to evaluate this information with only
an English Bible, and if we do not have the right tools
for evaluation, how will this information affect our
exegesis?    Commentaries often discuss such textual variation, though not consistently.    How many such variations
are there in the New Testament anyway?    What should a
student do here?    Studies in textual criticism will provide direction in answering questions of this nature, but
here again we will have to work with the text of the
Greek New Testament.    Currently there is no critical
edition of the English Bible which fully addresses such
issues.    Nor is there one which even comes close.

Again, why does the NASB translation of John 1:5 read,
"And the light shines in the darkness; and the darkness
did not *comprehend* it," while in the margin we are told
that "*comprehend*" could be rendered "*overpower*."    The two
meanings are quite different.    Which is correct?    Is it a
matter of one word appearing in some ancient manuscripts
and another in others?    Not here.    This is a case where
lexical semantics (a subject taken up in chapter five)
will have to be considered since we are dealing with
multiple translations of the single Greek word κατα-
λαμβάνω.    A correct understanding of the range of meaning
of this word, along with a knowledge of John's use of it,
is all-important if we are to arrive at the right answer.

So it is that we study Greek because we are concerned
with knowing precisely what the text is saying. We are
not satisfied with complete dependence upon sometimes
controversial English translations.    We want to work with
the "raw ingredients," really know what we're talking
about, fully understand our options, and present our conclusions with confidence.

No Easy Task.    The fruits born of textual study are
hard won, and they do not come in equal measure to all
students.    Nor are they always immediately "practical,"
nor easily seen as "relevant."    With time, it will even
become clear that a working knowledge of Greek can create
as many questions as it answers.

Add to this the fact that when one studies Greek, he or she does not merely study a language but studies that language with a view to incorporating it into an entire hermeneutical package. In other words, Greek students are both made to learn the language as such and do word and syntax analyses, textual criticism projects, and so on--an exceedingly tall order for any "language" course.

It is not a surprise then that Greek is less and less a factor in certain ministerial degree programs. Eighteen years ago Earl Ellis pinpointed the problem when he wrote, "American higher education tends to be 'higher' in name than in fact. In a climate where 'everyone has a right to a college degree,' it is understandable that the more demanding disciplines ... would be the first to be fudged or sacrificed." Ellis further cited "the pragmatic temper of American education" as a leading contributor to the demise of the formal study of Greek in seminaries.[5] Today, the merits of Greek studies are still being debated in Bible colleges and seminaries, often when schools need to make room for additional courses in other areas. What are we to make of this?

**Greek and Scripture.** If Greek studies are being deemphasized (or dropped), does this not tell us something about how the modern church thinks about the Bible? This may seem a harsh judgment, but in fact *any* deemphasis upon its teaching, whether it takes the form of deleting language studies, hermeneutics courses, or actual exegesis classes, may very well indicate that sound exegesis is increasingly less a factor in the modern church.

Perhaps more startling yet is the fact that while some modern Bible colleges and seminaries have either cut back on Greek, made it optional, or not required it at all, they have at the same time arduously promoted a very high

[5]Earl Ellis, "What Good are Hebrew and Greek?" *Christianity Today* 16 (May 26, 1972), pp. 8-9.

view of Scripture.  For those for whom this approach has become acceptable, we are forced to ask just how consistent an approach it is.  If the church is going to uphold a high view of the Bible, then it must also clearly uphold a consistently high regard for learning the languages in which it was written.

**Who Should Study Greek?**  This book is written with the conviction that the study of Greek is fundamentally important to the leadership ministry of the church of the 90's and beyond.  To be sure, it may not be easy, but ease has never been a criterion by which Kingdom service is judged.  In this age of frequently watered-down theology, preaching, teaching, and hymnody, persons training for a ministry of *proclamation* (in whatever medium) need to study Greek.

Granted, whereas some students (especially those who will be involved in frequent preaching and teaching) will need to be able to translate and analyze the Greek text often and in large doses, others (music ministers, for example, who will be writing lyrics to songs or analyzing the messages of already prepared lyrics) may need to know only how to utilize commentaries which employ some Greek, perform Greek-based word studies, and execute minimal translation skills.[6]

**The Right Approach.**  All students will need a *holistic* approach, whether studying Greek for a year or five years.  Greek is a language, and, as such, deserves to be studied in the context of how its parts relate to each other.  For example, too much emphasis on word studies in lieu of analysis of syntax or discourse structure will lead to unreasonable and artificial judgments which can-

---

[6]In over ten years of teaching Greek, it has been my experience that some of the very finest Greek students are music majors, but Greek is not often required of students majoring in music ministry.

not be supported.[7]   Words always have meaning in *con-texts*.   Then again, too much emphasis on syntax may obscure important meanings of individual words.   Balance is the key.   An approach which evenly incorporates forms, syntax, vocabulary, translation and exegetical procedure should be characteristic of most Greek classes.   Of course, in all of this the concern is that we use Greek as a tool for Christian ministry.   It must never become an esoteric, end-in-itself, kind of study.

**Linguistics and Linguistic Approaches.**   Currently, there is some movement in the direction of a successful marriage between the study of Greek and the application of principles of linguistics, the science of under-standing language systems.[8]   Since this book is primarily concerned with those areas where the study of Greek language makes a unique contribution to the overall exe-getical process, it will not take up detailed discussions

[7]James Barr's *The Semantics of Biblical Language* (Ox-ford: Oxford University Press, 1961; reprint ed., Lon-don:SCM Press, 1983), pp. 206ff., is replete with illus-trations of this kind of problem. See also D.A. Carson's *Exegetical Fallacies* (Grand Rapids: Baker, 1984), pp. 25ff.

[8]See especially David Black, *Linguistics for Students of New Testament Greek: A Survey of Basic Concepts and Applications* (Grand Rapids: Baker,1988).   Newer still is Peter Cotterell and Max Turner, *Linguistics and Biblical Interpretation* (Downer's Grove: Intervarsity Press, 1989).   The foci of the two books are somewhat different. The latter is broader and incorporates Old Testament as well as New Testament examples.   However, it (Cotterell and Turner) also includes a discussion of discourse analysis whereas Black does not.   David Kiefer's *New Testament Greek for Bible Students*, 3 vols. (Lincoln, Ill.: Lincoln Christian College Press, 1975) is a semi-programmed elementary Greek text which incorporates lin-guistic principles (e.g., surface and deep structures) in the discussions in helpful, nontechnical ways.

of linguistics.    Nevertheless, we cannot and do not wish to avoid those areas where linguistics will be helpful to our purpose.    The section on *discourse*, for example, is really a section about linguistic principles.    However, the aim of this chapter is to show how Greek studies make some unique contributions (not easily detected from English translations) to discourse analysis.    The chapter is not primarily then a primer in discourse analysis so much as it is a chapter on the place of *Greek* in analyzing discourse.    Please understand that such a limited discussion of elements of discourse only begins to scratch the surface of this emerging field of study. And, in keeping with the purpose of this book, I am not presenting a comprehensive model for analyzing Greek at the level of discourse, but rather, some guidelines for conducting this kind of research from the Greek text.

**An Overview.**    Already I have established the main purpose of this book, which is to introduce those phases of exegesis where a knowledge of Greek makes its greatest contributions to understanding the message of the New Testament.    Occasionally, there will be guidelines and examples which may be used with Greek or English Bibles but are best used with the Greek text.    In the section on word study, for example, it will be clear that some principles are quite general (e.g., how to select the right words to study), while others require the use of the Greek text (e.g., a study of the cognates of φρονέω). Again, we will focus most sharply on the latter. Granted, this will create something of an hermeneutical imbalance, but given the rather limited scope of this book, that is understandable.

In addition to demonstrating the usefulness of Greek for exegesis, there is also the matter of its importance in exposition.    Even when they understand what the Greek text is saying, students and ministers alike frequently have trouble knowing exactly what to do with this information in the pulpit and classroom. Choosing the simplest course, they often avoid it altogether. Granted, it is important not to burden congregations with technical explanations, but expositors who teach and preach biblically will need to learn how to present at least some of these technical points in nontechnical ways. This problem is addressed in nearly every chapter.

There are at least five critical areas where a knowledge of Greek plays a major role in successful exegesis. They are *textual criticism, morphology, word study, syntax,* and *discourse.* Other areas could be singled out. A chapter on phonology, for example, might have been included,[9] but phonology is not all that germane at the level of exegesis. Care has been taken to insure that we are working with areas of greatest contribution.

We will think of these five areas as building blocks, not entirely related, yet each in some way dependent upon the next for its contribution. The five areas appear below in figure 1.

**Figure 1: The Five Building Blocks**

D    I    S    C    O    U    R    S    E

S    Y    N    T    A    X

W    O    R    D        S    T    U    D    Y

M O R P H O L O G Y

T E X T U A L        C R I T I C I S M

*Textual criticism,* the first of the five areas, is the bedrock in this model. It is that discipline which seeks to determine the exact wording of the text of the New Testament through rigorous comparison of the various manuscripts and versions. As such, it is the foundation upon which all other investigation must rest. If we are

[9]See, e.g., Black, *Linguistics for Students of New Testament Greek,* pp. 23-52.

confident that the words we are reading are the words of Matthew or Paul or John, then and only then may we proceed to examine other matters of exegesis. Conversely, if those words do not belong in the text, then our exegesis, however apparently "reliable," is pointless. It is based on a reading which is in some way at variance with the original text.

The next three building blocks, though quite distinct from textual criticism, are nevertheless related to each other. *Morphology* is the study of bits and pieces of words. In this section we will see how observing these components within words may contribute to exegesis. *Word and phrase study* involves, much as this label suggests, detailed analysis of Greek words using various tools, including concordances, lexica, theological wordbooks, even commentaries, in an effort to determine the meaning of a given word within its contextual setting. *Syntax* is the study of how these words are combined to create meaningful units of thought. It goes beyond the level of mere word study to include phrases, clauses, and entire sentences.

A final chapter on *discourse* has already been described to some extent above. In this chapter I hope to show how certain Greek words may serve to mark specific pericopes, suggest given sequences, or point out certain structural features of the discourse. Admittedly, this will not be easy. Nor is it something elementary Greek students are expected to master. Still, the benefits of implementing elements of this approach, even at an introductory level, far outweigh the disadvantages of ignoring it altogether. As with the other chapters, the aim is to present numerous examples from the Greek text, and in so doing, show you just what to look for.

Each chapter (with the exception of chapter two) includes an introduction to tools and procedures, textual examples, an explanation of how the findings of your study from the Greek text may be explained from the pulpit or lectern without sounding unduly technical, other practical suggestions, a conclusion, practice problems, and selected bibliography with limited annotations. Charts and appendices help summarize and clarify various data. Because each new chapter builds upon the previous one, you should study a single chapter at a time, giving yourself adequate time to digest the principles and work through some of the suggested problems.

Textual criticism is probably the most demanding of the five areas covered in this book. In view of its intricacies, it has been given two chapters. The first lays the groundwork while the second examines procedures and suggestions both for the study and the pulpit. If you want to get right to the heart of how to practice textual criticism, skim the next chapter and go on to chapter three. However, if you do so you may find yourself referring back to chapter two for information more often than you would like. It is best to read both chapters.

## CHAPTER 2

## TEXTUAL CRITICISM:
## THE RIGHT PLACE TO START

Jigsaw puzzles fascinated me as a child. Although I was not always able to connect their sometimes frustrating interlocking pieces, it was fun to try. I would study the color patterns in the picture, the straight and rounded structures, and the ways in which the pieces themselves were shaped. It seemed to me that most puzzles consisted of rows and columns of pieces, and I could generally place these in the right segment of the puzzle, again, with the help of the picture on the box. After many matches (and *more* mismatches) I would eventually fit everything together, and the product would look exactly as it should.

Textual criticism is rather like an enormous jigsaw puzzle. Its pieces are the words contained in the numerous and often dissimilar manuscripts of the Greek New Testament. Its color patterns and structures are the books of the New Testament in all of their wonderful contextual, syntactical, and stylistic variety. Through careful, studied use of the principles of textual criticism the pieces of the puzzle eventually fall into place, and the result we call Scripture.

But there are also significant differences between textual criticism and jigsaw puzzles. For one thing, in textual criticism there are far more pieces than will ever fit into the puzzle. For another, there are times when more than one piece will fit or nearly fit a single opening. Determining which piece to use is sometimes a problem. But more important yet is the fact that we simply do not possess the box in which the puzzle came. We can only reconstruct the full picture through pains-taking, and at times conjectural, research. Do not be alarmed. Most of the pieces are already in place. They came to us that way. (Wouldn't it be nice if jigsaw puzzles were like that?) And, so far as we can tell, all or nearly all the remaining pieces are present. We simply have to fit them into their proper places.

If you are concerned to know how we received the exact words of Scripture as they appear in your Greek or English Bible, if you are not satisfied with variant translations among the modern versions, if you are frus-trated with unexplained marginal readings in English Bibles, then read on. This chapter is written with you in mind.

**The Need for Textual Criticism.** Textual criticism (sometimes called "lower criticism") is foundational to every other phase of exegesis. This is so because this discipline seeks to determine the actual words of the text of the New Testament,[1] the sayings of Jesus, the reminiscences of Luke, the details of Paul, all word for word as they came from these authors.

You are probably wondering what is meant by the use of the word *determine* in this context. Does the modern textual critic somehow establish what does and does not belong in the Bible, or didn't the New Testament writers do that well enough? Undoubtedly they did. Theirs, not ours, are the words which form Scripture. In no way do I mean to suggest that the textual critic has any part in editing the initial message of the Bible.

But he does have a part in determining just what that message was. Whereas we now have well over 5,000 manu-scripts (hereafter abbreviated mss) of the New Testament in Greek, in whole or (quite often) in part, of one kind

---

[1]The word "text" is used here in reference only to the *Greek* New Testament. Translations are called "versions."

or another, and hundreds of copies of ancient versions (thousands in Latin), we do not however possess even one *autograph* of a New Testament document. (An autograph is an original document as it came from the very hand of the New Testament author or his amanuensis. It is something like a modern master from which photocopies are made, though as regards their accuracy many of the manuscripts of the New Testament are far from being anything like modern photocopies!) In view of the facts that we possess no autographs and that we have so very many manuscripts whose actual wordings frequently differ, we are thus forced to determine the text of the New Testament only in the sense of *verifying* what the New Testament authors have already said.

In one sense this discipline involves science[2] inasmuch as science operates within the boundaries of strict controls and accepted principles. There are several clearly defined guidelines for textual criticism, and although the theories of some scholars disallow these, the guidelines which we will observe are widely accepted in the scholarly community.

But the discipline of textual criticism also involves art.[3] This is so because, unlike the similar results of

[2]Gordon Fee observes that textual criticism "is the science that compares all known manuscripts of a given work in an effort to trace the history of variations within the text so as to discover its original form," in "The Textual Criticism of the New Testament," in *Biblical Criticism*, ed. R.K. Harrison et al. (Grand Rapids: Zondervan, 1978), p. 127.

[3]See Bruce Metzger, who distinguishes between aspects of textual criticism as science and art in *The Text of the New Testament*, 2d ed. (Oxford: Oxford University Press, 1968), p. v. As a science, textual criticism works with "the making and transmission of ancient manuscripts, the description of the most important witnesses to the New Testament text, and the history of

two scientific experiments conducted in the same environments and in the exact same ways, in textual criticism the outcomes of separate investigations of the same problem, using the same guidelines, will not always be the same. One student may draw much attention to a variant which is in keeping with the author's style while the other points to outstanding contextual evidence which runs counter to the evidence of the first. It is not that these students have operated with different artistic media, but rather, that they have emphasized different strokes, one highlighting the sky and the other mountains. Learning when to highlight sky as opposed to mountains is learning the *art* of textual criticism.

In any case, *discipline* seems the right word for describing this whole enterprise. It is required of both scientist and artist. In all of your judgments about the text of the New Testament, you will be called upon to exercise the greatest care, proceeding with extreme caution. As you become increasingly familiar with the territory your proficiency will increase, but you cannot afford lapses. After all, you are deciding upon the very words of the likes of Jesus and Paul.

Understand, too, that textual criticism is a demanding field. With thousands of manuscripts and versions, no two of which (we are told) agree entirely, you will have to depend greatly on the scholarly literature and manuals on the subject. You may wonder, "Why bother? If the manuscripts are not available to me how can I make a decision? Even if they were available, would I be able to read them?" (The Greek of the nicely edited modern New Testament is a far cry from ancient mss where words were not separated and little or no punctuation appeared.) "And what of versions? Would I need to learn Coptic?

the textual criticism of the New Testament as reflected in the succession of printed editions of the Greek Testament." As art, textual criticism is "the application of reasoned considerations in choosing among variant readings."

Latin?     Syriac?     Isn't this a highly specialized field suitable only for scholars?"

Not really. On the one hand, there is a difference between knowing enough to publish detailed monographs, teach textual criticism in a seminary, and belong to learned societies of textual critics, and, on the other, knowing enough to follow basic arguments, comprehend essential principles, come to conclusions based on the right application of those principles, and explain these conclusions to interested students of the Bible in the local church.     Anyone who teaches the Bible regularly will at some point need to know something about textual criticism.     Marginal readings in study Bibles abound. Preachers are viewed as local "experts" on Scripture. Questions will come:     "Why is there a longer ending to Mark's gospel?     What about the woman taken in adultery? Why isn't it in my Bible?     And does the Lord's prayer (Matthew 6:9-13) really end with the terse, 'Deliver us from the evil one?'     Whatever happened to 'Thine is the Kingdom ....'?"     Some knowledge of textual criticism is necessary if you are going to be prepared to answer questions like these.

A word of caution is appropriate here. Those of us who grew up with the King James Version were somewhat surprised to find out that several of our most treasured readings, passages which we thought were as much a part of the New Testament as apple pie is American, were not present in the autographs.     Proceed with caution.     These are not often matters to be discussed in your first sermon in a new pulpit.     Such issues have nothing to do with being "liberal" or "conservative," but when handled in cavalier fashion do tend to bring out defensive feelings in all kinds of people.

Our inquiry begins with a look at the text-critical setup in the UBS 3rd edition (hereafter UBS3) as well as the Aland 26th edition (hereafter NA26) of the Greek New Testament. We will proceed then with brief discussions of selected kinds of mss and versions of the New Testament, kinds of errors encountered in these mss, and a brief history of the early transmission of the text.    Chapter three continues with procedures of textual criticism, examples, practical suggestions for preachers and teachers, practice texts, and bibliography.

**The UBS3 Apparatus.** Have you ever wondered about the seemingly cryptic symbols below the solid black line in UBS3?    For most first year students, the challenge of what lies *above* that solid black line is alone sufficient for hours of study.    But the task at hand is to tackle the text-critical apparatus at the bottom of the page.[4] Here we find the information which is necessary to determine why the editors have chosen the readings which appear in the text. It is important to note that they have provided a *full* apparatus, one which presents representative manuscripts, versions, and church fathers (when available) for each variant.    This evidences the fairness with which they have conducted their work and makes for a very usable Greek testament for purposes of exegesis. Still, you must realize that the editors have not chosen to include *every* textual variation inasmuch as there are so many, and those selected have been chosen with a view to their usefulness for Bible translators.    NA26, discussed below, provides additional textual variants.

The apparatus of UBS3 is generally easy to follow. Although you may not yet be familiar with many of its features and symbols, it will be helpful to get to know a few of them now.    In 1 John 3:1 there exists a variation of some importance.    It involves the presence or absence of καὶ ἐσμέν ("and we are") following the subordinate clause "in order that we might be called sons of God."

---

[4]There is also a punctuation apparatus at the bottom of many pages as well as a list of select parallel passages.    You will be able to distinguish the text-critical apparatus in several ways: (1) it is always first among the several apparatuses, (2) it is usually the longest of the apparatuses, and (3) it has several distinguishing characteristics including a rating system and manuscript symbols.

It asserts as fact that we are presently sons of God, not merely that we might be, as the purpose clause preceding it suggests.

Turn to the variant (p. 817), and follow along as we observe the features of the critical apparatus. First, note that just below the solid black line (which runs across the entire page), there is a superscripted "1." This is simply a footnote indicator. Such footnotes are renumbered (beginning with "1") at the first set of variants in each chapter of the New Testament. Next, there is a boldface numeral which corresponds with the verse number in which the textual variations are found, in our case, **1**. The verse number is followed by a bracketed A, B, C, or D, providing some indication of the relative certainty of the textual committee as to the reading at hand. {A} suggests that the text is "virtually certain" while {B} "indicates ... some degree of doubt." {C} signifies a "considerable degree of doubt" and {D}, a "very high degree of doubt" (p. xii). The system is not very precise, but it is especially helpful for those who do not have a strong background in textual criticism. At a glance, students are afforded a look at what leading scholars in the field have said about this or that variant. 1 John 3:1 has received a {B} rating; there is some degree of doubt though not a high one.

Before we discuss what follows the {B} in 1 John 3:1, it is appropriate to mention the fact that Bruce M. Metzger has summarized the textual judgments of the UBS3 textual committee, composed of Kurt Aland, Matthew Black, Carlo M. Martini, Bruce M. Metzger, and Allen Wikgren, in *A Textual Commentary on the Greek New Testament*, also available from the United Bible Societies. This tool will be of great value to you who are just beginning studies in textual criticism. It affords a rare, behind-the-scenes glimpse of scholarly discussions of variants. It is not, however, a replacement for your own independent evaluation of the manuscript and internal evidence (categories discussed below). Still, it comes highly recommended after you have completed your own investigation.

Following {B} we find the words καὶ ἐσμέν. This is the reading adopted by the committee. In other words, the editors of UBS3 feel that καὶ ἐσμέν was present in the autograph of this document. Manuscript support for καὶ ἐσμέν follows. It consists of a list of symbols (explained to some extent in the introduction to your Greek New Testament) which represents various kinds of manuscripts. These we will discuss at a later point in the chapter. Suffice it to say that those symbols prefixed with a p and followed by a superscripted numeral represent *papyri*, those in upper case (English or Greek as well as the Hebrew symbol א and numerals prefixed by 0) indicate *uncials*, and those assigned numbers (not begun with 0) signify *minuscules*. *Versions* are abbreviated as are the *church fathers*.[5] Again, full tables of abbreviations appear in the introduction to UBS3.

The slightly angular pair of vertical lines following the church father Theophylact is followed by a *second* possible reading. In this instance, five uncials, numerous minuscules, the majority of Byzantine mss (*Byz*), many lectionaries (*Lect*), and Ps-Oecumenius all favor omission of καὶ ἐσμέν. Once again, specific information on the manuscripts, versions, and fathers is available in the introduction to UBS3. At your earliest convenience read these data in survey fashion, pausing to spend time with the several paragraphs interspersed between lists of manuscripts and their dates. Simply become familiar with these pages. Know where to look for specific kinds of information.

**The NA26 Apparatus.** A more compact and somewhat harder system to master, this apparatus nevertheless contains far more variant information. For example, in researching John 21:20, UBS3 shows no variation following the participle ἀκολουθοῦντα ("following"). The text simply depicts the "disciple whom Jesus loved" as "following."

---

[5]We will cover papyri, uncials, minuscules, versions, and the fathers at a later point in this chapter.

It does not specify whom he was following (as in the NIV = "them"); it simply says that he was following. Upon examining NA26, however, we learn that ἀκολουθοῦντα is not present in several mss, including א* (the asterisk suggesting that the scribe who produced א did not include ἀκολουθοῦντα; a subsequent corrector apparently added it). Granted, the manuscript support for omitting ἀκολουθοῦντα is weaker than that for its inclusion, but the tendency of scribes was to add words, not delete them. It is just possible that ἀκολουθοῦντα was not present in the first place.

The variant is significant exegetically. Peter has already been commanded to follow Christ in verse 19 (ἀκολούθει μοι = "Follow me") and this, after the painful inquiry of Christ regarding Peter's love for the Master (vv. 15ff.). Later (v. 22), in response to Peter's turning to ask about the future of the beloved disciple, Jesus concludes, "What is it to you? You must keep on following me!" It seems then that following Jesus is the principal theme of the entire pericope, and if this is so, the presence or absence of ἀκολουθοῦντα becomes very important. If we accept the reading, the text is suggesting that the beloved disciple was at least following someone (perhaps several people; again, John is not specific on this). Could this be an indication that he was following Jesus *as a disciple*, not merely spatially, while Peter needed rather strong prompting on the matter?[6] On the other hand, if the reading is rejected, no such conclusion may be reached. The exegetical possibilities are limited, or at least altered. In any case, NA26 has alerted us to the options, while UBS3 does not mention them.

As for the actual layout of the NA26 apparatus, several items are significant. 1. Textual variants and only

[6]This conclusion is based upon the meaning of ἀκολούθει elsewhere in this passage, as well as John's tendency to play with words, at times giving them a double meaning.

textual variants are covered in the block of fine print at the bottom of each page of NA26. 2. The coverage is no longer full as was the case with UBS3. Only those mss which support the alternate reading, i.e., the reading not adopted in the text of NA26, are cited (unless the abbreviation *txt* is apparent; in such instances, those mss which follow *txt* support the reading found in the text). 3. The symbols which announce the particular kind of variation (be it addition of a word or words, omission of a word or words, transposition, etc.) must be mastered to use this critical apparatus effectively. A list of these symbols appears on p. 45 of NA26. 4. There is no system for rating the relative certainty of the reading adopted in the text. The reader is left to decide this for himself. 5. Sets of variants for each new verse are introduced by the presence of a conspicuous black dot, helping the reader locate his textual problem quickly. 6. Most importantly, there are generally several variants listed for each verse, far more than are found in UBS3. This is the chief value of this handy edition.

There can be no shortcuts with NA26. As with UBS3, you should read the introduction (several times) for detailed information about symbols and abbreviations. But the best results will be achieved only when you use the apparatus. In general, it is best to begin with UBS3. Then, studying the same variant, check NA26. Do this repeatedly. You will see that the information is quite to the point. You will also become increasingly comfortable with NA26. In time it may become more profitable for you to conduct much (even most) of your text-critical work in NA26, especially as it affords greater brevity and, at the same time, a glimpse at more variations among mss.

One word of caution. Neither UBS3 nor NA26 offers coverage of all mss. No handy edition is able to do that. Understand that the mss listed are only *representative* of larger groups of mss which frequently go without any mention in critical apparatuses. This is particularly true with NA26. For example, in 1 John 3:1

NA26 lists only three uncials, one minuscule, 𝔐 (for the vast majority of Byzantine mss), and a single manuscript of the Latin Vulgate as omitting καὶ ἐσμέν. No mss in favor of the reading are offered. It is therefore best to consult UBS3 for further help. (Though such help is not always available, it is in 1 John 3:1.)

**Manuscripts of the Greek New Testament.** There are four kinds of manuscripts of the Greek text. The first and earliest, the *papyrus*, is also the least easily preserved. Constructed of glued strips of a reed plant which grew in the Nile delta area, papyri have survived remarkably well, however, in the dry climate of Egypt. There are more than 90 such copies of parts of the New Testament today. Among them is the Rylands fragment ($p^{52}$), dated A.D. 125, the oldest known record of any New Testament document.

Papyri are listed first in support of a given reading. This is reasonable inasmuch as the papyrus scroll was likely the first material upon which the New Testament was written. Later New Testament papyri were written in codex form, somewhat like the pages of a modern book. The papyri with which textual critics work today are codices, not scrolls.[7]

New Testament papyri range from the second to eighth centuries, but most were produced in the third and fourth centuries. For the most part, *uncials* (a term used for parchment mss produced from the skins of animals and written with uncial or upper case characters) replaced papyri after the fourth century.

Many papyri are remarkably important. All deserve attention. You would do well to become especially familiar with $p^{45}$, $p^{46}$, and $p^{47}$ (the Chester Beatty papyri), and $p^{66}$, $p^{72}$, $p^{74}$, and $p^{75}$ (the Bodmer papyri). When performing textual criticism, consult the lists of mss in

[7]See Greenlee, *Scribes, Scrolls, and Scripture* (Grand Rapids: Eerdmans, 1985), p. 14.

Appendix A for specific information about these and other papyri.  See also Bruce M. Metzger, *The Text of the New Testament*, pp. 36-42, Harold Greenlee, *Introduction to New Testament Textual Criticism*, pp. 33-36, and Kurt and Barbara Aland, *The Text of the New Testament*, pp.96-101. The latter has a full list of all papyri, complete with their contents (i.e., which chapters of the New Testament are included), date, current location, bibliographic information, type of text, and category.  The last two items (type of text and category) are designations prepared by the Alands to assist the student in assessing the relative character of given mss, a subject to which we will return in the section on procedures of textual criticism. [8]  These categories are particularly helpful for beginners. [8]  A very recent work, *Early Manuscripts and Modern Translations of the New Testamnet*, by Philip W. Comfort, provides some of the most detailed information available on papyri.  It will repay close study.

*Uncials* were written on parchment or vellum. These prepared animal skins are generally more durable than papyri, which became brittle with age. There are nearly 300 uncials.

These mss appear after the papyri in the critical apparatus.  They are represented by upper case letters, Greek and English as well as Hebrew א.  A separate set of designations has these mss numbered from 01-0274.  (They are distinguished from the *minuscule* mss, which are also numbered, by the presence of a zero preceding the other digits.)

Scribes used uncial mss in the third to tenth centuries, though most were produced in the fifth and sixth. A number of early uncials (fourth and fifth centuries) are characterized not only by quality writing materials

[8]Explanations of these systems appear on pp. 59, 64, and 93 (types of papyri) and 105 (categories) of *The Text of the New Testament*, revised ed., translated by Erril F. Rhodes (Grand Rapids:  Eerdmans, 1989).

but by cautious scribes who were careful not to add, delete, or otherwise change portions of their *exemplars*
(i.e., the ms from which a scribe copied, his pattern or
example). Of course, this does not mean that *all* uncials
are equally faithful in preserving the text (as will be
illustrated in a moment), but, as a rule, certain uncials, especially *Alexandrian* uncials (a category discussed
below), should always be consulted in establishing the
text of the New Testament.

Specifically, several scholars see Codex Vaticanus (B)
as the most important witness (or at least among the most
important witnesses) of the Greek New Testament.[9] Such a
categorical statement may seem dangerous, but the high
value which experts place on this manuscript is worth our
careful attention. Codex B contains both testaments, although Revelation and portions of Hebrews are missing.
It dates from the middle of the fourth century.

Codex Sinaiticus (ℵ) is also extremely valuable. It,
too, comes from the mid fourth century and contains the
entire Bible, along with the letter of Barnabas and the
Shepherd of Hermas, both early Christian documents. Once
thought by some (especially Dr. Constantin von Tischen-
dorf, the man who secured it from the monastery of St.
Catharine on Mount Sinai)[10] to be the single most important manuscript of the New Testament, today scholars have
detected certain elements in parts of the text which
betray influences likely alien to the autographs. Still,
it is thought to be among the most important mss of the
Bible.

Codex D (known as Bezae, sometimes called Cantabrigi-

---

[9]See, e.g., Greenlee, *Scribes, Scrolls, and Scripture*,
p. 27. Metzger acknowledges that it is "one of the most
valuable of all the manuscripts" in *The Text of the New
Testament*, p. 47.

[10]The whole story is delightfully recounted in Metzger,
*The Text of the New Testament*, pp. 42-46.

ensis) dates from the fifth or sixth century. Its text is at times radically different from those of ℵ and B. In fact, Metzger remarks, "No known manuscript has so many and such remarkable variations from what is usually taken to be the normal New Testament text."[11]  According to Metzger, this is especially true of its text of Acts, which is almost 10% longer than it is in other mss.

Bezae reminds us that no single *kind* of manuscript (e.g., papyrus, uncial, etc.) necessarily stands above all others. Each manuscript, regardless of kind, must be studied on its own merits with a view to both its tendency to agree with the majority of apparently solid mss (sometimes called the "standard" or "normal" text) and its own distinctives, whatever they are. Whereas the alliance of mss B and ℵ in support of a given reading was at one time thought to stand against all other mss as representing the true text (if it actually came to this), such simple solutions are no longer acceptable to textual critics. Aland observes, "In the twentieth century the papyri have eroded the dominance of the uncials, and a group of minuscules presently under study promises to diminish it further."[12]  The point is clear: you should study uncials alongside, not in front of, all other mss.

As with the papyri, you should study Appendix A. in determining the date and significance of selected uncials. See also Metzger, *Text of the New Testament*, pp. 42-61, Greenlee, *Introduction to New Testament Textual Criticism*, pp. 36-42, and Aland and Aland, *Text of the New Testament*, pp. 106-125. Again, the latter has the most extensive list of mss along with helpful designations as to characteristics of particular mss. However, Metzger is especially readable and ought to be consulted not only for information necessary for making a textual decision, but also so that you may get a feel for the actual makeup of selected mss, how large they were

---

[11]*Text of the New Testament*, p. 50.

[12]Aland and Aland, *Text*, p. 102.

and what they looked like.[13]

The third group of mss, the *minuscules*, is also the largest by far. The Alands cite 2,795, compared with approximately 90 papyri and close to 300 uncials. This type of manuscript appeared late, in the ninth century. As a group, then, minuscules are generally less important in determing the text of the New Testament. However, certain minuscules, e.g. 33, contain a text-type (see below on church fathers) prevalent in far earlier and generally reliable mss. For this reason minuscules cannot be wholly dismissed as unimportant to the process of reconstructing the original text of the New Testament.

As previously mentioned, minuscules are numbered in critical apparatuses. They follow the uncials in order of appearance. Often, many minuscules are listed in support of a given reading in UBS3. Again, they are not all of equal value. *Byz* appears frequently in UBS3 signifying the fact that a large number of minuscules of generally poor quality supports a reading.

The following minuscules may be of some importance in establishing the text of the New Testament: 33, 36, 81, 322, 892, 1006 (Revelation), 1175, 1241, 1243, 1292, 1342 (Mark), 1409, 1506 (Paul), 1611 (Revelation), 1735, 1739, 1841 (Revelation), 1852 (general epistles), 1854 (Revelation), 2050, 2053, 2062, 2127 (Paul), 2329, 2344 (Revelation), 2427, and 2464.[14]

The characteristics of these and other minuscules are

---

[13]Also especially good for this is Jack Finegan's *Encountering New Testament Manuscripts* (Grand Rapids: Eerdmans, 1974). Finegan goes beyond simple explanations of textual criticism to actual plates with plenty of examples of various kinds of mss and the kinds of problems text-critics encounter.

[14]These mss were selected from the more extensive lists in Aland and Aland, *Text*, pp. 129-138.

available in Appendix A. For further comparison see Metzger, *The Text of the New Testament*, pp. 61-66, Greenlee, *Introduction to New Testament Textual Criticism*, pp. 42-44, and Aland and Aland, *The Text of the New Testament*, pp. 129-138.

Second only to the minuscules in terms of sheer numbers (over 2000) are the *lectionaries*, carefully arranged Scriptures read during daily or weekend services, dating from as early as the sixth century. In critical apparatuses, these generally follow the minuscules and are represented symbolically by the presence of an *"l"* followed by a number. *Lect* frequently appears in UBS3 to denote that the majority of lectionaries in the Synaxarion (the "movable year" calendar) and the Menologion (the "fixed year" calendar) agree.

Lectionaries are of limited value in determining the text of the New Testament. Most of them come from roughly the same period as the minuscules. There is a rather full list of lectionaries in UBS3, pp. xxviii-xxxi.

**Versions of the Greek New Testament.** As the gospel went to neighboring lands the need for translations of New Testament books arose. Latin *versions* (or translations) first appeared in and around Rome in the latter part of the second century, Coptic versions in various parts of Egypt in the second and third centuries, and Syriac versions in the lands surrounding Palestine as early as the second century. Versions in these three languages are generally the most significant for textual criticism. Others (Gothic, Georgian, Armenian, etc.) followed. Our English translations are themselves modern versions of the Greek New Testament.

Ancient versions frequently show up in the critical apparatuses of UBS3 and NA26. When there are so many Greek mss available, you may wonder why the editors have included versions alongside their sometimes extensive lists of mss. After all, versions are nothing more than translations and are therefore limited in several ways. For one thing, there may not be exact syntactical correspondences between languages.   For example, it has often been pointed out that the definite article is lacking in Latin, a feature which may create a lack of precision in unraveling certain textual problems. Second, just as we do not have autographs of the Greek mss, so it is with the versions.   We must first come to grips with the textual tradition of a given version before it may be of any significant service.

However, before we write off the benefit of versions completely, two points are particularly important: (1) Many of the versions of the New Testament arose quite early, and, where their syntax and vocabulary compare favorably with the text of the New Testament, their readings may prove helpful, and (2) because versions can often be traced to specific geographic locales, they aid us by providing some insight into the *geographic distribution* of a given reading.   That is, they may help us determine how widely a given reading was accepted.

Versions are listed after the lectionaries in the critical apparatus.   Often, however, no lectionaries are cited, and the versions follow the list of minuscules.

The symbols for versions are generally easy to follow inasmuch as they are simple abbreviations of appropriate languages.   The symbol for Coptic is cop; for Ethiopic, eth; for Syriac, syr.   However, this system of symbols is somewhat complicated by the fact that there are often numerous versions within a single language.   For example, in Egypt there was the Sahidic dialect of Coptic, spoken in the south, and the Bohairic dialect of Coptic, spoken in the north.   The symbols will reflect such distinctions in the critical apparatus.   Thus both cop$^{sa}$ and cop$^{bo}$ appear.   For a full list of these distinct symbols, consult the introduction to UBS3, pp. xxxii-xxxvi.

Significant versions are mapped out in Appendix B. You should use this map to help determine the geographical distribution of readings.   You will also want to consult Metzger, *The Text of the New Testament*, pp. 67-86, and Aland and Aland, *Text*, pp. 185-214.   For a delightfully simple but informative introduction to versions see Greenlee, *Scribes, Scrolls, and Scripture,* pp. 29-33.

**The Church Fathers.** Of somewhat limited value for textual criticism are the Scriptural citations in the writings of the church fathers. These great volumes of exhortation and polemic from the early Christian centuries contain nearly all of the New Testament, with multiple citations for many verses. Frequently the fathers would cite Scripture after Scripture in the form of catena[15] or some similar device.

Whereas we cannot always date mss with exact certainty or detect the geographical origins of each, records of the times and places of the fathers are much more certain (see Appendix C.). This provides a distinct benefit for textual critics inasmuch as it may help them trace the point of origin of *text-types,* that is, whole groups of mss organized much like a family tree, with one scribe copying another and still others copying the second. This process would go on and on until there might be tens and hundreds of copies which had a single early exemplar as their point of origin. Attempting to trace that exemplar to a probable time and place is helpful in the process of establishing the text-type's relative value for making textual judgments, though the process itself has not ever actually been accomplished for any New Testament text-type.[16]

[15]A literary technique involving a list or "chain" of Scriptures cited in support of an argument.

[16]Michael W. Holmes summarizes the problems well in "New Testament Textual Criticism," in *Introducing New Testament Interpretation* (Grand Rapids: Baker, 1989), ed. Scot McKnight, p. 54. Holmes calls special attention to the sheer proliferation of New Testament mss and what he calls "cross-pollination," the mixture of elements of various text-types in a single ms, making it very difficult to place that ms into a specific text-type.

Unfortunately, as with versions and mss, scholars may have to unpack a history of textual transmission for the works of the fathers. In other words, they may have to perform textual criticism on manuscripts of the fathers before these will provide any help in determining the text of the New Testament. Further complicating this is the fact that the fathers often quoted from memory, sometimes incorrectly. Origen was particularly notorious for disparate multiple quotations of a single passage of Scripture. Hence you may see a fraction by his name in textual apparatuses. Origen$^{2/5}$, for example, would be used to indicate that he quoted a given verse one way twice, and in other ways a total of three times. Given these limitations, you can see why the value of the fathers for textual criticism is limited.

The church fathers are cited frequently in UBS3. They will appear last, following the versions, in the apparatus.

Appendix C. provides a map of the Mediterranean world, complete with key fathers, their locations, and their dates. The map should help you get a feel for the geographical spread and time framework of the fathers. Notice that certain fathers appear in more than one place. Several were involved in extensive travels, a fact which complicates their helpfulness in categorizing families of manuscripts. You will also want to consult UBS3, pp. xxxvii-xl, and Bruce Metzger, *The Text of the New Testament*, pp. 88-89.

**Kinds of Errors in the Mss.** You should understand how variations in these mss, lectionaries, versions, and fathers arose. Although we would like to believe that no one ever deliberately altered his exemplar, the fact remains that some scribes did. On occasion, scribes would smooth out rough grammatical constructions, harmonize divergent accounts (especially among the gospels), clarify ambiguous Greek, or change what appeared to be misspellings. Many of the variations cited in UBS3 fall into one of these categories. You may read about them in

Metzger's *Textual Commentary*. Actually, these scribes were generally trying to refine, not corrupt, the message of the New Testament in some way. Still, it is important to keep these intentional changes in mind as you work with textual problems.

Many variations were not, however, intentional. Rather, they may have taken one of the following forms:

1. *Faulty Word Division*. As previously noted, early mss of the Greek New Testament did not have neat divisions among words. Later copyists and editors may have separated them erringly from time to time. In 1 John 3:20, the text begins with ὅτι ἐὰν ("that if") while the textual apparatus of NA26 indicates that some modern commentators read rather ὃ τι ἐάν.[17] The first option treats ὅτι as a single word and the second, as two. In early mss, the words appeared as ΟΤΙΕΑΝΚΑΤΑΓΙΝΩΣΚΗ ..., giving no distinct indication in favor of one reading or the other. Fortunately, contextual clues help us here. Beginning with verse 19, there are three instances of ὅτι. The first clearly means "that," as the English reads, "And by this, we know *that*...." The third (in verse 20) is either "that" or "because" (probably the latter), reading "*because* God is greater than our heart...." But the second ὅτι (or ὃ τι, if these commentators are correct) does not make sense as either "that" or "because." Hence the following translation of verses 19-20, based upon the division of ὅτι as ὃ τι, may be correct, "And by this[18] we know that we are from the truth and we will set our heart at ease *at which place* or *whenever* (ὃ τι) our heart condemns us, because God is greater than our heart and knows all things." "That" will not work here because it does not make

[17]From the neuter singular relative pronoun (ὃ) + the neuter form of the indefinite pronoun (τι).

[18]"This" refers to the test set up in verse 18, namely, whether we have loved in deed and truth.

sense. "Because" is out of place since the last part of verse 20 is already a causal clause. "Whenever" may very well be the best choice.[19]

2. At times, scribes omitted words and phrases, a mistake called *haplography*. Often, haplography occurred when a word or phrase appeared more than once in a text. The copyist looked at the ms, copied a word (or phrase), took a second look at the text, and, rather than fixing his eyes on the *first* occurrence of that word, skipped to the *second*, thus omitting all intervening words. The technical name for such ommisions is *parablesis*. Parablesis may have occured due to (1) *homoeoteleuton*, where the scribe left out a section between words of similar ending or, (2) *homoioarcton*, where there was an ommision between words of similar beginning.

There is an instance of parablesis in 1 John 2:23. The phrase τὸν πατέρα ἔχει ["(he) has the Father"] appears in that verse twice, both times at the end of a clause. A number of mss leave out the last half of the verse, presumably because at some point the eyes of a weary copyist skipped from the first τὸν πατέρα ἔχει to the second, thus eliminating ὁ ὁμολογῶν τὸν υἱὸν καὶ ("The one who confesses the Son also ...."). If we include the words (as the mss overwhelmingly suggest that we should), then it reads, "Everyone who denies the Son does not have the Father (while) *everyone who acknowledges the Son also has the Father.*" Leaving out the last clause is definitely not in keeping with the constant antithetical parallelism which John employs. Here, the longer reading is correct.

Or consider 1 John 3:13, where the end of verse 12 reads δίκαια and verse 13 begins either with μή or with καί μή. The scribe may have looked at the words

---

[19]Viewing ὅτι as a dative neuter form of ὅστις, meaning *at whatever point*, yields much the same meaning.

δίκαια καὶ and, having already copied the και in
δίκαια, skipped the separate word καί altogether.
There are additional instances of haplography in John
9:28 and 1 John 1:13.

3.    Related to haplography is *dittography*, the repetition of a phrase, word, part of a word, or a letter.
Greenlee[20] notes possible dittography in Mark 12:27,
where the text has οὐκ ἔστιν θεὸς νεκρῶν ("He is not
the God of the dead ....") while several mss (θ $f^{13}$ 33
1241) have instead οὐκ ἔστιν ὁ θεὸς θεὸς νεκρῶν ("God
is not the God of the dead...."). A scribe has presumably added ὁ θεός at some point in the transmission
of the text, either to clarify the subject of the
sentence or as a result of simple dittography.

4.    Confusing one letter for another, either as a result of mistakenly hearing a word read or seeing
similar letters on the page, sometimes led to inadvertent variations. This likely accounts for the
separate readings, καυχήσωμαι ("that I may boast") and
καυθήσωμαι ("that I may be burned"), in 1 Corinthians
13:3. Only one letter separates the two words, but it
is all-important for the meaning of this verb.

Of course there were other kinds of errors, but these
will suffice to demonstrate the sorts of problems which
arose in the history of the transmission of the New
Testament in Greek. You should become familiar with them.

**A Brief History of the Early Transmission of the Text,
Together with the Emergence of Distinct Text-Types.** It is
very important that you understand how the New Testament
achieved its remarkable proliferation in the early Christian centuries and how it did this in its varied forms.

Unfortunately, the earliest copies of the text are
also the ones about which the least is known. Prior to

---

[20]J. Harold Greenlee, *Introduction to New Testament
Textual Criticism* (Grand Rapids: Eerdmans, 1964), p. 64.

the arrival of the fourth century uncials, we are dealing largely with papyri (although there were of course some versions, especially Latin versions, in this period), many of which are rather like carpet remnants, bits and pieces, which together may help us substantially, but separately only give us a glimpse of what was happening with the transmission of this or that book (or books). Again, there are not that many papyri, and the ones that we have are generally quite fragmentary (with the notable exception of the Chester Beatty and Bodmer collections, both of which are extremely important in determining the text). Nor are they uniform in respect to their quality. Some, the Bodmer papyri, for example, seem to square nicely with the character and quality of later uncials such as Codex B, while others, especially the Chester Beatty collection, are somewhat freer in their approach to the text.

Given the early diversity of the church about the Mediterranean world, periods of local persecution which may have caused production of New Testament documents to go underground, and the fact that in this early period trained scribes were the exception rather than the rule, you should at once appreciate both the varying characteristics of these mss and the fact that the text of the New Testament was preserved so well.

*The situation changed* dramatically with the rise of the Emperor Constantine in the early fourth century. Christianity was officially recognized. Professional scribes now meticulously committed the books of the New Testament to writing. Evidence suggests that scribes began to compare mss, with some attempts to bring them into line with each other. The Emperor himself ordered 50 new copies of the New Testament.[21] It was during this period that the uncials ℵ and B came into existence.

We must, however, recognize that alien influences had

---

[21]Eusebius, *Life of Constantine*, iv. 36.     Cited in Metzger, *Text of the New Testament*, p. 7.

already crept into the text of the New Testament by this time, and that at points, no matter how early the manuscript or how professional the scribe, the exemplars were faulty.    Unless scribes made careful comparisons with other, more reliable manuscripts, these erring exemplars corrupted the copies which followed them.    It is not enough to have numbers of mss in your favor.    The characteristics of manuscripts must be examined closely.

The most reliable mss produced in this era were *Alexandrian* (so named for their apparent emergence in and around this city of Northern Egypt).    Outstanding mss from this text-type are Codex Vaticanus (B) and $p^{75}$.    Such mss are characterized by brevity and fidelity to what appear to have been good exemplars.    You should pay very careful heed to those mss which belong to the Alexandrian text-type.

But there were other, less reliable though still helpful, mss in these times.    Precursors of the fifth century Codex Bezae (D) showed up as early as the third century. $p^{48}$, for example, apparently betrays a tendency toward free addition and paraphrase by comparison with other text-types.[22]    This so-called "*Western* Text" (though in reality, it may have little to do with the mss of the Western Church of that time)[23] has not proven particularly useful in determining the actual words of the New Testament, although it may provide some insights into the theology of its creators.

At one time scholars also detected a "Caesarean text." Found only in the gospels (and perhaps Acts in $p^{45}$), there were not as many representatives in this family as

---

[22]The Alands, *Text*, p. 159, associate this ms with the D text.

[23]The Alands are particularly adamant about this.    See *Text*, pp. 54-55.    From the second century on, Latin versions were probably in use in the West as much as or more than anything.

in others.[45] Its earliest representatives were $p^{37}$ and perhaps $p^{45}$. It was considered a generally reliable text, second perhaps to the Alexandrian family, with less additions and paraphrases than the "Western" text. Says Greenlee, "It is often found in the company of the Alexandrian text, often with the Western text, and often with its own readings apart from the other local texts."[24] Recent studies have treated these "Caesarean" mss as mss of mixed character. Michael W. Holmes, for example, lists them simply as "Other Impotant MSS" in his text-type listings.[25] The Alands see the text-type as purely theoretical.[26]

*Another critical era* in the history of the trans-mission of the New Testament arose in the fifth and sixth centuries. It was later accompanied by the spread of Islam (which halted the important and generally reliable manuscript production in Egypt) and the now accepted *Byzantine* text-type, a text which held sway for some 1,000 years (and then some) as the predominant text-type. Mss from this group are characterized by free additions (some of them quite lengthy), smoothing of grammar, and the like. In other words, this manuscript tradition contains many *intentional* (as well as unintentional) errors.

Actually the Byzantine (or *Koine*, as it is sometimes called) text-type had been around for some time, its initial exemplar being traced to Syrian Antioch somewhere in the early fourth century.[27] In fact, tendencies of this text-type can be traced back as far as the turn of the second century, where the *Didache* (variously dated from A.D. 90 to 120) appears to add to the end of the

[24]*Introduction*, p. 90.

[25]"New Testament Textual Criticism," p. 59.

[26]*The Text of the New Testament*, p. 66.

[27]On this, see Aland and Aland, *Text*, pp. 64ff. and Metzger, *Text*, p. 170.

Lord's Prayer, "For Thine is the Kingdom ...," whereas other early mss do not contain this ending.

This Byzantine text ultimately served as the basis for our King James Bible, which is now recognized as an outdated translation due to its archaic English and the comparatively poor quality of the mss used in its translation. Granted, there are thousands of these Byzantine mss--Alexandria had no chance for such numbers in the face of Islam, which swept across North Africa in the seventh century--and some moderns argue on the basis of sheer numbers that the King James Bible is a superior Bible. But this ignores the early history of the transmission of text as well as the reasons for which the Byzantine tradition came to prominence. It is a poor argument.

## CHAPTER 3

## TEXTUAL CRITICISM:
## CHOOSING THE RIGHT READING

**Procedures of Textual Criticism.** Having surveyed the need for textual criticism, critical apparatuses, kinds of mss and versions, and a brief history of transmission along with the various text-types, we are now in a position to look at the proper criteria used for arriving at solid textual judgments. These criteria are largely well established in the scholarly community, many of them stemming back over one hundred years to the times of the Englishmen Brooke Foss Westcott and Fenton John Anthony Hort, whose *The New Testament in the Original Greek* appeared in 1881. However, the discovery of newer mss, especially the papyri, and the rise of advanced textual theories have altered the practice of textual criticism considerably in our times, and there are surely further advancements to come.[1]

[1]Kenneth W. Clark, "Today's Problems with the Critical Text of the New Testament," in *Essays in Divinity* (Chicago: University of Chicago Press, 1968), vol. 6, pp. 157, argues against what he calls "today's Textus Receptus," that is, today's *standard* text (much as the KJV was the standard translation for English readers for hundreds of years). He suggests that we need to dismantle the Wescott-Hort structure, with special new emphasis upon the church fathers outside Egypt (p. 168). He reminds us that it is important that we not accept the textual tenets of another age uncritically. Interestingly, the article preceding his, Ernest C. Colwell's, "Hort Redivivus: A Plea and a Program," pp. 131ff., pleads almost

Above all, that reading which, for whatever reasons (most of them discussed below), *best explains the presence of all others* is generally considered primary. To put it another way, the reading from which all others developed, whether by reason of addition, omission, paraphrase, transposition, substitution, or some other, is the preferred reading.

In Romans 8:28, the text reads πάντα συνεργεῖ, which may be rendered, "All things work together" (if πάντα is viewed as the subject) or "He works all things together" (if πάντα is viewed as the object). The ambiguity of the sentence seems to cry for some point of clarification. Hence, some mss (among them, p[46] A B 81 cop[sa]) appear to have added ὁ θεός ("God") as subject, thus offering the full reading, "And we know that for those who love God, *God* works all things together for the good." In spite of the weighty manuscript evidence for the inclusion of ὁ θεός as subject, it appears that the reading which best explains all others is the simple πάντα συνεργεῖ ("All things work together"). Alone, it is simply too vague (it would seem) for a scribe to resist some kind of refinement. After all, do "All things" work on their own in some naturalistic or pagan sense? The reading which includes ὁ θεός leaves no room for theological guesswork. On the other hand, it is just possible that some mss omit ὁ θεός in view of the fact that it is preceded by τὸν θεόν and is therefore somewhat redundant. Both options must be considered, but the former ("All things work together ....") seems more reasonable on balance.

In order to select that reading which best explains all others, the textual critic turns to two key kinds of evidence used in separating textual variations from original readings--*external* and *internal*. External evidence has to do with the *mss themselves*, their characteristics, points of origin, text-types, and so forth, while internal evidence is more concerned with the actual *readings*

the opposite case.

present in the mss and whether they are well-suited to the text at hand in view of such matters as style, scribal tendencies to add to the text, and so forth.

External Evidence. Areas of concern under this heading include *date, quality, geographical distribution,* and *genealogical relationship* of mss of the New Testament.[2] That the date of any ms, version, or father is important goes without saying.   Generally, earlier mss are of more importance in the process of establishing the text, although certain later mss (e.g., 33 and 1739) appear to follow good Alexandrian exemplars.   Even those papyri which exhibit tendencies toward intentional change rank high in importance simply because their dates are so early.   This is not to say that they are equal in all respects with all mss of the early period.   Rather, they are important in that they show us just how early variations began to show up in distinct manuscript traditions.   You should consult Appendix A. for dates of key mss.   There are also extensive lists of manuscript dates in the introduction to UBS3.

Manuscript *quality* is also important.   "Quality" is used here to indicate that those scribal characteristics which set one manuscript apart from another in some distinctive way are important in deciding the particular benefit of that manuscript in determining the text.   Is the manuscript given to recurring corrections at the hand of an editor?   Does it contain frequent and careless errors?   Are there numerous intentional errors, or are the errors few and of a nonintentional nature?

Some mss are of mixed quality.   For example, C (Codex Ephraemi Rescriptus, a palimpsest, see p. 45) appears to be an important manuscript for establishing the text.   It

[2]These categories are adapted from Bruce Metzger, *A Textual Commentary on the New Testament Commentary on the New Testament* (New York: United Bible Societies, 1971), pp. xxvff. They are well established among textual critics.

is generally Alexandrian.    However, it also bears the
marks of other text-types. It must be used with caution.
Even Codex Vaticanus (B) is less careful in the gospels
than in other parts of the New Testament, and Codex
Sinaiticus is also suspect, at points betraying a West-
ern-type hand.

The standard manuals of textual criticism are most
helpful in determining the quality of mss.    Consult
Metzger, *The Text of the New Testament*, pp. 36-92, and
Aland and Aland, *Text of the New Testament*, pp. 72-184,
for discussion of individual mss.    See also Comfort, pp.
31ff., for information on the papyri.

The *geographical distribution* of a given reading is
important in determining how well received it was.    If
early mss of good character from a wide variety of places
support a given reading, then the external evidence
clearly favors that reading.    However, proceed with caution.    In spite of the fact that the text-types bear
geographical names, this does not mean that all of the
mss in these groups necessarily come from the particular
locales whose text-type names they bear.    We have already
noted that the Western and Caesarean text-types are
dubious (especially the latter).    Nevertheless, the fact
remains that these text-types are in various ways distinct, and we can trace at least two of them (Alexandrian
and Byzantine) to specific places.[3]    Appendices B.
(versions) and C. (fathers) may be helpful in tracing the
geographical distribution (and perhaps text-type) of
various readings.

In all of this, the important principle to remember is
that readings with a wide distribution are preferred.    A
reading with support from Rome, Asia Minor, Caesarea, and
North Africa may be superior to a reading supported only
by Alexandrian texts if the confluence of all other

---

[3]At least the vast majority of Byzantine mss are
traceable to Asia Minor even if the origins of this text-
type are more elusive.

evidence, external and internal, so indicates. For further information on geographical distribution, see the following: Greenlee, *Introduction*, pp. 117-118, and Metzger, *Textual Commentary*, pp. xvi-xxiv and xxviii- xxxi.

I have saved *genealogical relationships* for last inasmuch as these are most difficult for beginners to tackle. Here, we are trying to find out who copied whom. Just as a tree has one trunk but many branches, up to thousands of manuscript "branches" may ultimately be traced to a single papyrus or uncial "trunk." Part of the text-critic's job is to determine which branches likely belong to the several textual trunks and which mss may fairly be called "trunks." Obviously, genealogical relationships are related to text-types, and, just as obviously, the earliest mss are much nearer *the* trunk (or autograph) than later ones. But, as noted earlier, determining whether later scribes in the Alexandrian tradition (for example, the scribe who produced 33, ninth century) copied from B (fourth century), $p^{75}$ (third century), or some other ms is virtually impossible. Thankfully, you will not have to unpack all this--it is already difficult for the expert--but you should be quite sensitive to it. Appendix A. may be helpful in a very general way.

Other matters, directly related to the manuscripts themselves, may be of some importance. What about the manuscript's state of preservation? Are its readings beyond verification at points? Is it a palimpsest, i.e., a manuscript of the New Testament once copied, then erased, and copied over with something other than the New Testament, thus forcing the textual critic to use ultraviolet or chemical technology in order to recover its rendering of the New Testament? Just how much of the New Testament does the manuscript contain? Can its text-type be adequately verified on the basis of a chapter or less? Such matters may make a difference in your conclusions about given texts.

<u>Internal</u> <u>Evidence.</u> Although it may seem that a care-

ful look at external factors is alone sufficient to determine the actual wording of the text of the New Testament, this is simply not the case.   If language were like simple math, completely predictable, with no room for variation, external evidence would be enough.   But the fact is that it is quite possible even for the best mss to contain errors simply because they were copied by human beings.

Hence we move into a discussion of internal factors which may influence textual decisions.   Specifically, we are concerned to know which reading is the *shortest*, which is the *most difficult*, which is at home with the *context*, and which best suits the *style* of the author.

Without doubt, the easiest of all criteria for establishing the text is determining which reading is the *shortest*.   No mental gymnastics are necessary here. Usually, it is simply a matter of counting words.   The rationale for this fundamental canon of textual criticism is rather simple, too.   Certain scribes had a tendency to add to their exemplars.   As we have already noted, tendencies toward clarification, paraphrase, and simple addition are fairly common in the Western and Byzantine text-types.

This does not mean that students should automatically adopt the shortest reading. Homoeoteleuton (omitting sections which appear between words of similar ending), for example, involves inadvertent omission. Still, the occurrences of addition probably outnumber those of omission, and you should watch for this.

Choosing the *most difficult* reading has often been a misunderstood criterion among beginning Greek students. Note carefully that "most difficult" does not mean the reading which is most difficult for the student to translate.     Instead, the "most difficult" reading is that reading which, if left unaltered, would have been the hardest for a scribe to accept--for whatever reason(s).

Consider, for example, Matthew 5:22.   The verse reads

either, "But I say to you that everyone who is angry with his brother will be liable to the judgment," or "But I say to you that everyone who is angry with his brother *without cause* (εἰκῇ) will be liable to the judgment." The former reading is clearly shorter. That much is easy. But the reading which omits εἰκῇ is also that reading which was more difficult for the scribe to accept. As it stands, this somewhat vague reading, rather like the one in verse 11, seems quite general. It almost sounds as though Jesus roundly condemns all anger. But aren't there times when anger is appropriate? Or will anger alone place disciples in jeopardy of judgment? Apparently, a scribe raised these questions or ones like them and concluded that the insertion of εἰκῇ was altogether appropriate. Likely, he thought that if anger was without cause (or perhaps, "haphazardous," another possible translation of εἰκῇ), then it was clearly sinful.[4] The significance of this variant should not be minimized. Our conclusion on the matter may affect the way we read the passage theologically--as either condemning or justifying anger.

A special case of the most difficult reading occurs when gospel accounts are brought into line with each other. The account which is *verbally dissident* from the others is likely the original account. Luke 6:20 has Μακάριοι οἱ πτωχοί ("Blessed are the poor") while א[2] (a "corrector" working with א), Q, θ, f[1.13], and 33 all have Μακάριοι οἱ πτωχοί τῷ πνεύματι ("Blessed are the poor in

---

[4]The external evidence is somewhat divided. Among those which lack εἰκῇ are the following: p[67] א B numerous fathers; among those which include it: א[c] (a so-called later "corrector" of Sinaiticus) D K L W θ f[1] f[13] 33 1241 1242 *Byz* numerous early versions). Although the shorter reading has strong Alexandrian support, the longer reading would appear to have wider geographical support, leaving us at an impasse as regards external evidence. In this instance the criteria of shortness and difficulty help sway the critic in favor of the reading without εἰκῇ.

Spirit"), apparently in an attempt to bring the Lukan account of the beatitude into line with Matthew's wording in 5:3.   As a rule of thumb, always compare such similar accounts among gospels when there are textual discrepancies.

You must pay attention to *context* at all levels of hermeneutics, textual criticism included.   It is vital, however, that you be able to see "context" in something of a different light when judging text-critical problems. Whereas exegetes typically want to know how things fit *together* when doing context studies, paying attention to such matters as repeated terminology, recurring themes, and important sequences, textual critics often see *disparate* readings within a single context as preferable. This is fully in keeping with the notion that scribes were apt to smooth out difficult grammar and bring diverse readings into line with each other.

This is not to say that text critics see no continuity in Scripture. It is to say that they have a keen understanding of scribal tendencies such as harmonizing divergent texts and clarifying ambiguity. But textual critics, like all other students of the Bible, look for the *literary* context to hold a passage together, not tear it apart, when it comes to exegesis.

You must therefore be careful to distinguish between those texts which call for a reading which seems to fit the context and those that do not.   In 1 John 1:4 the text reads either, "And we write these things in order that *your* joy may be fulfilled," or "And we write these things in order that *our* joy may be fulfilled." The Alexandrian text-type strongly supports the inclusion of ἡμῶν ("our") while a fairly diverse group of mss supports ὑμῶν ("your").    Neither reading is shorter than the other. "Our" may have been somewhat more difficult for a scribe to accept (seeming rather selfish or at least out of place). But this does not tilt the argument significantly in one direction or the other.

In this instance, an analysis of the context of the

readings in question is very helpful. In verse one, John speaks of what "*we* have heard, seen, beheld, and handled," all in first person plural. Verse two continues in the same vein: "And *we* have beheld and now testify and announce to you eternal life, which was with the Father and was revealed to *us*." Verse three repeats the pattern of oft used first person plural verbs and pronouns, and verse four concludes, "And *our* fellowship is with the Father and with his Son, Jesus Christ." Throughout, John has plainly and emphatically spoken of his active partnership in the gospel and its God. It does not seem strange then that he would speak of "*our* joy" being fulfilled. (Paul does the same in Philippians 2:2.) Thus viewed, "that *our* joy may be fulfilled" seems a most fitting conclusion to this introductory pericope. In this instance at least, that reading which best seems to *fit* the context is the most appropriate.[5] Suffice it to say that, given strong external support, *a reading judged thoroughly appropriate to the context ought to be accepted, in spite of the fact that it may not be considered the most difficult reading.*

Finally, there is the matter of *style*. Of all the criteria for evaluating textual variants, style is the most subjective, for if we say that the most difficult reading is preferred (and that reading which is at variance with the style of the author could easily be considered the most difficult) then how can style be considered *alongside* the most difficult reading as a canon for textual criticism? When inconsistencies among internal criteria arise--and they will--the student should give the greater consideration to external evidence. When *it* is equally balanced, decisions are hard to come by.

It is particularly hard for beginners to utilize the

---

[5]There is at least one other consideration. "Your joy" may simply be an accommodation to John 16:24, which has ἵνα ἡ χαρὰ ὑμῶν ᾖ πεπληρωμένη ("in order that *your* joy may be fulfilled").

criterion of style inasmuch as they have barely learned the rudiments of the language itself, much less its intricacies from author to author. But several tools may be of value: 1. A Greek-based concordance (see chapter 4) may help you find similar syntactical structures or groups of words. 2. The syntactical concordance (GRAM-CORD, see preface), though quite advanced, is likely the best tool available for surfacing stylistic elements. 3 Though brief, Nigel Turner's *A Grammar of New Testament Greek*, volume 4: *Style*, may be of some assistance. In the final analysis, there is no replacement for a careful reading of the various authors of the New Testament and discovering their respective styles.

Be careful. A survey of key variants in First John reveals that often the *variants* appear in accord with the style and message of the author. (See 3:14, for example.) This makes good sense since scribes likely wanted their intentional variations to agree with the tone of the author. Even *unintentional* variations may resemble the author's distinctive way of writing.

**Examples.** Throughout this chapter we have discussed a variety of examples of textual problems but largely in the context of particular scribal tendencies. In this section we will be applying external and internal evidence as we examine several textual problems in a book well suited to beginners.

First John does not have a particularly rich diversity of textual dilemmas. There are no sections quite like the disputed instance of the woman taken in adultery in John's gospel or the longer ending of Mark. Rather, 1 John offers sets of variations more like those you might encounter studying any book of the New Testament on a regular basis. As such, it is a good place to practice.

First John 1:4 has two variants noted in UBS3. We have already discussed the second in the section on context. Now take a look at the first. Initially, you should set up the various readings, along with their support, in the following manner:

1. καὶ ταῦτα γράφωμεν ἡμεῖς ("And we ourselves write these things")--אּ A* B P Ψ 33 it^z cop^{sa ms}

2. καὶ ταῦτα γράφομεν ὑμῖν ("And we write these things to you")--A^c C K L 049 056 0142 81 88 104 181 326 1241 1739 *Byz* *Lect*^m it^{ar,c,dem,div,p,t} vg syr^{p,h,pal} cop^{sa,bo} arm eth Augustine Bede Ps-Oecumenius Theophylact

You will notice that some minuscules found in UBS3 are not listed here. Sometimes the lists of minuscules are quite long. In such cases, only leading mss of this type (located in Appendix A.) are listed. You probably also noticed several special notations following various manuscript symbols. For example, A (supporting reading one) has ^{*vid} following it. In this case, ^* tells us that the original hand of this manuscript supports reading one. (The ^c following A in reading two tells us that a "corrector" has written ὑμῖν for ἡμεῖς, probably above ἡμεῖς). The superscripted abbreviation ,^{vid}, means that the state of the preservation of the manuscript at this point is such that this reading is beyond complete verification. These notations are fully explained in the introduction to UBS3 (pp. xlviiiff.). You should become thoroughly familiar with them.

External support for ἡμεῖς is strong. The first three mss all appear in column I (Alexandrian text-type) in Appendix A. Their dates are early, too. Actually, upon closer examination, nearly all mss and versions listed for this reading are Alexandrian, with the exceptions of P, which is Byzantine in the general epistles, and a single eighth century Italian version.

Reading two has limited Alexandrian support in its favor, though it comes in a mixed package (C).[6] Uncials

---

[6] Codex Ephraemi Rescriptus (C) is considered Alexandrian but betrays elements of other, less reliable, text families present at points in the manuscript. Hence its

K and L are Byzantine, as are many of the minuscules. However, mss 81, 104, and 1739 are Alexandrian, there are numerous Italian (and thus, Western) versions, and this reading has strong support from the other two groups of early versions, Syriac and Coptic. Church fathers will not be a strong consideration here.

On balance, the external evidence is strongest for reading one. In spite of fairly wide geographical distribution for reading two, the mss and versions listed there come from equally wide time periods. Most are late. Time alone would help account for the wide geographical dissemination of this reading.

Internal factors also seem to favor reading one. Neither reading appears shorter, though reading one in a sense is. ʽΗμεῖς simply duplicates and makes emphatic the subject already stated in the verb γράφομεν, whereas the second reading, ὑμῖν, provides an indirect object and may therefore in some sense be considered the longer of the two readings. The first reading also appears the more difficult. Both in verses 3 and 5, John says ἀναγγέλλομεν ὑμῖν ("We proclaim to you"). It is very probable that a scribe would tend to accommodate verse four to this language as well.

The text thus reads, "And we (*ourselves*) are writing these things in order that our joy may be fulfilled." John has already said that he is writing "to you." That much would be clear even if no variation existed. The difference between the two readings is one of emphasis, with the first (the reading we have chosen) bringing out the "who" of the epistle and the second, the "to whom." From the outset then, the author emphatically establishes the fact that none other than he who has heard, seen, even touched the Word of Life, *he* is writing this letter. Understood in this way, the variation is of some significance.

enclosure in parenthesis, an indication of mixed character.

First John 2:20 reads either,

1. καὶ ὑμεῖς χρῖσμα ἔχετε ἀπὸ τοῦ ἁγίου καὶ οἴδατε πάντες ("And you have an anointing from the Holy One and you *all* know")--ℵ B P Ψ 398 1838 1852 co^sa Jerome Hesychius, or

2. καὶ ὑμεῖς χρῖσμα ἔχετε ἀπὸ τοῦ ἁγίου καὶ οἴδατε πάντα ("And you yourselves have an anointing from the Holy One and you know *all things*")--A C K 049 056 33 81 88 104 1739 2412 *Byz* *Lect* it^ar,c,dem,div,h,p,z vg syr^(p),h cop^bo arm eth Didymus Ps-Oecumenius.

Clearly the two readings are quite distinct, though the difference between them in Greek is only in the spelling of πάς. The first reading has the masculine plural, πάντες, while the second has the neuter plural, πάντα. Which is correct? Finding out will not be easy. UBS3 gives this one a D rating, indicating a very high degree of doubt.

We begin with external evidence, and, as with reading one in 1 John 1:4, the manuscript evidence for reading one in 1 John 2:20 is quite strong though basically limited to the Alexandrian tradition. The twin fifth century Alexandrian mss, A and C, along with mss 33, 81, 104, and 1739 (also all Alexandrian), support reading two, "all things." But the base of support is much wider here than for reading one. There are numerous Byzantine mss and plenty of versions from around the Mediterranean world, early and late. The distribution of this reading appears to be wider than the distribution of reading one. As external evidence goes, we are in something of a deadlock, though the strong Alexandrian support for reading one is very significant.

Turning to internal evidence, we note the following: 1. Neither reading appears shorter. 2. Both readings may be considered difficult; the first, because we might expect ὑμεῖς (the second person plural pronoun, "You") to appear with οἴδατε, and thus the reading, "You yourselves know" (as opposed to πάντες οἴδατε, "*All* of you know," a less frequent construction); and the second, because "truth" (verse 21), not "all things," would appear to be the proper object of their knowledge in this passage.

One possibility is that a scribe has changed πάντα to πάντες in view of the occurrence of the latter near the end of verse 19. Yet another is that a scribe altered πάντες to πάντα in order to provide an object for the normally transitive οἴδατε.

With such grand difficulties before us, we are forced to return to the important evidence of the manuscripts themselves. Though this evidence is fairly divided, preference goes to reading one, πάντες. The reason? An alliance of early Alexandrian witnesses indicates solid external support for this reading. Still, this can be only a tentative decision. If you deem it necessary to discuss the matter from the pulpit, you should acknowledge both readings, adopt one, and briefly explain your reasons for the choice.

In sense the readings are quite different. The first tells us that all Christians know (presumably "the truth"; see verse 21). (Interestingly, Metzger[7] reports that the textual committee understood this passage to be directed against the claims of a few who thought themselves the owners of esoteric knowledge.) The second indicates that Christians know "all things," considerably broadening the base of Christian understanding. If πάντα is accepted, we must after all inquire as to what this all-encompassing knowledge actually is, a difficult decision.

Our final problem, in 1 John 4:3, is more a curiosity than a variation worthy of great attention. This is so in view of the outstanding quality of the external evidence. The reading is supported by numerous mss from a variety of text-types as well as a diverse group of

[7]*Textual Commentary*, p. 710.

versions, early and late, and geographically diverse fathers. It reads,

1. καὶ πᾶν πνεῦμα ὅ μὴ ὁμολογεῖ τὸν Ἰησοῦν ἐκ τοῦ θεοῦ οὐκ ἐστιν. ("Every spirit which *does not confess* Jesus is not from God.")--ℵ A B K Ψ 049 33 81 88 104 1241 1739^txt *Byz*, etc.

while the apparent variant reads,

2. καὶ πᾶν πνεῦμα ὅ λύει τὸν Ἰησοῦν ἐκ τοῦ θεοῦ οὐκ ἐστιν. ("Every spirit which *annuls* (λύει) Jesus is not from God.")--1739^mg numerous Italian versions and fathers.

The second reading has much weaker external support, though a variety of fathers and several Latin versions do contain it, and this may be helpful in tracking down the origins of the reading. It is possible that the fathers have strengthened μὴ ὁμολογεῖ for polemical reasons. That is, they may have inserted λύει ("annul" or even "destroy") so as to show exactly what, in their understanding, takes place when someone verbally denies Christ. The language is quite strong, but so were the heresies of the times, among them a teaching which re- garded Jesus as not at all human, but altogether divine.

**A Word About the Place of Textual Criticism in Preaching and Teaching.** This entire subject may be a delicate matter among some audiences. In particular, preachers should handle textual criticism with greatest care. Sunday School teachers have the distinct advantage of being able to field questions, provide lengthy explanations (if necessary), and even teach whole lessons on the subject. Given their limited time, diverse audiences, and Scriptural themes, preachers generally cannot afford such luxuries.

However, this does not excuse the preacher from ad- dressing particularly significant textual variations. There will always be some people who will want to know why there are marginal readings in their Bibles, and they may walk away from the sermon dissatisfied with an apparent lack of scholarship should the preacher neglect to address these issues. It is therefore very important that preachers pay special attention to *marginal readings* which show up in the versions from which they normally preach.

In the New International Version of Matthew 6:13, the words, "for yours is the kingdom and the power and the glory forever" do not appear in the translation itself but in the margin, along with the explanation, "some late manuscripts (read) ...." However, these words do appear in the King James Version, without any notice of their absence in early mss. If you were preaching the Lord's Prayer from the New International Version and failed to comment on the absence of this ending, those of your audience reading the King James Version might very well wonder why you neglected the rather spectacular ending contained in their Bibles. Conversely, should you treat the ending as though it were undoubtedly a part of the prayer, readers of modern translations which do not contain this ending in the translation proper would wonder why you had obviously neglected the evidence of the "early manuscripts" about which their footnotes tell them. In both cases you would have failed your audience. Some explanation is needed. I recommend one similar to the following:

"How does the Lord's Prayer end? Some of your Bibles include the words, 'for Thine is the kingdom and the power and the glory forever,' but others end with the prayer, 'Deliver us from the evil one.' The reasons for this difference in endings are good ones, and you should be aware of them. Generally, older translations, especially the King James Version, include the longer ending. In the days when these early English versions were produced, translators worked diligently with a small number of manuscripts. They were careful to translate as best they could what lay before them. However, modern discoveries of a significant body of older, more reliable mss, have given us reason to believe that this longer ending of the Lord's Prayer was not original to Matthew's gospel. The prayer itself is *Biblical* all right. It shows up in 1 Chronicles 29:11-13. But *Matthew* did not write it. Apparently, a scribe (or copyist) added this Old Testament ending to round out what appeared to the scribe an unusual way to end a prayer. This would have made the Lord's Prayer easier to pray, adapting it to a larger variety of prayer applications in private and public worship.

"I sincerely doubt that the scribe thought of himself as *adding* to the Word of God. He simply had a practical concern in mind. But other scribes copied him, and still others copied them, and *their* copies did eventually become accepted as a part of *some* Bibles.

"You may be wondering whether all this makes any difference at all. 'If the longer ending does come from the Old Testament, why worry about it? After all, it is at least Scriptural,' you may reason. But it does make a difference, and a rather large one at that. First, if there is overwhelming evidence that the words do not belong in *this part* of the Bible, then we should not put them there. To accept them simply because they seem to fit the context or because they provide a smoother ending and transition is simply not right. We are not dealing with a hymn or reading like those in the backs of your hymnals, but with God's Word. We must treat it with all respect.

"Second, if Jesus *ended* the Lord's Prayer with the words, 'Deliver us from the evil one,'[8] (as he apparently did) then it would appear that this part of the prayer is particularly relevant for the disciples. Theirs would be difficult ministries. Satan would seek to destroy them even as he had their Master. Jesus knew firsthand how vital this prayer was. He had seen the evil one after his baptism. He knew of his power to tempt. The disciples must not forget the enemy. Viewed in this way, the ending seems altogether fitting, and we ought to pray

---

[8]Or "evil," but that's another discussion altogether.

this prayer, with this emphasis, for ourselves and the modern church constantly."

Not all explanations will follow these lines. At times you may need to discuss such difficult matters as dittography or haplography, or the internal criteria of style and difficulty. Whatever the textual problem, remember:

1. *Keep it simple.* You are addressing people who likely have not studied any Greek at all.

2. *Keep it short.* The attention span of your audience is a vital factor. You may lose their concentration in a detailed explanation of numerous criteria for selecting the appropriate reading.

3. *Make it interesting.* Note that in the illustration above, relevant facts from the history of translation of the text show up at critical points. People want to know where the Bible came from. Do not obscure important facts with simplistic explanations. This may be insulting.

4. *Make it relevant.* The final two paragraphs of the illustration above seek to bring the significance of this variant home. If the variant you are working with is *not* exegetically or expositionally relevant, then do not mention it in your sermon. It will be viewed as esoteric and may do damage to your overall presentation.

5. *Be flexible.* There are many kinds of variants, and they call for varied explanations. Write out your comments, word-for-word. Read and reread them. Make sure that the explanation fits the variant.

6. *Pay special attention to readings in the margins of English Bibles and comment on them.* However,

7. *Do not limit your comments to variants in the margins.* When other variants make a difference in

your exegesis and exposition, *especially when you choose a reading which the translators of your Bible did not adopt,* include limited discussions of them as well.

**Conclusion.** Textual criticism is a demanding and intricate field of study, but it is *not* an impossible field, even for beginners. In this chapter I have attempted to survey the principal concerns of this discipline. Begin now to use them. Frequently consult the bibliography listed below. It is deliberately limited to titles suitable for beginning students. I have referred to these titles (and few others) frequently throughout this chapter in the hope that you will really *use* these books.

Remember to weigh the evidence evenly, giving equal consideration to all matters (both external and internal), with special attention to the reading which appears to explain the origin of all others. But if in the end you are still undecided, you should pay special heed to *external* evidence. In the final analysis it is less subjective and, therefore, more reliable, at least for beginners. Always consult the *Textual Commentary* when it addresses the problem you are considering.

Much work remains to be done. There are quite possibly other mss yet to be unearthed. New methods are being tested. Better and fuller critical apparatuses are systematically being developed. Keep watching. Listen to the experts. But do not be afraid to step out and study the critical apparatus on your own. There is a wealth of information in it, an entire history of the development of the text of the New Testament. From it we gain some understanding of what was going on in the emerging church of the early Christian centuries; from it we discover how that church thought of its book, the New Testament; but above all, from it, with tirelessly careful scrutiny, we can unlock the actual words of the New Testament canon. Never underestimate the importance of this discipline!

**Practice.** The following texts contain major textual variations. Using the criteria outlined in this chapter, together with Appendices A.-C., analyze them, and explain your conclusions as though you were addressing a congregation or Sunday school class. Be sure to check your conclusions against those in Metzger's *Textual Commentary*, but only *after* your independent research is complete.

1. Matthew 17:21. Does this verse belong in the text?
2. Mark 16:9ff. Which ending is correct? Compare Metzger, *Text*, pp. 226ff.
3. Luke 4:4. Does the verse end with ἄνθρωπος?
4. John 7:53--8:11. How would you explain the presence of this passage in the text of John? Or would you need to at all?
5. Acts 8:37. Does it belong? How best explained?
6. 1 Corinthians 2:1. μυστήριον or μαρτύριον? Significance?
7. Ephesians 1:1. Was this letter initially sent to the Ephesians or some others?
8. 1 Thessalonians 2:7. νήπιοι or ἤπιοι? Significance?

**Bibliography.** For the most part, these are *standard* texts which have served students for some time. The text by Kurt and Barbara Aland is much more recent and especially helpful, if at times controversial. Its copious lists of mss are the best available to beginners. Students would do well to purchase both it and Metzger's *Text of the New Testament*, with Greenlee's *Introduction* running a close third. Comfort is particularly helpful with the papyri.

Aland, Kurt and Aland, Barbara. *The Text of the New Testament*. Second ed. Translated by Erroll F. Rhodes. Grand Rapids: Eerdmans, 1989.
Comfort, Philip W. *Early Manuscripts & Modern Translations of the New Testament*. Wheaton, Ill.: Tyndale House Publishers, Inc., 1990.
Fee, Gordon. "New Testament Textual Criticism." In *Biblical Criticism: Historical, Literary and Textual*.

R.K. Harrison, ed. Grand Rapids: Zondervan, 1978.

Finegan, Jack. *Encountering New Testament Manuscripts.* Grand Rapids: Eerdmans, 1974.

Greenlee, Harold. *Introduction to New Testament Textual Criticism.* Grand Rapids: Eerdmans, 1964.

_____. *Scribes, Scrolls, and Scripture.* Grand Rapids: Eerdmans, 1985.

Holmes, Michael W. "New Testament Textual Criticism." In *Introducing New Testament Interpretation.* Scot McKnight, ed. Grand Rapids: Baker, 1989.9.

Metzger, Bruce. *The Early Versions of the New Testament: Their Origin, Transmission, and Limitations.* Oxford: Clarendon, 1977.

_____. *A Textual Commentary on the Greek New Testament.* New York: United Bible Society, 1971.

_____. *The Text of the New Testament.* New York: Oxford, 1968.

Pack, Frank. "New Testament Textual Criticism." In *Biblical Interpretation: Principles and Practice.* F. Furman Kearley, Edward P. Myers, and Timothy D. Hadley, eds. Grand Rapids: Baker, 1986.

## CHAPTER 4

# MORPHOLOGY:
## LOOKING FOR CLUES WITHIN THE WORD

**What are Morphemes?** The *morpheme* is to a word what the arm is to a body; it is a part of the word, distinguishable from all others by its unique makeup and function. But whereas all normal bodies have exactly the same components (arms, legs, heads, etc.), not all words have exactly the same numbers and kinds of morphemes. In fact, many words contain only a single morpheme (perhaps even a one-letter morpheme, though morphemes generally consist of several letters). Such is the case with ἐκ, which generally means "out." Longer words, like ἀνακε-φαλαιώσασθαι ("to bring to a head, summarize"), contain numerous morphemes, and frequently each in some way contributes to the meaning of the word.

**The Relationship of Morphemes to Other Elements in the Sentence.** Since a morpheme generally constitutes only a part of a word, it is of utmost importance that you go well beyond the level of morphological analysis in studying vocabulary. We certainly do not read sentences in morphemes. If we did, a part of the last sentence you read would look like this, "It is of ut most im por tance."

No, we read sentences at the word level, and that is why you look up words, not morphemes, in a lexicon. Can you imagine how difficult it would be to look up the separate morphemes of "im-por-tant," for example, and then somehow piece them together? For this reason, *the final court of appeals for the meaning of an entire word will be the lexicon, not the combined meanings of the several morphemes present in the word.* Language is not math--it involves high levels of creativity and change--and the meanings of words which have gone through something of a lengthy "evolutionary" process may differ greatly from the combined meanings of their several parts. Moreover, words must be carefully studied in specific *contexts* in order to ascertain their meanings correctly.

Therefore, reading and understanding this chapter will be of little value to you if you do not spend greater time with the chapters to come, especially the next chapter, "Words and Phrases: Determining the Meaning of New Testament Vocabulary." In fact, you may spend more time *eisegeting* (reading into a passage the meaning you want to find) than you do *exegeting* (determining what the author intended to communicate to his initial audience) if you stop with morphology. Still, even such basic components as morphemes may be helpful in discovering the message of the New Testament. The trick is in learning what to look for and what not to look for.

**Morphemes and Phonemes.** Morphemes are not the smallest units of speech and must be distinguished from *phonemes*, "the minimal unit of speech sound in a given language that distinguishes one utterance from another."[1] Phonemes are represented symbolically by letters. Their chief function lies in the formation of words, or at least parts of words. The ways in which phonemes are combined must vary from utterance to utterance in order to insure that speakers will be able to distinguish one word from the next. For example, the English phonemes "p" and "l" alone distinguish the two words, "pie" and "lie," whose meanings are obviously quite different. The proper identification of each phoneme is vital to the accurate identification of the whole utterance.

---

[1]F.B. Huey and Bruce Corley, *A Student's Dictionary for Biblical and Theological Studies* (Grand Rapids: Zondervan, 1983), p. 150.

Aside from the fact that morphemes are generally longer than phonemes, one key difference between the two is that while phonemes do help differentiate one word from the next in terms of raw spelling, they do not contribute to overall meaning. Morphemes, on the other hand, may help furnish the meaning of a word in one way or another. They are the "minimum units of speech conveying a specific meaning (concept) in a language."[2]

Some morphemes help furnish *lexical* meaning. Words built on the δικ root, for example, generally have something to do with "pointing out what is right." Others point toward *grammatical* distinctions. For instance, when ω appears at the end of a verb it tells us that the verb has as its subject an individual person who is speaking (or being quoted) in first person in active voice. Still others, especially noun suffixes, may indicate whether a word represents a process, result, or quality. The σις suffix, for example, often suggests a process.

In a way, exegesis begins with morphology. This may sound like something of a contradiction in view of the fact that I have entitled chapter two, "Textual Criticism: The Right Place to Start." But it is important to think of the relationship of textual criticism to morphology as a builder would think of the relationship between *verifying* that he has the right materials with *inspecting* the materials themselves. If in doing textual criticism we affirm that we have the right words to work with, as a builder would make sure that he has chosen only the proper boards and nails fit for the job, in studying morphology we are no longer verifying that we have the right materials, but closely beginning to look at the boards themselves to see just what they look like and how they function. Some provide support for walls; others serve as door frames; still others end up in trusses. Similarly, some morphemes supply essential meanings;

[2]David Alan Black, *Linguistics for Students of New Testament Greek*, p. 53.

others modify these meanings spatially, temporally, and otherwise; still others supply grammatical information such as person and number or case and gender. Interestingly, some do not affect the meaning at all (though they may have at an earlier point in the language). With these variegated morphemes we are actually beginning to see how the house is built, and in *this* sense exegesis begins with morphology.

Of course, we will need to view the house from multiple distances to get the full effect, and this we will do in chapters to come. In the chapter on syntax, for example, we shall look at entire rooms at a time, and in the chapter on discourse, the completed house. But for now we begin with the most basic building materials.

**Important Terminology.** Several key terms appear throughout this chapter. In fact, you have already seen some of them. You may already know the others, but if you do not, please commit them to memory now. It will make the rest of your reading much easier. A *prefix* is a morpheme (generally a preposition) which comes at or near the beginning of a word. There may be more than one prefix, as in the case of ἐξαποστέλλω (where ἐξ and ἀπό are prefixed to στέλλω for the meaning "I send away"), but most prefixed words will have only one prefix (e.g., κατακρίνω, "judge against, condemn," and ἐκβάλλω, "I cast out").

The *root* morpheme is that morpheme which typically constitutes the center around which other morphemes (when present) revolve. In the examples in the previous paragraph, the root morphemes are στέλ ("send") and κρίν ("judge"). Prefixes have altered the meanings of these words by way of restricting the "where" of the sending ("I send *away*") and the "how" of the judging ("I judge *against*"). The root notions remain intact.

*It is of primary importance that you understand that root meanings do not always remain intact, however.* Some time ago A.T. Robertson argued that ἐκκλησία, which has καλ as its root morpheme (here κλη), associated with a call or summons, no longer retains its apparent *etymological* or original notion of calling in the New Testament, but means "assembly" or "body of Christ."[3]  In other words, the focus is no longer on the process of calling but on the result of that activity, namely, the *body* of believers thus assembled.  There will be more about this kind of shift in meaning in the chapter on word and phrase study.  One all-too-common mistake among preachers is the assumption that the combined meanings of the several morphemes of *any* Greek word provide the "real" or "literal" meaning of that word.  Although Greek vocabulary is frequently *transparent*,[4] this is simply not true.[5]  Remember to verify meanings lexically and contextually, not simply morphologically.

A *suffix* consists of a letter (or letters) added to the end of the word, usually to suggest inflection (i.e., indicating a grammatical relationship to the rest of the sentence, as with nouns and verbs).  The ει in βλέπει, for example, tells us that the verb is third person, singular, and active; ος indicates that χείρος is genitive singular, and so on.

An *affix* is any addition to a word, whether it comes at the beginning, in the middle, or at the end.  It is inclusive of both prefixes, roots, and suffixes.

Finally, *free* morphemes may stand alone as whole words (καί = "and"; τε = "both"; γάρ = "for").  *Bound* morphemes may not stand alone but have meaning only when attached

---

[3]A.T. Robertson, *A Grammar of the Greek New Testament* (Nashville: Broadman Press, 1934), p. 174.

[4]That is, the meanings of many Greek words are clear from their morphological makeup, e.g., ἐξέρχομαι means, "I go (ερχ) out (εκ)" and εἰσέρχομαι, "I go (ερχ) into (εις)."  In this sense you can almost "see through" them; they are transparent.

[5]See the examples of this fallacy in D.A. Carson's *Exegetical Fallacies*, pp. 26ff.

to other forms.   For example, the ω in λύω ("I free") has meaning only because it provides person, number, and voice when affixed to the root morpheme, λυ.

**Scope of the Inquiry.**   The plan for this chapter is simple.   We will examine the Greek word thoroughly, beginning with the root and then exploring other kinds of morphemes which appear in nouns and verbs as well as other parts of speech.   The primary focus is on the place of morphology in exegesis, and there are numerous examples.   Bibliography and practice problems round out the study.   In all of this I will attempt to limit technical linguistic terminology.[6]

**The Root Morpheme.**   Our study begins with that morpheme which lies at the heart of the word.   The root morpheme is generally easy to detect in verbs, nouns, and adjectives.   In the case of verbs, remove the augment (when present), any prepositional prefixes, prefixes and consonantal suffixes added to form principal parts (e.g., σ for future and aorist; reduplication and κ for perfect and pluperfect), and the personal ending.

For the verb περιεβάλομεν, for example, remove the preposition (περι), the augment (ε), the thematic vowel (ο), and the personal ending (μεν).   The remaining letters (βαλ) constitute the root of this *compound* verb.   (A "compound" is a word composed of two or more free morphemes, in this case, περι and βαλ).   This root means "to throw."   When compounded with περι, it means "to put on, clothe."   We might be tempted to say that the final product means "to throw on your clothes," but this strains the lexical evidence.[7]

---

[6]However, for a helpful approach to the place of modern linguistic theory in the study of Greek morphology, the student should consult Black, *Linguistics for Students of New Testament Greek*, pp. 53-95.

[7]W. Bauer, *A Greek-English Lexicon of the New Testament and Other Early Christian Literature*, trans.

Παρακλήσις, a compound noun, consists of three morphemes: the preposition παρα, the root καλ (in its altered form, κλη), and the suffix σις. Again, in order to isolate the root we simply have to remove a prefix and a suffix. Of course, this is not the case with every Greek word. In fact, most do not have prepositional prefixes, and not all have distinct suffixes.

When you are in doubt as to whether you have actually found the root morpheme, consult Appendix D., "Some Common Root Morphemes Found in the New Testament." If you are still not sure see Bruce Metzger, *Lexical Aids for Students of New Testament Greek*, pp. 49ff., Thomas Rogers, *Greek Word Roots*, or Harold Greenlee, *A New Testament Greek Morpheme Lexicon*, pp. 149ff. (The latter is far more extensive in its treatment of Greek roots, but Metzger and Rogers are still quite serviceable, especially for beginners.) Each of these books contains a list of Greek words, listed by root, complete with compounds built upon these roots. Appendix D. includes both root morphemes and variant forms of root morphemes in an effort to assist you in locating various morphemes with minimal effort.

It is important to become somewhat familiar with principal Greek roots so that you can spot them both when they are obvious and when they are not.[8] As already noted, they are sometimes obscured by compounds and often

---

W.F. Arndt and F.W. Gingrich, rev. and ed. by F.W. Gingrich and F.W. Danker (Chicago: University of Chicago Press, 1979) p. 646, hereafter referred to as BAGD, allows that the word is used of "an encircled city," though not in the New Testament. There is also the nuance "of plunging someone into torture," though (again) not in the New Testament. Clearly, the New Testament writers prefer "to put on (articles of clothing)."

[8]The list in Metzger, *Lexical Aids*, pp. 49-72, is very helpful for this purpose.

seen in variant forms (βλη for βαλ; κλη for καλ). Train
your eyes to look for them by carefully inspecting each
part of the word (sounding it out if necessary) and
checking the probable root against your mental dictionary
of Greek roots. Of course, you will have to use a
printed dictionary until you have become familiar with
essential Greek roots. Fortunately, there are not that
many basic roots to learn.

Correctly locating the root morpheme is important.
But what about the *exegetical* significance of these Greek
roots? I hope to demonstrate this in the following examples, most of which emphasize the importance of *repeated*
root morphemes in a single pericope.

Ephesians 2:19-22 contains a single root which shows
up in six lexically distinct words. (A word which is
*lexically* distinct from another is one which has its own
dictionary form. E.g., πλήρης and πληρόω, both built on
the πλα root, are nevertheless lexically distinct.)
These words (in their inflected forms) are: πάροικοι,
οἰκεῖοι, ἐποικοδομηθέντες, οἰκοδομή, συνοικοδομεῖσθε, and
κατοικητήριον. Do you see the repeated root? It is
οικ, and it has to do with a dwelling, in this case the
dwelling Paul has labeled "The Household of God." You
will notice that four of these six words are prefixed
with prepositions (παρ, επι, συν, and κατα). Two of the
prefixed words are verbals and two are nouns. The two
words which do not have prefixes are both nouns, though
with distinct emphases.

Paul's point is that converted Gentiles, once distinct
from Israel, are now God's people as well, and he uses
this "house" (οικ) imagery to show this in several ways.
In verse 19 he says, "You are *members of God's house-*

---

[9]οικ is not listed as a separate root in Thomas
Rogers, *Greek Word Roots*, but there are several οικ words
in Metzger, *Lexical Aids*, p. 64.

*hold,*" a dynamic translation[10] of οἰκεῖοι τοῦ θεοῦ. In the next verse he uses an adverbial aorist participle (ἐποικοδομηθέντες) to suggest that these dwellers in God's house have already been *built* on the "foundation of the apostles and prophets"; it is an accomplished fact. In verse 21 Paul says that the whole *edifice* (οἰκοδομή) will grow into a holy temple in the Lord, and in verse 22 he concludes, "You yourselves *are being built together* (συνοικοδομεῖσθε) into a *dwelling-place* (κατοικητήριον) of God in the Spirit." Not only does the οἰκ root appear with some frequency; it appears in various syntactical settings, representing the perspectives of past, present, and future. Summarizing, we might say that the Gentiles *have* become a part of God's household, *are* a part of that household, and, together with others, will *continue* to be a part of that household--a very comprehensive description of their part in the "building" process.

Notice that several English words get at this: "dwellers," "building," "being built together", and "dwelling-place." But unlike their Greek counterparts, these English words do not all share a common root. In fact, the typical English rendering of πάροικοι (verse 19) as "aliens" seems to obscure the οἰκ root and the "dwelling" concept altogether. Originally, the word meant something like "alongside the house" or "away from the house," a nuance not present in the translation "aliens." This is not to say that "aliens" is an improper translation of πάροικοι in view of the fact that lexical study bears this meaning out.[11] It is to say that it is necessary to study the *Greek* text in order to see just how tightly the repeated οἰκ root holds this passage together, as well as the possibility of a pun with πάροικοι.[12] To put it

---

[10]That is, a translation which seeks to translate syntax for syntax and idiom for idiom, not simply word for word.

[11]BAGD, p. 629.

[12]Perhaps Paul *was* saying the the Gentiles were only "alongside the house." The repition of οἰκ in so many

another way, we might say that "aliens" is a *semantically* ("semantics" is the science of determining *meaning*) correct translation, but the repeated οικ root is nevertheless *morphologically* obscured in this translation.

2 Timothy 3:2-4 contains five separate instances of the φιλ root, a morpheme which is associated with "love." In every one of these instances the New International Version includes "lovers" in its translation: "lovers" of themselves, "lovers" of money, not "lovers" of good, "lovers" of pleasure, and "lovers" of God.    A sixth mention of "love" appears at the beginning of verse three ("without love" in the NIV), but this time there is a different Greek root (στοργ, from στεργ) and, quite possibly, a different emphasis.[13]    While the φιλ root generally has to do with setting one's affections or longings on this or that (often of things, though also used of people), στεργ has more to do with the natural affection of parents and children.    Hence, ἄστοργος, according to one major lexicon,[14] pertains to "a lack of love or affection for close associates or family."    It depicts a conscience numbed not only to material gain at the expense of others in general (as with the φιλ words), but numbed to the most essential of relationships, the natural ties between parent and child.    So much may be lost in translation, however.

A pair of φιλ words appears in Titus 1:8, where we have φιλόξενον φιλάγαθον. The first of these is often translated "hospitable," and this translation is accept-

and such different words suggests the likelihood of such a possibility.

[13]Cf. the several translations: "unloving" (NASB), "unkind" (TEV), "inhuman" (RSV), and "without natural affection" (ASV).    The last may come closest to the sense of ἄστοργοι.

[14]Johannes P. Louw and Eugene A. Nida, *Greek English Lexicon of the New Testament* (New York: United Bible Societies, 1988), 25.42.    Hereafter, LN.

able inasmuch as it clearly communicates the intent of this adjective.[15] However, it obscures the morphological relationship of φιλόξενον φιλάγαθον, and thus the heavy emphasis on *love* in this juxtaposition. The English reader is not left with the same impression as his ancient Greek counterpart. It will be up to the preacher/teacher to make this connection clear.

The same thing happens in Hebrews 13:1-2, where the text reads ἡ φιλαδελφία μενέτω. τῆς φιλοξενίας μὴ ἐπιλανθάνεσθε ("Brotherly *love* must remain. Stop neglecting stranger-*love*"). Here again φιλοξενίας may well be (and is) rendered "hospitality," so long as we do not obscure the fact that it is related to strangers, which this context makes plain,[16] and so long as we acknowledge the morphological connection with the preceding verse (φιλ appearing in both). The issue in Hebrews 13:1-2 is unbiased *love*, shown both to those who are familiar brothers in the Lord and those who are not so familiar, but (again) this is not always plain in English versions.

The plain inference from all of these examples is that students should pay careful attention to the presence of root morphemes, especially when a given root shows up repeatedly in a single text. There are numerous instances of this in the New Testament (καλ in 2 Corinthians 1:3ff.; κριν and δικ throughout the book of Romans; παν in Philippians 1:1ff.). Always be on the lookout for others. Such study may contribute richly to

---

[15]In this instance the second morpheme, ξεν ("stranger"), is not brought into the translation in the NASB, NIV, TEV, or ASV. BAGD, p. 868, renders φιλόξενος, "hospitable."

[16]Cf. NASB, "Do not neglect to show hospitality to strangers." Unlike φιλόξενον in Titus 1:8, where the "stranger" (root = ξεν) element may be altogether lost in the meaning "hospitable," strangers are clearly in view in Hebrews 13, where some are said to have "entertained angels" without knowing it.

your exegesis.

**Prefixes.**    Many morphemes appear as prefixes in compounds.   Of these, quite a few (though not all) are prepositions.    As with repeated root morphemes in the examples above, words sharing a common prepositional prefix may dominate a passage of Scripture.

Such is the case with Romans 8, where the preposition συν ("with") appears in compounds nine times and once by itself.   The verses which include συν, along with the compounds in which it is found, are 16 (συμμαρτυρεῖ, "bear witness together"), 17 (συγκληρονόμοι, "joint-heirs"; συμπάσχομεν, "we suffer with"; συνδοξασθῶμεν, "we may be glorified with"), 22 (συστενάζει, "it groans with"; συνωδίνει, "it suffers with"), 26 (συναντι-λαμβάνεται, "He takes part with"), 28 (πάντα συνεργεῖ, "all things work together"), 29 (συμμόρθους, "share a form with"), and 32 (συν αὐτῷ, "with Him").

This clear preference for "with" words is exegetically significant.   In order to see why, we need to establish the context.   Romans 7-8 forms something of a unit, providing us with two separate ways of attempting to live for God, one based on law and the other, on Spirit.   In the first (chapter 7), the commandment which was intended to bring life only brought death (v. 10), sin sprang to life (v. 11), and the result was failed attempts at doing what is right, what God desires (vv. 15-20).   In the second (chapter 8), the Spirit of God invades the world of people, their minds (v. 5), their lives (v. 11), their obligations (v. 12).   It is in this context of Spirit-directed living that Paul takes up the συν or "with" vocabulary.   The frustrated life of failures before God in chapter 7 is problematical precisely because the Spirit does not enter into the picture at all.   He is not *with* the person who attempts to do God's will there.   Rather, there is only impersonal law.

Chapter 8 then proceeds to show us that we cannot please God by human efforts based on law alone.   For example, verse 26 indicates that the Spirit assists us in our prayer lives, working with us (συναντιλαμβάνεται) where we are weak, offering our prayers to God in the form of groans when words simply will not do. In verse 16, Paul remarks that it is the Spirit whose testimony confirms and works with ours (συμμαρτυρεῖ) that we are in fact God's children, providing assurance of our place as heirs of the Kingdom.

Yet it is not *just* the Spirit with whom Christians live and work. Verse 17 links us as joint-heirs (συγκλη-ρονόμοι) *with* Christ, provided that we suffer *with* Him (συμπάσχομεν) with a view to being glorified, once again, *with* Him (συνδοξασθῶμεν). The implications of this "withness" are remarkable. It is one thing to realize that we are saved *by* His grace *through* faith *in* Him (Ephesians 2:8), but quite another to see ourselves as *joint*-heirs and *fellows* in glory. In all of this Christ becomes less remote, faith becomes more vibrant, and hope looms larger on the horizons of our thought. Of course, all of this is contingent on the equally remarkable fact that Christians suffer *with* Christ as well. If faith and hope are ours, so is the cross; if we are with Christ in the good times, we will be with Him in the bad. It is a tension-filled experience, this Christian life, but in various ways we are with Christ at all times and through all experiences.

Yet this does not go far enough. In verse 29, the "predestined" are said to be "conformed to the likeness (συμμόρφους) of His Son" (an extraordinary thought!), while in verse 32 Christians are, once again, viewed "with Him" (σὺν αὐτῷ), this time in the context of His giving (NEB, "lavishing"; from χαρίσεται) the church "all things." The mood of the verb is indicative and the anticipated response to the question, "Will he not lavish on us all things?", positive. The chapter provides be-lievers with every assurance that God has done all that He can for the church, that He has made every provision for sustaining believers and transporting them into glory.

This is significant in face of the fact that "All creation groans *together* (συστενάζει) and suffers great pain *together* (συνωδίνει)" (v. 22). It will be observed that the "withness" of pain is experienced by everything affected by the fall ("all creation"), but especially and particularly, by the church (vv. 23ff.). That Christ and the Spirit are with the church throughout this ordeal is more than a little comforting.

Not all prefixes are prepositions. For example, the letter α is frequently prefixed to various kinds of words in order to reverse their meanings. If δίκαιος means "righteous" or "just," then ἀδίκος means "unrighteous" or "unjust"; if κάρπος means "fruit," then ἄκαρπος means "unfruitful," and so on. This use of *alpha privative* is common in the New Testament. Occasionally, its presence is obscured in translation, as in the NIV in Romans 12:1, where ἀνυπόκριτης (lit., "without hypocrisy") is rendered "sincere," thus turning a negative meaning into a positive one and leaving the English reader with no morphological clue that the word has anything to do with hypocrisy.

Other important prefixes are listed in Appendix E., "Important Affixes and their Meanings." Familiarize yourself with these prefixes and suffixes. This kind of learning facilitates both vocabulary acquisition and exegesis.

**Suffixes.** The New Testament is filled with exegetically significant suffixes which often go completely ignored by beginning exegetes. Obviously, *inflectional* suffixes (i.e., those suffixes which provide such designations as tense, voice, person, number, case, and gender) are important to exegesis. That the verb ἐγείρω ("to raise") repeatedly ends with passive voice endings (ται, νται, etc.) when used in connection with Christ's resurrection has obvious significance. Christ did not singularly raise himself. Acts makes it quite clear that God raised Him (Acts 3:15, 4:10, 5:30, etc.). Hence, when we sing the hymn, "Up From the Grave Christ Arose," we should not think of Christ's resurrection as though it were all His doing. To be sure, He did say to the Jews, "Destroy this temple, and in three days I will raise it again" (John 2:19), but the vast majority of texts which speak of His resurrection depict Him as being raised *by* God.

Verbal suffix morphemes also provide person (first, second, or third) and number (singular or plural). This is especially important in second person, where the single English pronoun "you" can be either singular or plural. As you probably know this is not the case in Greek. Greek always distinguishes between singular and plural in all three persons. This distinction is very important in the correct application of a number of texts, one of which is Philippians 4:3-4. In verse 3 Paul uses a singular pronoun (σε) to enlist the help of a fellow believer in bringing together two apparently estranged women in the church. But in the very next verse he switches to second person plural (χαίρετε), calling upon the entire congregation to continue to rejoice in the Lord. The distinction is not at all obvious in English versions.

Earlier in chapter 2 (verse 4), the inflected morphology of an adjective plays an important role in focusing our attention in the right place. Literally, the verse reads, "Each (ἕκαστός, singular) of you not noticing your own things, but all (ἕκαστοι, plural) of you noticing the things of others." The shift from singular ἕκαστός to plural ἕκαστοι is not easy to detect in modern versions, but is quite noticeable in Greek.[17] Paul begins his focus here on the individual, drawing

---

[17]There is some question as to whether ἕκαστοι is the correct reading. K 88 181 326 *Byz*, several versions, Chrysostom, and Jerome all read ἕκαστος for ἕκαστοι. p[46] ℵ A B 33 81 104 1241 1739 and numerous Fathers, however, read ἕκαστος. Such external testimony is significant. In view of the fact that ἕκαστοι is also the more difficult reading, we are inclined to agree with UBS3 that it is the correct reading in the latter part of verse 4.

attention to private, selfish attitudes. But he concludes his thought with a rare plural of ἕκαστός[18] (which normally means "each") in an apparent attempt to emphasize that the entire congregation must jointly notice the concerns of all other people. Problems like those in Philippians 4:2ff. may be avoided should the congregation as a whole adopt this servant attitude, shifting the focus from the individual to the entire church.

So much for inflectional suffix morphology. Actually, it is as much a concern of *grammar* as of morphology, and there will be more about this in the chapter on syntax. But at this point it is important to take a look at another kind of suffix, the *derivational* suffix (i.e., suffixes which distinguish words lexically).[19] Such suffixes are often overlooked in exegesis. This is unfortunate since these morphemes often contribute to meaning in significant ways.

Long ago, Greek grammarians observed that certain nouns in their nominative case forms shared similar endings. For example, the nouns κλέπτης ("thief"), προφήτης ("prophet"), and μάθητης ("disciple") share the της ending, an ending which seems to indicate a class of people, vocation, or perhaps agency. A number of similar patterns were detected and classified.[20] There is a particularly helpful list in David Black's *Linguistics*

---

[18]In fact, out of 82 occurrences of this adjective in the New Testament, this is the only plural form. All others are singular. This is why we consider ἕκαστοι the most difficult reading.

[19]On this, see Black, *Linguistics*, pp. 60-61.

[20]See Robertson, *A Grammar of the Greek New Testament*, pp. 143ff., James Hope Moulton, *A Grammar of New Testament Greek*, vol. II, *Accidence and Word Formation*, by Nigel Turner (London: T.&T. Clark, 1963), pp. 332ff., and F. Blass and A. Debrunner, *A Greek Grammar of the New Testament*, trans. and rev. by Robert W. Funk (Chicago: University of Chicago Press, 1961), pp. 58ff.

*for Students of New Testament Greek,* pp. 64ff.

We do the same in English. Think of the Biblical nouns ending in "ation": "salvation," "expiation," "propitiation"; or of such nouns as "consternation," "interrogation," "calculation," "incubation," and "intimidation." Each may be considered a process noun. This is not to say that all "ation" nouns reflect a process. "Notation" frequently refers not to the process of note-taking (though it may), but to the actual result of that process, that is, the note itself. Still, these "ation" words are frequently related to some kind of process.

In this section I will list and illustrate several noun suffixes whose meanings grammarians generally agree upon. The suffixes are listed in order of their relative exegetical significance.

*Nouns of Action or Process Nouns.* Numerous grammarians agree that third declension nouns whose nominative case forms end in σις should be included in this group. The following nouns are representative:

ἀνάγνωσις--"reading"
ἀνάστασις--"resurrection"
ἀποκάλυψις--"revelation"
αὔξησις--"growth"
βρῶσις--"rusting" or "eating"
δέησις--"intercessory prayer"
δόσις--"giving"
θλῖψις--"tribulation"
κλῆσις--"calling"
ταπείνωσις--"humility" or "humiliation"

That such nouns may indicate a process is clearer in some cases than in others. Βρῶσις, for example, refers to the process of corrosion in Matthew 6:19, where "moth and *rust*[21] corrupt." A process is also in sight in Romans

---

[21]or "corrosion" (BAGD, p. 148).

14:17, where "the Kingdom of God is not βρῶσις καὶ πόσις ('eating and drinking')," but "righteousness and peace and joy in the Holy Spirit." However, a process is not as clearly in view in John 4:32, where Jesus says, "I have food (βρῶσις) to eat you do not know." To render this, "I have eating to eat ...." would not be sensible. Here John apparently refers not to the process of eating but to the food itself. As with other kinds of morphological study, it is important to verify your conclusions about suffix morphology lexically and contextually as much as possible.

James 1:17 should probably read, "Every good (act of) *giving* (δόσις) and every perfect gift (δώρημα) come from above." That δόσις may mean "giving" is confirmed by its only other use in the New Testament (Phil. 4:15), where Paul says, "No other church shared with me in the matter of *giving* and receiving[22] except you only." What James gives us is a comprehensive statement of God's gracious giving. Not only does He give gifts in process (δόσις), but he also gives them specifically (δώρημα), as NEB reads, "All good *giving*, every perfect *gift*, comes from above" (emphasis mine).

Endings other than σις may also indicate a process. Among them are μος and εια. Hence, we may render βασιλεία "rule" (as in "His rule was mighty") in certain contexts rather than "kingdom," which may suggest geographical boundaries more than the process of reigning. Similarly, ἁγιασμός may be something like "the process of becoming holy," not merely "holiness."[23]

*Nouns Which Indicate Result or a Thing Itself.* This group of nouns consists largely of those whose suffix is μα in the nominative case or lexical form. Consider the following examples:

---

[22]λήμψεως, from λήμψις, also a process noun.

[23]Both meanings are attested in BAGD, p. 9.

ἁγίασμα--sanctuary
ἀπόκριμα--official report
βάπτισμα--baptism
γράμμα--letter
δόγμα--decree
θέλημα--will
κατάκριμα--punishment[24]
καύχημα--a boast
κρίμα--verdict
πνεῦμα--spirit
ποίημα--what is made
σπέρμα--seed
στόμα--mouth
σχίσμα--division (as a tear in a garment)
σῶμα--body

It is instructive to compare several of these nouns with others built on the same root but which contain the σις suffix.[25] Contrast the meanings of the following:

κατάκρισις--condemnation    κατάκριμα--a specific punishment
καύχησις--boasting          καύχημα--a boast
κρίσις--judging[26]            κρίμα--a specific judgment

κατάκρισις conveys the process of condemnation and κατάκριμα, the result of that process, a certain punishment. καύχησις generally indicates the act of boasting; καύχημα, the boast itself. κρίσις often means, "judging"; κρίμα, on the other hand, the specific result of the action of judging. Thus, when Paul announces that there is no "condemnation" (κατάκριμα) for those who are in Christ Jesus (Rom. 8:1), he is really saying that

---

[24]BAGD, p. 412, notes: "probably not 'condemnation,' but the punishment following sentence."

[25]Note that we have included only one meaning for each word, generally the primary meaning.

[26]Though this word frequently means "judgment" as well, BAGD, p. 453.

there will be no specific "punishment following sentencing" for believers. The sentence has already been spelled out all too clearly in Rom. 6:23 ("The wage sin pays is death"), but Christ has removed this terrible obstacle to glory (Rom. 7:25). Chapter eight highlights some of the results of His accomplishment on the cross (e.g., life in the Spirit, gifts of service, purity, etc.).

κήρυγμα presents special problems.[27] In 1 Cor. 1:21 it seems to mean, "what is preached," focusing on the result of the act of preaching, that is, the message itself. But in 2:4 the meaning seems rather to be "preaching," with emphasis upon the activity of delivering the message. This same understanding of κήρυγμα is possible in other texts, including Matt. 12:41, where the Ninevites repented at "the preaching of Jonah." However, in this text the "preaching of Jonah" is paralleled by the "wisdom of Solomon" (verse 42). Thus the emphasis appears to be one of content, not activity. The people of Ninevah repented at "what was preached." This is an important distinction inasmuch as it places the emphasis not upon a man, but rather on God's message. Moreover, it is in keeping with what has been said about the μα ending.

— *Nouns Which Indicate a Class or Type of Person, or Agency.* The της suffix indicates a class of persons. It does so on a very regular basis throughout the New Testament. Since class or type distinctions are quite apparent in English renderings--no one would mistake a prophet (προφήτης) from preaching (προφητεία) in Greek or English!--this category is not as helpful as the previous

---

[27]Friedrich observes that κήρυγμα "has a twofold sense ..., signifying both the result of proclamation (what is proclaimed) and the actual proclaiming. In other words, it denotes both the act and the content. In many cases it is hard to say where the emphasis falls" (Friedrich, *Theological Dictionary of the New Testament*, vol. 3, p. 714. On the use of this tool, see chapter 4).

two in terms of distinguishing among *cognates* (words built upon the same root). Still, it is a helpful distinction since in the singular it represents an individual who is either: (1) a member of an entire class of people, and who may for that reason be associated with a whole host of class affiliations, or (2) an agent working on behalf of another.

Consider the following examples:

βαπτίστης--baptizer
γνώστης--an expert
δεσπότης--lord, master
δότης--giver
ἐργάτης--worker
εὐαγγελιστής--evangelist
κλέπτης--thief
κρίτης--judge
μαθητής--disciple
προφήτης--prophet
ὑπόκριτης--hypocrite
ψευδοπροφήτης--false prophet
ψεύστης--liar

Other suffixes included in this category are ευς, γος, and ων. Examples:

ἀρχιερεύς--high priest
βασιλεύς--king
γεωργός--farmer
ἄρχων--ruler

*Various Categories.* As with the class or agency suffix (της), the suffixes listed in the following categories are generally significant only at the level of making broad distinctions among groups of words. Still, it is good to be aware of these endings.

*Nouns Which Indicate a Quality.* ια and συνη nouns often indicate quality. The following are representative:

ἀδικία--evil
ἀκροβυστία--uncircumcision
ἁμαρτία--sin
ἀπιστία--unbelief
ἀγαθωσύνη--goodness
δικαιοσύνη--righteousness
εὐφροσύνη--gladness
ταπεινοφροσύνη--humility

*Nouns Which Indicate an Abstraction.*    Linguists classify words as either concrete, relational, abstract, or relating to an event.    Abstract nouns, words like "truth" and "love," whose meanings are conceptual rather than tangible, are often formed with the α or η stem.    The following are representative:

ἀνατολή--east
ἀρχή--beginning
ἐντολή--commandment
ὀργή--wrath
τιμή--honor
ἀγάπη--love
εἰρήνη--peace
λύπη--grief
νίκη--victory
χαρά--joy
δόξα--glory
ἡμέρα--day

But some first declension nouns, especially names, are concrete:

γλῶσσα--tongue
κεφαλη--head
πόρνη--prostitute
ἀδελφή--sister
Γολγοθᾶ--Golgatha
Γόμορρα--Gommorah
Λύστρα--Lystra

*Other Concrete Nouns.*    Concrete nouns (those representing items known to the senses) are often formed with the omicron or second declension stem. Examples:

λαός--people
μάγος--wise man
λύχνος--lamp
ναός--temple
οἶκος--house
οἶνος--wine
υἱός--son
χρυσός--gold

**A Word about Morphemes in Preaching and Teaching.**
Unless you are teaching a class of Greek students or
preaching to people who know Greek, detailed discussions
of Greek morphemes from the pulpit or in the classroom
will be terribly out of place.   Try not to call attention
to words like "morpheme" or "suffix."   In fact, *try not
to call undue attention to the mechanics of Greek language at all!*

This may sound odd to students who have invested
countless hours memorizing paradigms, translating New
Testament texts, and learning vocabulary.   Yet you need
to realize that for all your good learning, congregations
do not generally appreciate an elaborate excursus into
the intricacies of Greek language.   They are not in a
position to appreciate such luxuries.   They have come
expecting to worship and learn, and they will do so best
in language and thought forms which they understand and
relate to.   It is entirely possible to communicate the
findings of your detailed study from the Greek text
without becoming involved in lengthy, technical explanations.

If, for example, you are preaching the "house" text
from Ephesians 2, you might say something like this:

"Paul has carefully and consistently chosen vocabulary
which emphasizes the central fact that the Gentiles
are now a part of God's *household*:   In verse 19 he
says, 'You are *members* of God's *household*'; in verse
20, that these same Gentiles have been *built* on the

foundation of the apostles and prophets; in verse 21, that the entire *edifice* will grow into a holy temple in the Lord; and in verse 22, that 'you yourselves *are being built together* into a *dwelling-place* of God in the Spirit.'    In effect, Paul says that the Gentiles *have* become a part of God's household, *are* a part of that household, and, together with others, will *continue* to be a part of that household--a very full description of their continuing and vital place in God's great 'building program.'"

This explanation comes almost directly from an earlier section in this chapter.    It has been stripped, however, of technical morphological explanations.    Notice that certain words are emphasized with italics.    One of the ways to communicate the importance of the repeated οικ root is to emphasize it in your sermon or lesson.    Simple voice inflection will help to highlight adequately what was so obvious to you as you began to detect just how many times this root was repeated.    *The important thing is not that your audience understands morphology like you do, but that you effectively communicate what you saw in the text to the extent that you leave them with the same impression that you had when you first saw it.*

There is another example of how you might present the findings of your morphological study in a palatable form on page 75.    Reread the paragraph which begins, "Yet is is not *just* ...."    Of course, you would not need to mention the Greek words given in parentheses there. Simply read the English.

**Summary.**    Careful analysis of root morphemes, prefixes, and suffixes may provide increased understanding of individual words, sentences, and even entire paragraphs.

What to look for:

1.    *Train yourself to spot important morphemes, especially high frequency morphemes.*    These may give an indication of a recurring idea or a pun. Remember,

however, that certain infrequent morphemes may also be significant. Do not gloss over any morpheme simply because you are not familiar with it.

2. *Inflectional suffixes provide such classification as voice, person, and number, all of which are vital to exegesis.* It is not enough to know that a verb is aorist active, first plural. What significance might this have for translation? Exegesis? Preaching?

3. *By all means, remember that notable Greek morphemes are frequently obscured in English translations.* You may miss a critical thematic connection if you rely solely upon the English text in doing exegesis.

What to avoid:

1. *The tendency to look at morphemes too closely may result in "nearsighted" exegesis.* We do not speak with morphemes but with words. Do not spend more time with morphological analysis than you do words and syntax. If anything, you should spend more time with the latter.

2. *The final court of appeals for the meaning of a Greek word is the lexicon, not the morpheme.* Morphemes may help furnish lexical meaning, but they are not alone sufficient to determine the meaning of a word. It must be studied in context and with a critical lexicon.

**Conclusion.** As with textual criticism, much work remains to be done in the area of morphology. Noun and adjectival classification by suffix stands in need of some refinement. This is also the case with verbs. The widely spread notion that simply compounding a verb by the addition of a prepositional prefix intensifies its overall meaning needs further evaluation and refinement. The maxim seems true but too generic to be of much value. The advent of computer technology and works like Harold

Greenlee's *A New Testament Greek Morpheme Lexicon* will assist in this endeavor. It is quite possible that there will be significant improvement in our understanding of morphology in the near future.

**Practice Problems.** Admittedly, some of the problems below will require investigation at the word (not morpheme) level for full answers. You may wish to pursue further investigations of these roots and the words built with them after you have finished the next chapter, but as much as possible simply study the morphemes for now.

1. There are several conspicuously repeated root morphemes in 2 Corinthians 1:3-11. Scan that text. You do not have to know the meanings of all Greek words present. Simply look for significant morphological connections. Jot down the frequent morphemes. Using Metzger's *Lexical Aids for Students of New Testament Greek* (pp. 49ff.), get a feel for the meanings of these morphemes by looking at several words built on their roots. Now look up the lexical forms of the words which contain these repeated morphemes Paul used in 2 Corinthians 1:3-11, paying special attention to any suffixes, especially noun suffixes. What do you make of the frequent repetition of the root morphemes in this text? Are the noun suffixes you looked at significant in determining the particular emphasis of certain words? How?

2. The τελ root appears twice in Philippians 3:12-16, once in verse 12 and again in verse 15. In what two words does this morpheme appear, and what do these words mean? Do you detect any tension in Paul's use of these words which contain the same root? (You will probably need to read the passage in an English version in order to get the sense.)

3. What theologically significant root appears four times in 1 Corinthians 1:1-2 and three more in vv. 8-10? In your estimation is this repetition a coincidence or is it planned? Comment on each of the seven occurrences separately. The repeated root may be planned in some instances though not in others. It is your job as a

responsible exegete to determine which occurrences, if any, are planned and which are not, which are significant for exegesis and which are not.

4. Romans 12:9 begins with these words: ἡ ἀγάπη ἀνυπόκριτος ("Love is without hyposcrisy" or "Let love be without hypocrisy"). Some scholars read verses 9-13 as expounding on the theme of Christian love. Is there any further morphological support for this? If so, what is it?

5. Study the ways in which the δυν root is translated in Ephesians 3:20. Do the same with πισ in Romans 3:22 and δικ in Romans 3:21-26. Compare several English translations. Which seem best? Why? How will you explain these morphological connections without sounding technical? Or should you?

**Bibliography.** Only those titles of the greatest significance for what you will do with morphology at an introductory level are included. Each is helpful.

Black, David Alan. *Linguistics for Students of New Testament Greek.* Grand Rapids: Baker, 1988. Especially helpful in two ways: introduces the language of morphology, including technical and linguistic terminology, and includes complete lists of significant suffixes for nouns, verbs, adjectives, adverbs, etc.

Greenlee, J. Harold. *A New Testament Greek Morpheme Lexicon.* Grand Rapids: Zondervan, 1983.

Metzger, Bruce M. *Lexical Aids for Students of New Testament Greek.* Princeton, N.J.: by the author, 1975.

Rogers, Thomas. *Greek Word Roots: A Practical List with Greek and English Derivatives.* Grand Rapids: Baker, 1981.

## CHAPTER 5

## WORDS AND PHRASES:
## DETERMINING THE MEANING
## OF NEW TESTAMENT VOCABULARY

**A Widely Used Approach.** You would undoubtedly be met with a wide range of responses were you to survey former Greek students on whether and how well they have kept up with their Greek. A recent national survey of preaching ministers indicated that 42% consult the Greek text at least "once a week," 27% consult it "once a month," and 31% consult it "rarely or never."[1] While these statistics may seem fairly encouraging, we must recognize that the survey did not ask about such specific matters as whether these ministers had kept up with syntax, or what books they had used (grammars, lexica, word study books, etc.), or how extensively they had used them. Its sole concern was to find out whether they continued to use Greek *in one way or another*, and many (if not most) probably use Greek in connection with word studies more than any other phase of exegesis.

This is understandable. There are scores of books which contain already prepared word studies, many of them written by reputable scholars, and not a few are far from technical. Concordances and lexica of all types abound, and for the student who really wants to get a feel for

[1]The survey was conducted by Tom Tanner, Librarian at Lincoln Christian College, Lincoln, Illinois, in 1989. The statistically valid sample of 700 Christian Church/ Church of Christ ministers yielded a relatively high response rate of 50%.

the vocabulary of Scripture there are multivolume theological encyclopedias whose frequently lengthy articles are based upon theologically significant words. Word studies are relatively easy to prepare, and, most importantly, their fruits, unlike those of some textual criticism studies, are frequently immediately applicable.

**A Definition.** So just what *is* a word study? It is a thorough analysis of a single *lexeme* (a word in all of its inflected forms), using concordances, lexica, and word study books, in an effort to determine (1) what the word means in a *particular* passage, and (2) its attested *range* of meaning in all the passages where it occurs. By all means, remember that the primary focus of any word study is to find out what a word means in a specific setting. This maxim flows from the conviction that we study one book and passage at a time--and sometimes one word at a time--paying constant heed to the contextual, literary, historical, and grammatical milieu of our text. That we may also discover the complete range of meaning for a given word will be helpful as we make lexical decisions in future translation and exegesis. But this is only a secondary goal of word study. After all, the lexicon is always as close as the bookshelf.

*When performing a word study, always do so with a single text in mind. Any other approach may lead to dangerous conclusions,* as we will see later in this chapter.

**The Need for Word Studies.** So much for what word studies are. The question is, "Why do we do them in the first place?" There are good reasons:

1. *Words frequently change their meaning over time.* "Suffer," for example, has gone through significant changes in English. Once meaning "allow" or "permit" (see Matthew 19:14 in the KJV), it now means "to experience pain" or "hurt," a very different nuance.

Often, figures of speech are responsible for changes in meaning. The disciples surely did not think of themselves as literal "salt" and "light" upon hearing Jesus' teaching in the Sermon on the Mount. The literal meanings of both words were extended into metaphors. Moreover, meanings were altered, refined, particularized, even created as speakers experimented with fresh ways of communicating their ideas. Word study is frequently necessary in order to determine which meaning was most current and which was most suitable.

2.   *As a result, many words have multiple meanings.* Τέλειος is a good example. Among its several meanings are "perfect," "whole" or "complete," and "spiritually mature." Commentators have run into all kinds of snags in understanding its exact meaning in passages like Matthew 5:48 and 1 Corinthians 13:10. It is particularly nice to know all the available options before making a weighty decision which will significantly affect your exegesis.

3.   *Words often share meanings with other words.* An entirely new lexicon, based upon *semantic domains* (words related to a single *concept*, grouped together for comparative purposes), specializes in this very thing.[2] It offers the student an informative cross-listing of the *meanings* of New Testament vocabulary, with words listed under meaning headings rather than meanings listed under words, as is the case with most other lexica. It should prove helpful in refining the meanings of specific words as well as analyzing New Testament concepts. We will explore its possibilities for exegesis (along with those of more traditional lexica) at a later point in this chapter.

4.   *Since some words appear quite infrequently in the New Testament (as little as one time), it will be necessary to study them in non-New Testament litera-*

---

[2]Johannes P. Louw and Eugene A. Nida, eds., *Greek-English Lexicon of the New Testament Based on Semantic Domains* (New York: United Bible Society, 1988).

*ture when that is possible.*   Paul was particularly good at adopting these seldom used words in his letters.   We will spend some time discussing what to do with *hapax legomena* (words found once in the New Testament) and other words of slight frequency.

5.   *Words often have a specially influenced meaning.* The influences vary.   Some words and phrases seem to have strong roots in the Old Testament, e.g., "Son of Man," "lamb," and "Spirit."   Others have been influenced by literature roughly contemporary with the New Testament.   In fact, the language of the New Testament *is* the language of Hellenism.   It is not a unique language designed exclusively for Christian people.   We need to study it not only as it appears in Scripture, but outside as well.   Theological wordbooks are particularly helpful in this task.

**Additional Benefits.**   Naturally, there are important byproducts which come from word studies. First, any number of *contextual associations* may help you to see how the meaning of a specific word is closely related to certain themes in Scripture.   Κοινωνία ("fellowship"), for example, is closely associated with a Christian's *relationship* to God, Christ, the Holy Spirit, and Christian people in such passages as 1 John 1:1ff., 1 Corinthians 1:9, and 2 Corinthians 13:13.   But κοινωνία does not necessarily *mean* "relationship"; it is simply *associated* with the notion of relationship in a high percentage of its occurrences.

Second, a word study may help us to understand a Scriptural idea or theme in new ways.   From a complete word study of κοινωνία we might conclude that the general *concept* of fellowship involves sharing the gospel (Philippians 1:5), giving money (2 Corinthians 8:4), and acceptance (Galatians 2:9).   But this does not mean that κοινωνία means all of these things in every text where it appears.   The word study has merely served as a springboard into a *topical* study of the Biblical notion of sharing.   Nor will this concordance study of κοινωνία alone suffice to help us see all that the Bible has to say on the subject. You will need to study passages which do not even include κοινωνία (e.g., Acts 4:32-37) and others which include similar but different vocabulary for sharing, e.g., words like μετοχή ("partnership") and φίλος ("friend, associate").

Further, word studies often open the door to signi-ficant *parallel texts*. A concordance study of δέω in Mat-thew 16:19 leads us to examine the same word in Matthew 18:18. In fact, we discover that the entire verse reads very much like Matthew 16:19, though the pronouns and verbs are now plural. Whereas Peter is said to "bind and loose" in 16:19, it is the disciples whom Jesus addressed in 18:18 as having this same capacity. The scope of the words has been broadened in the specific case of a brother who sins--a very important indication that it is not Peter who singularly "binds and looses" among the disciples.

**Unique to Greek?** Actually, any student of the English Bible can perform a word study. In fact, he can even look up, sound out, and study the translations of a Greek word, all without knowing even the first bit of Greek. Modern concordances, whose words are keyed to brief Hebrew and Greek dictionaries (supplied with the concor-dance), make this possible. So what is the use of spending all this time talking about word studies in a book about the significant contributions that *Greek* affords a Bible student?

Just this. Although you can study Greek words without knowing Greek, *you will save countless hours, study with greater understanding, and conduct your research using some of the finest, most scholarly tools available* if you will follow the procedures outlined in this chapter, procedures which assume that you know at least some Greek. More than this, there is something quite awkward about studying a word whose language you do not understand. It is true that English Bible students can study one Greek word at a time, but that does not mean that they will understand how that word fits into the syntax of the sentence in which it appears, at least not the *Greek* syntax, and this syntax may affect the word's meaning as much as the findings of a concordance or lexical study.

For example, Romans 3:22 speaks of πίστεως 'Ιησοῦ Χριστοῦ ("the faith of Jesus Christ").  Many translations render the phrase, "faith *in* Jesus Christ," understanding the genitive ("Jesus Christ") to be the *object* of faith, and this is altogether possible for the genitive case. However, recent scholarship has reminded us that it is entirely possible to render the phrase "the faith *of* Jesus Christ," thus setting the verse's teaching in an entirely new light.  In this view, the righteousness of God comes in part, at least, through Jesus' faithfulness to the mission God gave Him.  That we must believe or have faith is the evident teaching of the latter part of the verse, which makes plain that God's righteousness comes only to those who "keep on believing."  This under-standing does not seem to undermine the importance of personal faith; rather, it enhances it. If Jesus has been faithful to His mission, believers should be faithful to Him.  Unfortunately, the decision on the meaning of these words is not so simple as this.[3]  In any case, we must carefully discern the Greek phrase in order to see what options lie before us.

[3]This problem has lately been the subject of a rather extensive scholarly debate.  See, e.g., James D.G. Dunn, *Romans 1-8*, The Word Biblical Commetary, David Hubbard and Glenn Barker, gen. eds. (Dallas: Word, 1989), pp. 166f., who sees the genitive as objective but cites others who do not, and Moises Silva, *Philippians*, The Wycliffe Exegetical Commentary, Kenneth Barker, gen. ed. (Chicago: Moody, 1988), pp. 186-87, who (with Dunn) suggests that Paul never "speaks of Jesus as faithful ... or believing ... while he certainly speaks of individuals believing in Christ," a point worthy of consideration.

<u>Phrase Studies</u>?    Examples like this one suggest why I have entitled this chapter, "Words and Phrases: Determining the Meaning of New Testament Vocabulary."  Whereas most word studies focus upon a single word at a time, it may be very important to study a word as part of a larger phrase.   In Romans 3:21, we would not study δικαιοσύνη ("righteousness") alone, but δικαιοσύνη τοῦ θεοῦ ("the righteousness of God").   Similarly, where the gospels speak of the "Son of Man" (ὁ υἱὸς τοῦ ἀνθρώπου) we would not simply study "son," but the entire phrase, "Son of Man."   In  each  case  the  genitive  case  qualifier  is important  in  determining  the  exact  significance  of  the word which precedes it.   The "righteousness of God" is not the same thing as an act of righteousness (see, e.g., Matthew 6:1) any more than the phrase "Son of Man" means the same thing as "son."[4]

In fact, no word study can be conducted without a context.  So it is that we study phrases, clauses, sentences, paragraphs, books.   Each word must be correctly understood  in  the  literary  and  syntactical  framework  within which it was placed.   Again, the New Testament sometimes speaks of the  "Holy  Spirit"  (τὸ ἅγιον τὸ πνεῦμα);  at other times of the  "Spirit"  (τὸ πνεῦμα);  at still others of the "Spirit of God" (πνεῦμα τοῦ θεοῦ); and at yet others of the "Spirit of Jesus Christ" (τοῦ πνεύματος Ἰησοῦ Χριστοῦ).   Is there any significance to these combinations?   Careful students will see distinctions in some instances.   For example, Paul uses τοῦ πνεύματος Ἰησοῦ Χριστοῦ in Philippians 1:19, where he appears to be discussing his possible imminent release from prison. Why "the Spirit of Christ Jesus?"   He may use these words

---

[4]BAGD, pp. 195-96, places δικαιοσύνη and δικαιοσύνη τοῦ θεοῦ in separate sections under δικαιοσύνη.   The former means "uprightness" while the latter "approximates *salvation*."  As for the meaning of ὁ υἱός τοῦ θεοῦ, **BAGD** (pp. 842-43) makes it clear that the words form a title for Jesus which was used exclusively by Jesus.   Thus, in the New Testament these words refer not to *any* son, but to Christ.

for one of several reasons, but two seem most promising:
(1) that Jesus had himself been unjustly handled by
government officials and would be uniquely capable of
ministering to Paul in his imprisonment and upcoming
trial, and/or (2) that, as the context following verse 19
suggests, Paul was determined to bring glory to *Christ*,
understood well that living is *Christ*, and knew equally
well that dying meant being "with *Christ*." Viewed in
this way, the "Spirit of *Jesus Christ*" as the source of
Paul's deliverance (or "salvation"; σωτηρία can be understood both ways) seems quite appropriate and natural.

(Note: From this point on "word studies" will be used
in reference to word and/or phrase studies.)

**Selecting the Right Words to Study.** Regardless of the
length of the passage you are studying, you will need to
pick your words carefully. The following guidelines may
be of some help.

1.  *Read your passage once through in a literal English translation* (NASB or RSV) *to get a feel for its
content and flow.*

2.  *Read the passage a second time in the Greek text*
(*using an interlinear as necessary*), *noting the Greek
words and syntax, paying special heed to words which
are unclear to you in their meaning.* Study these
first.

3.  *Pick those words which have a clear theological
orientation*, *words like grace, salvation, hope, peace,
God, Christ, Spirit, heaven, hell, justification,
judgment, wrath, atonement, and redemption.* Although
you may know quite a bit about these words, you probably stand in a position to learn a good deal more.

4.  *Pay special attention to words which are repeated
frequently.* These may signal an important theme. Be
sure that you are studying the *Greek* words at this
point. English translations tend to translate one

Greek word several ways, even within a single passage.

5. *Study those words whose meanings appear to be similar but slightly different.* There may be subtle, undetected shades of meaning which could alter your understanding of the text.

6. *Be selective.* This may sound cruel after suggesting that you should study words which are unclear, theological, repeated, and similar, but it isn't. You will have only so much time to prepare your lesson or sermon. No preacher would last very long should he deliver his sermons on Monday morning due to the fact that he had to perform so many word studies! Do not overload your precious time for exegesis with word studies. This is a common fallacy which leads to improperly balanced exegesis, which is nothing more than a euphemism for *poor* exegesis.

**The Basic Tools of Word Study.** The complete or exhaustive *concordance* (an alphabetically arranged verbal index of Scripture) is indispensable here, especially if you are studying a very frequent word or phrase. It is true that a concordance can be as exhausting as it is exhaustive, especially in the study of high frequency vocabulary, but there are some shortcuts which take the sheer drudgery out of concordance work, and we will explore these in the complete and brief word/phrase study guides which follow.

There are several Greek concordances available. W.F. Moulton and A.S. Geden's *A Concordance of the Greek Testament* was the best choice for many years. It is exhaustive (the 5th edition even includes lists of prepositions) and numerically codes selected phrases, allowing you to study theologically significant word combinations. But it does have some flaws, among them: (1) the amount of text for each entry is too slight to be of any real help, and (2) it is based upon a Greek text which is outdated.

A better choice for the modern student is the *Computer-Konkordanz zum Novum Testamentum Graece*, edited by H. Bachmann and W.A. Slaby. This newer concordance is based upon the most recent critical editions of the Greek New Testament (NA26 and UBS3), is quite readable, and (most importantly) includes a generous amount of text for each reference. The work is expensive, but if you plan to spend several years studying Greek, this is the concordance for you.

If, however, you will only be studying Greek for a year or two, you would be well advised to look into George Wigram's *Englishman's Greek Concordance of the New Testament*. Although this volume is dated, uses brief entries for each reference, and is based upon outdated manuscript traditions, it has tremendous merits for those who do not feel at ease with sight translation of the text. Its chief value for the beginner is that it allows him or her to look up words in *Greek* and quickly browse through the places where they occur in *English*. Thus, all you really have to know is the properly spelled Greek word, and you will be in business.

Of course, the *Englishman's Concordance* has its limitations. As I have already pointed out, it includes an all-too-brief amount of text for each reference. If you plan to do a serious word study, you will have to spend excessive time recovering the Biblical context of each reference. Actually, you will have to spend some time doing this with *any* concordance. After all, you are only using the concordance as an aid to understanding Scripture. However, you will have to spend a disproportionately large amount of time recovering the context of certain passages with the *Englishman's Concordance.*

It will also be necessary to check and recheck for textual differences between references in the *Englishman's Concordance* and UBS3. You should be able to do this fairly easily by using the NASB or RSV alongside your *Englishman's.* Simply look for differences in the text of the concordance and these modern translations.

When you find them, go to the textual apparatus in the UBS3 in order to find out why these differences exist. If the apparatus in UBS3 does not list the difference, you will need to consult NA26.

At this point you may be wondering whether the *Englishman's Concordance* is really a significant improvement over such English-based concordances as Strong's *Exhaustive Concordance of the Bible* and Young's *Analytical Concordance*. The answer is an unequivocal "Yes!" In Strong's scheme of things, each Greek word is assigned a number which the student looks up in the Greek dictionary in the back of the concordance. Once you find the number (and the Greek word assigned to it), you must look through the entire lexical entry to find all the ways in which this single Greek word is translated in the King James Version. In order to study this Greek word in all of its occurrences in the New Testament, you must then look up each English translation of the Greek word in the main concordance and, making sure that the number in the right hand column matches the number of the Greek word you are studying, manually compile a list of occurrences of that Greek word. Now you are ready to *begin* your word study. Enough said? If you have taken even a year of Greek, you are much better off purchasing the *Englishman's Concordance* than you are continuing to use concordances which may allow you to find every place where a Greek word occurs but take twice as much or more time to use.

A second major tool of word and phrase study is the *lexicon.* You have probably been using a brief lexicon in your study of beginning Greek, but it will not suffice for exegesis. The lexica used in exegesis are *expanded* dictionaries of the New Testament, complete with articles for each word used in Scripture, articles which sometimes take up several pages.[5] The major lexicon for study of

[5]I use the word "article" loosely here as referring to descriptions of meaning and usage of New Testament vocabulary. An "article" in a lexicon will have many

the text remains Walter Bauer's *A Greek-English Lexicon of the New Testament and Other Early Christian Literature.* This volume is in its second edition in English now and has been translated, edited, and revised by William F. Arndt and F. Wilbur Gingrich (first edition) and F. Wilbur Gingrich and Frederick W. Danker (second edition). It is without peer in modern lexicography, and you should have a copy of it. *BAGO*

I have already made mention of a newer lexicon based upon semantic domains, the *Greek-English Lexicon of the New Testament*, edited by Johannes P. Louw and Eugene A. Nida. This lexicon serves as a complement to Bauer and should help in the process of clarifying and refining the meanings of individual Greek words, as well as delineating the relationships of similar words. The lexicon is far less expensive than Bauer, comes in two volumes (the first, containing the 93 domains, and the second, an index of Greek and English words), and is well worth the money. It was especially designed for Bible translators (though its merits for exegesis will become plain enough) and has many fascinating notes on cultural idiosyncrasies which affect translation in one way or another.

Finally, there are two *theological wordbooks* of special merit.[6] The task of such volumes, broadly speak-

abbreviations, use choppy speech, and include numerous parenthetical remarks. All of this is done in an apparent effort to keep the book as short as possible, though New Testament exegetical lexicons are generally quite lengthy.

[6]A third, *Exegetical Dictionary of New Testament Theology*, ed. Horst Balz and Gerhard Schneider (Grand Rapids: Eerdmans, 1990), promises to be very helpful, especially in terms of its careful attention to distinctions in meanings represented in the New Testament itself. Unfortunately, only the first of three volumes was available at this printing.

ing, is to bridge the gap between lexicography on the one hand, and exposition on the other. Theological wordbooks are not lexica, though their articles are arranged around Greek words. Nor are they commentaries, though they often provide outstanding commentary on individual passages of Scripture. Rather, the authors and editors of theological word books wish to put a useful tool into the hands of the preacher and teacher, one which evidences thoughtful use of the concordance, which takes into full account the findings of lexicography, and which presents these in a palatable, theological form.

The wordbooks we shall be using are the *Theological Dictionary of the New Testament*, abridged in one volume by Geoffrey W. Bromiley, and *The New International Dictionary of New Testament Theology* (three volumes), edited by Colin Brown.[7] The first is a condensed version of the 10 volume TDNT, edited by Gerhard Kittel and Gerhard Friedrich and first written in German, a monstrous work of erudition and painstaking research. Its linguistic fallacies (which we shall discuss later) notwithstanding,[8] TDNT remains a constant factor in scholarly exegesis of the New Testament (as well as the Old Testament). But for our purposes the shorter, abridged edition will suffice.

NIDNTT came later and reflects a more current view of the nature of language. It, too, is quite scholarly and contains a helpful glossary of theological vocabulary in the first section of volume 1. It emerged out of twin convictions, stated here from its preface:

"On the one hand, theology at its deepest level is concerned with the revelation of God--the God who has

[7]I will abbreviate these as TDNT and NIDNTT, respectively, through the rest of the chapter.

[8]The latter volumes are more up to date than the former as regards their understanding of the nature of language.

revealed himself in Scripture. On the other hand, this revelation came to man over a period of many hundreds of years. It was expressed in ancient languages, employing the thought-forms of bygone civilizations. In order to understand the meaning and significance of Scripture, it is necessary to understand the meaning and use of its language against the background of its history and social structures."[9]

One of the most significant features then of this wordbook (and TDNT as well) is its intense interest in understanding the Greek language in the larger context of its entire social and cultural environment. Language has not proceeded within a vacuum. To study words with a concordance and lexicon may help us to understand them as components of literature, but such study runs the risk of ignoring the entire range of forces (political, religious, educational, philosophical, familial, etc.) which may have had some bearing on their meanings.

You will do well to purchase an appropriate concordance, Bauer's lexicon, and TDNT. You will do much *better* if you are able to purchase an appropriate concordance, both lexica, and both wordbooks.

So much for what word studies are, why we need them, what their purposes are, how to select the right words, and basic tools. The big question is, "How do I go about *performing* a word study?" And it is to this question that we now turn our attention.

**The Full Procedure.** The following steps are provided as general guidelines for conducting complete word studies. (Later we will observe what steps to take when you don't have time for so thorough an analysis.)

Please note that this model assumes that you should discover as much information as possible on your own,

[9]NIDNTT, vol. 1, p. 9.

formulate your own conclusions, and then check these against the conclusions of scholars in a variety of reference works. Of course, this does not mean that you are more knowledgeable than the various scholars whose books you will use, but you may discover something they did not mention for one reason or another. In any case, you come to the study seeking to understand a word's meaning in a very specific context, whereas they have attempted to summarize its meaning in all of its Scriptural (and at times, extra-Scriptural) contexts. Your focus is naturally more narrow.

1. Consult **Bauer's** lexicon (BAGD). It will not be necessary to read the entire article at this point, especially if it is a long one. Simply get an idea of the *range of meaning* of the word you are studying, carefully noting and jotting down the several major meanings for your word (listed as 1., 2., 3., etc.). If you are working with a phrase, see whether BAGD lists it as a major "meaning" or under some other heading. In either case, see what the lexicon has to say about the phrase. Remember, you are not looking up specific passages at this point. It is the general range of meaning you are after.

A word of caution. BAGD is not consistent in its approach to lexicography. Whereas some words are treated by *usage*, that is, by the grammatical constructions in which the word regularly appears, others are treated by separate lexical meanings. If you are not satisfied with the information you find in your initial investigation in BAGD, consult Louw and Nida, volume two, and (as needed) volume one.

2. Go to the **concordance**. See how many times your word appears in the New Testament. Is it frequent or infrequent? (You should already have some indication of frequency from lexical study, but it is much easier to look for this kind of information in the concordance. The *Computer-Kondordanz* provides exact frequencies for every word it lists.) Find out who uses your vocabulary the most often, and the least. Make some general notations. These may become significant at a later point in the

study.

    a.   It is especially important to get a feel for *your author's* use of the terminology. Together with a literal translation (NASB is good; two translations would not hurt) or the Greek Bible (if you can handle sight translation) and the concordance, first study the word as it appears in the book whose passage you are exegeting. The basic principle at this stage of the study is the *principle of immediacy*, namely, *the more immediate the context, the more relevant.* Think of it this way. When you throw a rock into a pond the ripples nearest the point of entry are tallest. As they move away from that point, they become less visible and grow farther apart. Of course, they are wider than those nearest the center and there may be quite a few of them, but this does not alter the fact that they are less visible as they grow increasingly distant from the point of entry.

So it is with word and phrase study. Study the nearest verses, chapters, book, author, genre, and testament (in that order) which utilize the vocabulary whose meaning you seek to uncover. Those passages nearest the one you are exegeting are generally the most significant. For example, if you were studying σοφία in 1 Corinthians 1:19, you would examine the word first in 1:17--2:7, where it occurs some 14 times. Next, you would examine 2:13, 3:19, and 12:8. You might then go to the lone occurrence in 2 Corinthians 1:12 (since it is a *Corinthian* correspondence), then Romans, Ephesians, and Colossians. Next, you may want to go to Acts since it contains some of the speeches of Paul (though none of them contains σοφία). After that you should go to the general epistles, James and 2 Peter (even Revelation), or you might go to the synoptics. The principle of immediacy lends itself to the general epistles (same genre), but Paul was especially prone to rely upon the teachings of Jesus in certain instances, and it might be more important to go to the gospels at this point.

b. You may have noticed that I have become a bit less precise in selecting texts to analyze toward the end of this concordance study.    Actually, once you have perused the word in your author's writings your most critical work is done, assuming of course that there is a sufficient base of data to work with.    It is a good rule of thumb to study your vocabulary, using the principle of immediacy, in *as many passages as seem necessary to provide enough data to answer your questions about its meaning.* But remember, if you do not study every occurrence of a word, you may miss a critical connection.    It is a risk every exegete runs. You simply do not have time to inspect every occurrence of a word each time you do a word or phrase study.    Here are some very specific rules which will help maximize your time.    You may want to modify them in time.

1. If the word occurs less than 25 times in the New Testament, study (or at least look at) every occurrence, again, using the principle of immediacy.

2.    If it occurs 25-50 times, at least look at its usage in the author whose book you are exegeting and, depending upon how few times it appears in his writings, the writings of other authors as well. Try to study it in some 25 distinct texts.

3.    You should always look at at least 50% of all occurrences for any word which appears from 50 to 100 times.

4.    If the word appears more than 100 times, simply study it in your author, unless he uses it infrequently, in which case you should study up to 50 passages using the principle of immediacy.

c.    As you study the word in a concordance, begin to compile two lists: (1) a list of *possible lexical meanings* (which may or may not be completely aligned with your previous notes from Bauer) for each Scripture reference, and (2) a list of _contextual associ-ations_ (ideas, themes, persons, and events which tend to show up when your word is present), again, for each Scripture reference. Carefully note the contextual associations which regularly accompany specific lexical meanings. There is a direct correlation between the two. In fact, contextual associations largely determine lexical meaning. Often, the two cannot be neatly divided. In the same vein, it is worth noting that a single meaning will frequently appear with the same set of contextual associations in a high percentage of texts.

Such is the case with δικαιοσύνη (generally translated "righteousness") in Romans 3:22. From Bauer's lexicon we observe the following meanings: (1) "justice," (2) "uprightness" (in a moral sense), (3) "the righteousness of God" as a gift which approximates salvation (a Pauline use). Concordance study clearly indicates that Paul employs δικαιοσύνη more than any other New Testament author and that the word appears most frequently in Romans (34 of 92 New Testament occurrences), especially in 3:21--4:13. If we adopt BAGD's rendering of δικαιοσύνη as a "gift" or "salvation" for Romans 3:22, then we should expect to see the same sets of contextual associations in 3:21--4:13 in general as we see in 3:22 in particular, and in fact we do.

In 3:21-22 the righteousness is apart from law, has God as its source, comes through faith,[10] and is attested in the Old Testament. It is no different in chapter 4, where Abraham's belief is credited as righteousness prior to his circumcision (4:9-10), is an apparent gift from God (4:4), is precisely what

---

[10]Regardless of our understanding of πίστεως Ἰησοῦ Χριστοῦ (the faith "of" or "in" Jesus), this righteousness comes "to all who believe" (εἰς πάντας τοὺς πιστεύοντας), and thus requires personal faith.

causes him to be counted righteous (4:3), and is plainly announced in the Old Testament (Genesis 15). There are other contextual associations which do not show up in both chapters (Christ as "propitiation" in chapter 3, Abraham as "father of many nations" in chapter 4), but the four we have observed are sufficient to help establish the meaning of δικαιοσύνη in Romans 3 with some degree of precision. It is a gift from God which approximates salvation and comes to believers.[11]

This understanding will further assist us in grasping the meaning of Romans 1:17, where δικαιοσύνη τοῦ θεοῦ also shows up, "For the righteousness of God has been revealed in it (the gospel) from faith to faith." The contextual associations here include salvation from God (v. 16), belief (vv. 16,17), and Old Testament attestation (v. 17), as in chapters 3 and 4. A further association, that the righteousness is "revealed" (ἀποκαλύπτεται, v. 17), compares well with 3:21, where the righteousness has been "manifested" (πεφανέρωται). For these reasons, the meaning of δικαιοσύνη τοῦ θεοῦ in 1:17 is likely the same as that in 3:22.

d. Formulate preliminary conclusions about the meaning of your word in your passage. Which meaning is most appropriate and why? Take careful notes.

3. Time now to return to **BAGD**, but in this phase you should spend considerable energy reading and studying what the lexicon has to say about your vocabulary. In fact, read the entire article.

a. First, look at the preliminary references (listed

---

[11]Of course, this is not all there is to be said about δικαιοσύνη. Further study in lexica and word study books will lead you to see that scholars are divided on whether this salvation is accomplished in a legal context (i.e., "to acquit") or a covenantal context ("to be put right with"). See, e.g., LN, 34.46.

parenthetically at the beginning of the article).    Get
a feel for the range of attestation outside the New
Testament.   For example, the article on νικάω (p. 539)
lists "Hom.+; inscr., pap., LXX, Philo, Joseph., Test.
12 Patr."   These abbreviations are explained on pp.
xxix through lv in the introduction to the lexicon.
They represent Homer (forward), certain inscriptions
and papyri, the Septuagint, Philo of Alexandria,
Josephus, and the Testaments of the 12 Patriarchs (a
pseudepigraphical document), respectively.

This rather widespread evidence for the ancient and
prominent use of νικάω indicates that the word was not
unique to Christianity.   It is also a good indicator
that the theological wordbook may help us get a feel
for the meanings and uses of νικάω in step 5 (use of
the wordbook) inasmuch as TDNT covers New Testament
vocabulary as it was understood in Classical Greek,
the LXX, the papyri, rabbinic Judaism, and other
areas.   Be sure to make a note of this.

Appendix F. lists the names, dates, and places of
origin of important authors and books cited in BAGD in
a convenient, alphabetically arranged format. Use it
to get a feel for the people who used the vocabulary
of the New Testament, their times, and occupations.
The list is by no means exhaustive--you will have to
consult the introduction to BAGD for authors and
titles not covered--but it does contain those authors
and titles most frequently cited in BAGD.

b.   At times you will be informed that your word is an
Aramaic, Hebrew, or Latin loanword (i.e., a word
borrowed and transliterated from another language).
Such is the case with Νίγερ ("Niger"), a Latin term
which serves as a surname for Simeon the prophet (Acts
13:1).   In such instances use whatever references are
available for study.   Fortunately, many such loanwords
are proper names and therefore will not require close
scrutiny in order to determine their meaning.

c.  You may also find references to grammars, information on variant forms of the word you are studying, even irregular forms.  These may be important to your study, but do not feel obliged to investigate every one of them.  At this point you probably do not have the time or resources to conduct such a thorough study, and generally it is not all that helpful anyway.

d.  If your word is highly infrequent in the New Testament but frequent outside it (a fairly common circumstance), you will need to study all available New Testament passages and any others you can find:

--Study the word in Classical Greek using Liddell and Scott, *A Greek-English Lexicon.*
--Study LXX occurrences with Hatch and Redpath, *A Concordance to the LXX.*
--Study the papyri with Moulton and Milligan, *The Vocabulary of the Greek New Testament Illustrated from the Papyri.*  (BAGD will indicate whether Moulton and Milligan include the word by the presence or absence of "M-M" at the end of the article.)[12]

As you consult these tools remember to continually employ the principle of immediacy both temporally *and* theologically.  A reference from a first century papyrus would be far more immediate (and therefore important) than a reference in Homer (eighth century) or some other early Greek writer.  A reference in the LXX (2d or 3rd cent. B.C.) might be of greater theological impact than that of a Greek author writing at about the same time.  In general, Hatch and Redpath

---

[12]If available, you may also wish to peruse *New Documents Illustrating Early Christianity*, 4 vols., published by The Ancient History Documentary Research Centre, Macquarie University.  These volumes are far more recent that Moulton and Milligan, though they are not as comprehensive.

(LXX concordance) and Moulton and Milligan (papyrus lexicon) are far more important for New Testament exegesis than Liddell and Scott (Classical Greek lexicon). There are lists of authors and dates in the introductions to the several lexica. Consult them to find out just when a particular author lived and wrote.

e. If your word is used frequently in the New Testament (unlike those we talked about in 4.d.), proceed through the article, reading carefully and checking at least some of the Scriptural references for each meaning. Constantly ask yourself whether the meaning you are studying is appropriate to the passage you are exegeting. *It is especially important that you be on the lookout for your passage.* Under which numbered meaning does the lexicon list it, if in fact it does list it?

You will find John Alsop's *An Index to the Bauer-Arndt-Gingrich Greek Lexicon* especially helpful here. Alsop lists those passages which BAGD cites in a convenient verse-by-verse format, providing the Greek word, its meaning, the number of the meaning under which it is located, and the page number (even the quadrant of the page) on which it appears. This is especially helpful for words whose articles are quite lengthy. For instance, it might take half an hour to find out whether BAGD lists 1 Corinthians 4:4 in its article on κύριος, but using Alsop you would simply turn to this verse, look at the list of words for which BAGD does cite a reference to 1 Corinthians 4:4, locate κύριος, observe that the Corinthians text is listed under meaning 2Cγ on page 460, and turn to that page (first quadrant). Purchasing this tool will save you untold hours in the long run.

f. Once you have found your passage in BAGD, see whether the meaning Bauer assigns to the word agrees with your findings in step 2.d. Is his decision reasonable? Different from yours? Acceptable or unacceptable? Why? Take good notes.

4.   Now you are ready to examine your vocabulary in the appropriate *semantic domain* in **Louw and Nida (LN)**. A semantic domain consists of a group of related words, e.g., *find, know, see,* etc., or *arm, leg, hand,* and *ear*. There are 93 domains altogether. Broadly speaking, they fall into four categories: (1) concrete items (e.g., 3. Plants, and 6. Artifacts), (2) events (e.g., 42. Perform, Do, and 45. Building, Constructing), (3) abstracts (e.g., 72. True, False), and (4) relations (e.g., 89. Relations).

Using volume two, the *Greek-English Index,* you need to locate your word and carefully note the domain(s) in which it appears. Based on your previous research, decide which domain is appropriate for your word in the passage you are studying. You can do this by making a guess from the glosses listed for your word. Once you have done this, and you may have to compare several domains in volume one before you arrive at a final decision, see what added information LN provides relative to the meaning of your word. As you have time, you may also want to look at the entire domain. If it is relatively brief, e.g., *Psychological Faculties* (domain 26), peruse the words and meanings of all vocabulary listed. If lengthy, e.g., *Possess, Transfer, Exchange* (domain 57), at least study the subdomain which contains your word. (There is a list of subdomains at the beginning of each domain study.) The key question in this step is whether LN helps *sharpen the focus* of the meaning of your vocabulary. Ask yourself:

a.   Whether the full meaning given by LN clarifies or refines the definition you saw in BAGD.

b.   Whether other words listed in the (sub)domain show up in the text you are exegeting. If so, what are their precise meanings? How do they compare with your vocabulary? Do you suspect that they are being used almost interchangeably with your word, or is there a significant difference between their meanings and the meaning of the word you are studying?   Why or why not?

c.   Whether you understand your word any better now that you have a clearer picture of what it does *not* mean.   LN often lists opposites in the various domains.   One of the best ways to understand what a word means is by comparing it with what it does not mean.

d.   How all of this affects your understanding of the word in question in the text at hand. Again, take good notes at every step.

5.   At this point you have spent considerable time investigating your word.   You should have a good working knowledge of its several lexical meanings, range of attestation, contextual associations, and the semantic domain(s) to which it may belong. You have probably already decided what it means in your passage and how you will translate the verse.   There is still one remaining step, however.   It involves the use of the **theological wordbook**, in this case TDNT (abridged).

a.   Locate your word in the transliterated index of Greek words, pp. ix-xix.

b.   Survey the article.   If your word is rare and the article is accordingly short, read it in its entirety. If the word is frequent, pay special attention to its Biblical (not just New Testament) usage.   But be careful to notice:   (1) whether the author has transferred an Old Testament, Classical, or other meaning into New Testament texts without carefully analyzing the New Testament contexts in which the word appears, (2) whether he has assigned multiple meanings to a single word in a given pericope, and (3) whether he has assumed that the etymological meaning (if such a meaning may be accurately determined) is almost everywhere present with this word.   These three errors tend to show up with some regularity in certain wordbooks.[13]

c.   Pay special attention to New Testament contextual associations.   This is one of the greatest strengths of the abridged TDNT.

d.   See whether the article has anything to say about your word in your passage, paying special attention to possible outside influences (e.g., Old Testament and intertestamental meanings and associations).   How do its findings square with your earlier decisions?   Have you learned anything new in this phase of the investigation?

e.   Take good notes throughout the entire process.

f.   As you have time, use the procedures outlined in step 6 with NIDNTT.

6.   Finally, taking into special consideration the immediate and remote contexts of the passage you are exegeting, the meaning(s) most clearly attested in your author, sensitivity to his intentions, any important Old Testament or contemporary cultural influences, and above all the principle of *literary and theological immediacy*, select that meaning which is the most sensible, being careful not to overlook the general and special principles of hermeneutics.[14]

---

[13]D.A. Carson has prepared a particularly thorough summary of word study fallacies in *Exegetical Fallacies*, pp. 25ff.   These three problems, and many others with them, are cataloged there.

[14]The scope of this book will not allow us to cover all of the general and special principles of the entire hermeneutical process.   You will need to purchase other books to do that.   E.g., T. Norton Sterrett discusses context, words, grammar, author's intention, background, and intrepreting Scripture by Scripture as "general principles" and figures, symbols, types, and prophecy as

Fortunately, the decision is not usually all that complicated and, mercifully, you will not generally have to go through all of these procedures. But in view of the fact that the meanings of some words will be hard to determine, this model for a full word study is provided in the hope that you will learn how to use the right tools to discover what possibilities lie before you and how to choose from among them correctly. For your convenience, table 5.1 summarizes the steps used in a full word study.

## TABLE 5.1: Full Word Study Guide

1. Consult **BAGD** for the range of lexical meaning.
2. Consult the **concordance.**
   a. Get a feel for *your author's* use of the terminology using the *principle of immediacy.*
   b. Study additional texts as necessary.
      (1) If the word appears less than 25 times, study every occurrence.
      (2) If 25-50, study in your author and, as needed, others. Study at least 25 distinct texts.
      (3) If 50-100 times, at least 50%.
      (4) If 100+ times, study in your author and others, as needed.
   c. Compile separate lists of *possible lexical meanings* and *contextual associations.*
   d. Formulate preliminary conclusions about meaning in your text.
3. Return to **BAGD.**
   a. Consider the preliminary references in BAGD for non-NT attestation.
   b. Look for information on whether your word is a loanword.
   c. Look for other special information.

"special principles" in *How to Understand Your Bible*, 2d ed. (Downer's Grove: Intervarsity Press, 1975).

  d. If your word is highly infrequent, study it in Liddell and Scott, the LXX, and M-M.

  e. If your word is frequent continue in BAGD, looking to see where he lists your passage.

  f. Compare BAGD's findings with yours in step 2.d.

4. Consult **LN**. Ask:

  a. Whether LN clarifies or refines BAGD's definition.

  b. Whether LN's lexical conclusions are true to your contextual setting.

  c. Whether other words given in the (sub)domain show up in your passage.

  d. Whether you understand your vocabulary any better.

5. Consult **TDNT**.

  a. Locate your word in the index.

  b. Survey the article.

  c. Pay attention to contextual associations.

  d. Be on the lookout for your passage and what TDNT says about it.

  e. Do the same with **NIDNTT**.

6. Make a final decision as to the correct meaning.

Some examples of word and phrase study follow. The first involves detailed study of a fairly common and very significant word. It will involve you in nearly every phase of word study. The second presents our conclusions on a rare but significant word. The third consists of the study of several words specially influenced by the LXX as well as an explanation as to how these words help us understand the focus of the entire pericope.

**A Study of** φρονέω **in Philippians 4:2.** This text begins a very specific thrust directed at two women in the Philippian congregation. Whereas Paul speaks to the entire church with second person plural forms through 4:1, he now speaks in the singular. And he nowhere mentions the names of individuals within the Philippian congregation in such a confrontational, though pastoral, way as he does here. His obvious concern for their welfare, and that of the church, is singular. He repeats παρακαλῶ ("I urge ...") along with each of their names and enlists the help of a specific individual[15] in the process of helping them to "think the same thing."  But just what does Paul mean by this?  Were they to agree at all points, allowing no room whatsoever for specific differences on detailed matters of day to day Christian living and corporate church life?  Just how were they to agree?  Is there a more specific point of agreement in mind?  This is the quest of our study of φρονεῖν in Philippians 4:2.

1.  BAGD lists the following meanings for φρονέω:  (1) *think, form* or *hold an opinion, judge,* (2) *set one's mind on, be intent on,* (3) *have thoughts* or *(an) attitude(s), be minded* or *disposed.*  We will use these to get our bearings in the preliminary investigation in the concordance.

2.  Turning to the *Computer-Konkordanz,* we first observe that φρονέω appears some 26 times in the New Testament.  It is not particularly frequent, though neither is it infrequent.  A quick count indicates 3 occurrences in the synoptics, 1 in Acts, and 23 in Paul's letters, 10 alone in the book of Philippians.  We immediately make mental note of the fact that the word is clearly Pauline and that nearly 40% of all New Testament occurrences appear in the four brief chapters of his letter to the Philippians.  It is too early to draw detailed conclusions about φρονέω on the basis of statistics alone, but, at the same time, the statistics do speak loudly.  Why the use of *this* verb?[16]  Why in Philippians?  Does this book have much to say about how Christians ought to think?

[15]Though Moises Silva sees σύζυγε as a possible reference to several members of the Philippian church in *Philippians,* p. 222.

[16]In fact, the New Testament employs several other verbs for Christian thinking, several of them in Philippians.  We will study these in LN later in this analysis.

Next, we begin to study φρονέω employing the principle of immediacy. Since the word appears 26 times in the New Testament, we will study nearly all of its occurrences.

Use three columns for your notes, one each for text reference, lexical meaning, and contextual associations. You may wish to underline special words in the third column, as we have below. In this case, the object of right thinking is underlined. Note that we have applied this chart format only to those passages where φρονέω appears in Philippians. There simply is not time to do this for every text we shall study.

| Text | Lexical Meaning | Contextual Associations |
|------|-----------------|-------------------------|

Philippians:

| 1:7 | have an *opinion* | Paul's confidence in their con-tinued good work |
| 2:2 | either *have an attitude* or *set your mind on* | completing Paul's joy; thinking the same or one thing; mutual concern |
| 2:5 | *have an attitude* or *set your mind on* | same as for 2:2; thinking this thing which was in Christ sacri-fice and service of Christ |
| 3:15 | *set your mind on* | Paul not perfected; singular concern for the upward call of God in Christ |
| 3:19 | *set your mind on* | earthly things; enemies of the cross; contrast our heavenly citizenship |
| 4:2 | *have an attitude* or *set your mind on* | continued corporate stand in the Lord; think the same thing; help enlisted to do this |
| 4:10 | *show concern* or *set your mind on* | right thinking (vv. 8-9); con-cern for Paul; contentment |

Using the meanings set forth in BAGD, "set your mind on" seems right for 3:15 and 3:19 inasmuch as these verses have specific goals in mind (though very different ones, "resurrection" and "earthly things"), while "show concern" appears appropriate for 4:10. 1:7 is pretty clearly "have an opinion." But you will note that there is some question about 2:2 and 5, and 4:2. In each case the meaning could either be "have (the same or one) attitude" or "set your mind on (one thing)." Actually, the difference appears slight.

It is important to notice the "one" or "same" thing and ἐν Χριστῷ wording is strikingly similar in a number of verses. Consider the following comparison of 2:2, 2:5, and 4:2:

| | | | |
|---|---|---|---|
| 2:2 | τὸ αὐτὸ | φρονῆτε | |
| | τὸ ἓν | φρονοῦντες | |
| 2:5 | τοῦτο | φρονεῖτε | ἐν ὑμῖν    ἐν Χριστῷ |
| 4:2 | τὸ αὐτὸ | φρονεῖν | ἐν κυρίῳ |

Since there is a regular emphasis on a singular thing (τὸ αὐτὸ, ἓν, and τοῦτο are all neuter singular) in these texts, we are tempted to see some correlation among them, especially the last two, where the phrases ἐν Χριστῷ Ἰησοῦ and ἐν κυρίῳ appear following the injunction to "think the same thing." The fact that Paul uses such similar phrases, first of the congregation, and later of Euodia and Syntyche, may serve to drive home clearly that what is true of the church in general is also and especially true of these women in particular. One can well imagine that Euodia and Syntyche might have felt somewhat uncomfortable upon first hearing Philippians 2:5, but particularly uneasy upon hearing 4:2.

But just what is that outlook? Are they to agree on all points, or is there some more general point of agreement? The immediate context of 4:2 does not offer easy answers. There is a call for the entire congregation to continue to stand in the Lord in 4:1, but this seems more a general summons than the specific object of Christian thinking which Paul appears to have in mind. Further, it is worded with second plural, not first singular, verbs as in 4:1.

Perhaps the rejoicing of 4:4 is what Paul is after. After all, it is a constant theme throughout the book and has everything to do with how Christians think. In fact, Paul writes in 2:2, "Complete my joy by thinking the same thing." In this way he seems to suggest that joy is dependent upon a shared Christian perspective and lacking when that perspective is not shared. But he goes further. Christians are to have *the same love*, be *united* in person, and, once again, think the *one thing*. Verses three and four appear to spell out just how this is accomplished. Believers "do nothing in accord with selfish ambition or empty conceit," but humbly consider others more important than self. They do not notice their own concerns but the concerns of others. They think *this thing* in them which was in Christ.[17]

We will never know the specific point(s) of disagreement between Euodia and Syntyche--Paul simply does not tell us what they are--but based upon the remarkably similar phraseology between 2:5 and 4:2, it is entirely possible, even probable, that Euodia and Syntyche needed to adopt the very attitude which Paul so clearly spells out in 2:2-4, that attitude which looks to give, not take, which finds its greatest good in demonstrating clear concern for others rather than seeking good things for self. If this is so, the meaning of τὸ αὐτὸ φρονεῖν in 4:2 is *to set the mind on a single servant outlook*, or *to share the attitude of concern for others as a goal*. The immediate context (4:3) confirms this understanding as Paul calls upon a close friend to demonstrate concern for these women in developing such an attitude.

[17]Or the sense may be, "Think this thing among yourselves which you think in your relationship to Christ Jesus," understanding the ἐν Χριστῷ phrase to indicate the sphere of Christ's Lordship, in which believers dwell. See NIDNTT, vol. 2, p. 619, and Silva, *Philippians*, pp. 107f. For a totally different view, see Hawthorne, *Philippians*, pp. 80f.

One other contextual consideration is relevant. Paul spells out in no uncertain terms what Christians are to think in 4:8. Though he uses a different word for thinking (λογίζεσθε), he uses it in fairly close proximity to his mention of Euodia and Syntyche; they could not have missed the point. Nor does the fact that he uses a different word throw 4:8 into a completely separate realm. This may simply be an instance of synonymy.[18]

At this point you will want to peruse the concordance quickly, noting any other passages where Paul mentions thinking *the same thing*. There are three: Romans 12:16 and 15:5, and 2 Corinthians 13:11. The first appears in the midst of a variety of exhortations, but it is especially noteworthy that the immediate context following reads, "Not thinking haughtily (ὑψηλὰ φρονοῦντες), but associating with the humble." This verse contains contextual associations very much akin to those of Philippians 2:2ff. and confirms the association of Christian thinking with humility as Pauline. It provides some "outside" strength for our understanding of the meaning of φρονεῖν in Philippians 4:2. The other two (each located very near the end of the book) appear as general exhortations to agreement in Christian thinking.

Finally, you should look at two gospel texts, Matthew 16:23 and Mark 8:33, where Jesus says to Peter, "You are not thinking the things (thoughts) of God but of men." These passages are reminiscent of Philippians 3:19, where the enemies of the cross are setting their minds on "earthly things." They help us understand what right thinking is by showing us what wrong thinking is. Peter's obstinate refusal to accept Jesus' destiny in

---

[18]Louw and Nida comment on the subject in the introduction to the *Greek-English Lexicon*, volume 1, pp. xvf. Though there are no true synonyms, i.e., words which have "the same meanings in all of the contexts in which they might occur," there may, nevertheless, be "variation for the sake of rhetorical purposes."

Jerusalem was clearly at variance with God's will.     He had to be rebuked.

3.   Now it is time to check our conclusions against those in BAGD.   Using the lexicon we note the following:

   a.   That φρονέω is used widely outside the Bible and in the LXX, and, therefore, that TDNT and NIDNTT may be helpful with this word.   We will consult these later.

   b.   That BAGD lists Philippians 4:2 under meaning 1., *think, form an opinion,* specifically, *be in agreement, live in harmony.*

   c.   That in some passages BAGD identifies the meaning of φρονέω just as we have (e.g., 1:7, 4:10, 3:19, and 2:5), though in others in ways other than we might have expected (e.g., 2:2 and 3:19).

This last point evidences the fact that there are differences in how we see the meanings of words, but it should be observed that the differences in this instance are not that great and that in no event do BAGD's classifications undo our observations about contextual associations and word order, items we might not have seen had we begun this study with the lexicon rather than the concordance.   In this case the concordance study helps refine the "attitude" or "harmony" (using BAGD's language) about which Paul speaks by pointing out that it is one of concern for others in the context of humility. Viewed in this way, the lexicon and concordance are rather like elements in a picture, the lexicon suggesting general shapes and the concordance filling in fine detail.   Understand that your conclusions may not always line up with those of the lexicographer, and you should always take a stand based upon the best evidence available.   But, at the same time, consult the lexicon at some point in every word study you perform.   After all, the lexicographer has studied all the vocabulary of Scripture.   He is in a very good place to make semantic judgments.

4.　　Turning to LN, we observe the following glosses provided in volume two:

φρονέω
| | | |
|---|---|---|
| a have attitude | ........... | 26.16 |
| b ponder | ................. | 30.20 |
| c hold a view | ............. | 31.1 |
| d honor | .................. | 87.12 |

φρονέω: unit
ύψηλὰ φρονέω
| | | |
|---|---|---|
| be haughty | ............. | 88.209 |

Letters a ("have attitude") and c ("hold a view") seem most appropriate for Philippians in light of our previous investigation.　　Turning to the first of these (in volume one), we discover the rather full meaning, "to employ one's faculty for thoughtful planning, with emphasis upon the underlying disposition or attitude--'to have an attitude, to think in a particular manner'" (p. 325). Interestingly, LN cites Philippians 2:5 as containing this meaning and provides further insight on the proper translation of the verse:

"In some instances it may be appropriate to render Php 2.5 as 'you should think the way Christ Jesus did' or 'how Jesus Christ thought about things is the way you should think about them ....' It is also possible to understand φρονέω in Php 2.5 as referring specifically to the attitude of people to one another."

What is particularly helpful in LN and new to our study of φρονέω is the component of *thoughtful planning*. It may assist in understanding both what Paul intended in 2:2-5 and 4:2, of course, insofar as the contextual associations will allow.　　The deliberate nature of Christ's decisions to become incarnate, take the form of a slave, and submit to the cross (2:6-8) certainly bespeaks thoughtful planning.　　Perhaps this component is present in Paul's thought as he commends the Philippians to "Think (φρονεῖτε) the same thing in you which was in Christ Jesus" (2:5).　　One wonders if Euodia and Syntyche are not encouraged to engage in similar selfless planning as they mend their fences (4:2-3).

A study of the entire domain, *Psychological Faculties*, together with a concordance, indicates that a significant percentage of the words in this domain show up in Philippians. Of course, you will have to determine whether they appear as psychological faculties. Among those which do are καρδία (26.3), ψυχή (26.4), the hapax legomenon ἰσοψύχος (26.5), another hapax, σύμψυχος (26.6), σάρξ (26.7), πνεῦμα (26.9), σπλάγχνα (26.11), νοῦς (26.14), and φρονέω (26.16). In fact, of the 16 words in this domain 9 show up in the 104 verses of Philippians, several of them more than once. The domain helps us to see just how thoroughly Paul treats Christian *thinking* in this book.

Further help comes our way upon investigating 31.1 ("hold a view"). In spite of the fact that this meaning, as LN presents it, does not have direct application for φρονέω in Philippians 4:2, the domain does however list words whose meanings overlap with φρονέω significantly, among them ἡγέομαι (which appears six times in Philippians) and λογίζομαι (which appears twice). Of course, each of these deserves its own study, but the general emerging picture is one of dire concern as regards Christian thinking. The church was at odds with itself (2:2-4, 12-14; 4:2f.). One wonders if Euodia and Syntyche weren't the principals in this dispute.

5.   TDNT indicates that φρονέω "usually means 'to think' or 'to plan' in the Greek-Hellenistic world" (p. 1277). In the Old Testament there is no one Hebrew word underlying this group (words built on the φρεν root). φρονέω is used negatively for idol worship (Isaiah 44:18-19), while its cognates are associated with divine wisdom in places in the OT (p. 1278). This pattern holds for Qumran and Philo as well. As regards their impact on Paul's use of φρονέω in Philippians 4:2, Old Testament and Hellenistic considerations are not paramount.

More importantly, the article states that Paul's goal in Philippians 2:2 is "a common mind, for which confession of Christ is the norm (2:5), in a fellowship that Christ himself has instituted (cf. 4:2)," (p. 1279). The words draw attention to the Christology of chapter two and the phrase ἐν κυρίῳ in 4:2. That Euodia and Syntyche are to "think the same thing *in the Lord*" is apparently viewed as an indication of their relationship to Christ and his lordship over their minds and thoughts.

NIDNTT (on similar grounds) adds,

"... at least 6 times his (Paul's) readers are commanded to 'be of the same mind' ... Such exhortations, which are frequently linked with warnings against arrogance ... do not spring from a pragmatic outlook which on purely practical grounds puts church unity above all else. Paul argues back to the fact of Christ, since he it is upon whom the church is built and by whom it is sustained" (2:618).

The theological word books have clearly drawn attention to the Christological setting of φρονέω, and helpfully so. Euodia and Syntyche, and everyone else in the Philippian church, for that matter, are to share a common servant attitude precisely because they are "in Christ/the Lord." The congregation is called to much more than "sticking it out" for its own sake. It is called to an obedience which involves mutual concern and servant thinking in *every* dimension of Christian experience since Christ's presence permeates every dimension of that experience.

6.  Time now to summarize, and I will do so as if presenting our conclusions to a congregation or Sunday school class.

"Why did Paul counsel Euodia and Syntyche to 'think the same thing'? Although we may never settle on their precise point(s) of disagreement, some things are clear. Paul was not telling these ladies that they had to agree on every detail in their thinking. If he were, he would likely have spelled out precisely what some of those details were. As it stands, he simply said think 'the same thing,' and not many verses later told the entire church to think about what was 'true, worthwhile, right, pure, agreeable, and praiseworthy,' all of which are quite general categories of thought. Moreover, there is no explicit reference in the immediate context to a particular problem between Euodia and Syntyche. In fact, Philippians 4:2 is the only verse in the entire letter that tells us anything about them by name. The important matters are that they are to think 'the same thing' and that they are to do so 'in the Lord.'"

"And just what was 'the same thing' which they were to think? In keeping with the teaching of Philippians 2, whose vocabulary and subject matter are very similar to Philippians 4:2ff., Euodia and Syntyche were to share the attitude of a servant, to look out for the interests of each other and the congregation, to pattern their lives after Christ's precisely because they were His to begin with. They were to allow selfish ambition to yield fully to humility, and they were to learn to give up some things in order to become what God desired they become. In a word, they were to think *Christianly*. In so doing, these women would certainly find a large measure of agreement on specifics, but more than this, they would demonstrate remarkable concern for each other even when their thinking about specific matters was *not* completely aligned."

"Please understand that Christians don't do this simply to hold churches together; they do it because they belong to the Lord, even as Euodia and Syntyche were to share this Christian perspective *in the Lord*. So many times we urge warring parties within the church to agree with each other, regardless of what is at stake, so as not to ruffle feathers. This is *not* Paul's teaching. He would no more have these women sacrifice Christian principle for a cosmetic 'healing' than preach circumcision for salvation. The presence of Christ in every believer is what governs his or her every thought, as the apostle says elsewhere, 'We take captive every thought and make it obedient to Christ'" (2 Corinthians 10:5).

More could be said. Had you worded this, you might have talked about the frequent and varied vocabulary for "thinking" in this epistle. LN would be of great service in such a discussion. Or you could have pointed out the component of "thoughtful planning," again with the help of LN. Perhaps you would choose to show specifically how you arrived at an explanation of "the same thing"--it would not be inappropriate--but remember to keep the explanation interesting and to the point. Else, you may lose your audience.

As it stands, the above explanation is fairly simple, employing elements of lexical study and contextual analysis, especially the contexts of Philippians 2:2ff. and 4:2ff., in keeping with the findings of our research.

**Epaphroditus the Gambler?** Elsewhere in Philippians (2:30), Paul praises his compatriot, Epaphroditus, as a "fellow worker" (συνεργόν) and "fellow soldier" (συστρα-τιώτην). (Note the repeated συν prefix.) In his desperate illness he served Paul well but was ready to return to the Philippians, who apparently sent him in their place (2:30). Near the end of his praise for this man, Paul mentions that Epaphroditus "neared death because of the work of Christ when he *risked* his life..." to do what the Philippians could not. Our question concerns the meaning of παραβολευσάμενος, translated "risked" ("risking" in the NIV). Precisely what kind of risk had Epaphroditus taken? Was he "gambling" with his life, as Harrington C. Lees suggested long ago?[19] Finding out is complicated by the fact that this word, the subject of

---

[19]"Entre nous," *Expository Times* 37 (1925-26):46. Lees observed that "Epaphroditus" sounds very much like "Aphrodite," the Greek goddess of gambling. He sees a pun in Paul's choice of παραβολεύομαι. "He (Paul) says Epaphroditus gambled with his life, but won, because God was there and 'had mercy on him.'"

our second example of word study, occurs only once in the New Testament and once outside it.

BAGD (p. 612) immediately alerts us to the fact that παραβολεύομαι is rare. In fact, the only attestation given in the parentheses immediately following it is a single second century inscription. The lexicon then provides the meanings "expose to danger" and "risk," followed by the Greek and English of the ancient inscription, "but also to the ends of the earth witness was borne to him that in the interests of friendship he exposed himself to dangers by his aid in [legal] strife, [taking his clients' cases] even up to the emperors." The translation is followed by a reference to Adolf Deissmann, *Light from the Ancient East*, whose research turned up this reference, together with a number of references to παραβάλλω, a word whose meaning is similar to παραβολεύομαι. Finally, BAGD lists Philippians 2:30 and closes with "M-M.*" ("M-M" telling us that Moulton and Milligan cite παραβολεύομαι in *The Vocabulary of the Greek New Testament*, and the asterisk indicating that BAGD's article lists every reference to παραβολεύομαι present in the literature examined in the preparation of this lexicon).

Several procedural conclusions are obvious. 1. We will have to go beyond BAGD in search of any other leads as to the meaning of παραβολεύομαι. 2. In view of the the fact that BAGD lists *every* reference to παραβολεύομαι in the New Testament and related literature, the Septuagint (LXX) will not be of any assistance here. BAGD does not list it. 3. We should at least consult Liddell and Scott, *A Greek-English Lexicon*, and Moulton and Milligan, *The Vocabulary of the Greek New Testament* (per step 3.d. in the guide for full word studies).

Liddell and Scott (p. 1305) do not cite any references beyond those we have already seen in BAGD. However, because of the convenient morphological arrangement of entries in this lexicon, we can see at a glance that παραβολᾶνοι were "persons who risk(ed) their lives as sick-nurses," whereas παραβολεύομαι simply means "venture, expose oneself." Comparing these meanings with the inscription BAGD cites from Deissmann, we observe that physical risk appears to be a feature of the παραβολ-vocabulary.

Moulton and Milligan (p. 480), like Liddell and Scott, do not cite any new references to παραβολεύομαι, but they do provide some interesting details. For example, they observe that the Olbian inscription cited by Deissmann was "under no suspicion of appropriating a coinage of a NT writer," thus indicating that the author of the inscription had probably come by this vocabulary in non-Christian circles. M-M further indicate that παραβολεύομαι "is from παράβολος, 'venturesome,' the verbal part expressing the energy of βάλλω, instead of being static as in παραβολή."

When we place the observations from BAGD, Liddell and Scott, and M-M into the grid of contextual associations present in Philippians 2:30, answers are forthcoming. In both Philippians and the second century inscription, the subject of παραβολεύομαι risks his life for a friend; in both, he has travelled extensively to do so; in both, he apparently exposes himself to a life threatening situation. Thus, we conclude that παραβολεύομαι means "to place one's physical well being at extreme risk," with emphasis upon extensive travel for the sake of a friend. Further confirming this understanding is the observation of LN, namely, that παραβολεύομαι means "to risk one's life" (21.7).

Does παραβολεύομαι ever mean "gambling"? Not in any literature that I could find. Lees' claim appears to be unsubstantiated. Only upon researching further references to this word, references which do not appear to be forthcoming, can we conclude that the word means "to gamble." It is best to stop short of conjectural conclusions of this sort.

**Old Testament Influences.** The New Testament is filled with quotes from the Old Testament, but it also contains many allusions, some of them clearer than others. Words like "lamb" and "servant" plainly have a distinctive background in the Old Testament, while the significance of "earthquake" and "stone" may not be so obvious. A glance at any of these words using Hatch and Redpath[20] will turn up several passages for examination. Often, you will discover that these Greek words have more than one Hebrew counterpart in the Old Testament.[21] It is not crucial that you study the Hebrew word(s), though such a study may prove helpful, especially as you continue to refine your skills. What really matters at this level is that you carefully examine the Greek vocabulary as it was employed and shaped by Septuagintal translators in the second and third centuries B.C.

Rather than performing a study on a single word in the Septuagint (or LXX), we will be looking at several words in this third study, an examination of significant ideas present in Matthew 24 and its parallels, Mark 13 and Luke 21. Concordance analysis suggests that these words (war, distress, famine, sword, etc.) form a regular vocabulary of enormous distress, employed by various Old Testament prophets, used to pronounce judgment upon Israel, Judah, and/or the nations, and especially on the city of Jerusalem. Our conclusion? Jesus employs the regular prophetic terminology of judgment to inform his hearers that Jerusalem will again be destroyed (as it turns out, in A.D. 70) in view of her sinfulness (Matthew 23:37-39; Luke 21:20-22). The language of Matthew 24:4ff. is a voice from the prophetic past, one that should plainly be

---

[20]*A Concordance to the Septuagint and Other Greek Versions of the Old Testament*, 2 vols (Graz: Akademische Druck-u. Verlagsanstalt, 1975; reprint, Grand Rapids: Baker, 1983).

[21]See, e.g., Leon Crouch's study of ἁρπάζω in "Greek Word Studies" in *Biblical Interpretation: Principles and Practice*, Furman Kearley, Edward Myers, and Timothy Hadley, eds. (Grand Rapids: Baker, 1986), pp. 230-31.

understood by its ancient readers.[22]

Obviously, Matthew 24 also speaks of Christ's second coming, especially in verses 36ff.[23]   There are other indications in verses 14 and 29-31, and chapter 25 is no doubt eschatological.   So Jesus prophesies on two fronts in this chapter, the destruction of Jerusalem in A.D. 70 *and* the second coming.   What will happen to Jerusalem appears to foreshadow a later coming, the return of the Lord, and the events accompanying the end of time. Apparently, this is why Jesus has woven these two events together into a single discourse.

In verse 2, after the disciples have drawn attention to the buildings of the temple, Jesus remarks that there will not be "stone upon stone" (λίθος ἐπὶ λίθος; cf. Habakkuk 2:16) which will not be destroyed.   The words are reminiscent of Lamentations 4:1, "The sacred stones have been poured forth at the top of all the streets,"[24] as the prophet laments the awful condition of his beloved Jerusalem after the destruction in 586 B.C.   Jesus' similar emphasis upon the fallen stones of the temple sets

---

[22]Matthew 24:15 even reads, "Let the reader understand," in reference to the "abomination of desolation," a clear reference to Daniel 9:27 et al.

[23]See practice problem number 2 on page 214.

[24]Quote from C.L. Brenton, *The Septuagint with Apocrypha: Greek and English* (London: Samuel Bagster & Sons, 1851; reprint ed., Peabody, Maryland: Hendrickson Publishers, 1986).   (Future LXX quotes will also come from this edition.)   This is the LXX edition that you should use in connection with your studies in Hatch and Redpath.   It is not a critical edition, but it will do nicely for word studies in the LXX, and, of course, it contains an English translation for your convenience. Never use a standard English translation of the Hebrew text, such as the NIV,   when doing word studies from the Greek Old Testament.   There are significant differences between the Hebrew and Greek Old Testaments.

the tone for what follows.

He speaks of "wars" in verse 6, obviously a primary idea in this destruction matrix. What is interesting is the fact that the prophets regularly couple war with other elements present in Matthew 24. Among these couplings are war and false prophets (Micah 3:5), war and famine (Jeremiah 18:21), and war, pestilence, famine, and fleeing to the mountains (Ezekiel 7:16). Especially significant is Daniel 9:25ff., where war appears alongside the "abomination of desolation" (mentioned in Matthew 24:15), the destruction of the city and sanctuary, and other atrocities. Moreover, the words "nation upon nation and kingdom upon kingdom" (Matthew 24:7) are closely paralleled in 2 Chronicles 15:6 and Isaiah 19:2, both of which are descriptive of divine judgments which took place in Old Testament times.

"Famine" (Matthew 24:7) is everywhere present in the Old Testament destruction vocabulary. See especially Jeremiah 5:12, 14:12, 15:2, 16:4, 18:21, 21:7, 24:10, 39:24 (LXX),[25] 45:2 (LXX), 42:16, 44:12-13 (LXX), 49:16, and 52:6. In each of these passages λίμος or λίμοι is in some way seen in connection with possible or actual judgment upon Judah and/or Israel for a variety of sins.

Other elements present include "earthquake" (σείσμος, verse 7) in Amos 2:13-16, 5:18-20, Isaiah 2:6ff., and Jeremiah 10:22, "tribulation" (θλῖψις, verse 9) in Jeremiah 6:24 and Ezekiel 12:18, "false prophets" (ψευδοπρο-φῆται, verses 11 and 24) in Jeremiah 6:13 (LXX), 33:7-16, and 34:9, "lawlessness" (ἀνόμια, verse 12) in Zephaniah 1:9, Jeremiah 36:39 (LXX), Lamentations 4:6, Ezekiel

[25]The reference numbering systems in the LXX and English translations from the Hebrew Old Testament differ frequently. Hatch and Redpath alert you to this by first indicating the LXX reference and then the appropriate chapter and/or verse from the Hebrew text in parentheses, e.g., Jeremiah 39(32):24.

8:6-17 et al., "the abomination of desolation" (τὸ βδέλυγμα τῆς ἐρημώσεως, verse 15) in Daniel 9:27 and 11:31, and in 1 Maccabees 1:54ff.,[26] "fleeing (from Jerusalem)" (φευγέτωσαν, verse 16) in Isaiah 22:3 and Jeremiah 4:6, and "hills (as a place of refuge)" (τὰ ὄρη, verse 16) in Ezekiel 7:16. Still others could be mentioned, but these should be enough to establish the existence of this prophetic vocabulary employed by Jesus. The conclusion that Jesus was saying that Israel would be humbled again seems reasonable in view of the fact that this judgment language was likely familiar to the Jews of his day and that Jerusalem did indeed fall to the Romans in A.D. 70.

The study is significant inasmuch as some students of Matthew 24 par. see verses 4ff. as referring exclusively to events associated with the end of time, especially the worldwide Great Tribulation which will transpire just prior to Christ's return.[27] That there will be such a tribulation is much clearer from 2 Thessalonians 2:1ff.

[26]Hatch and Redpath concord the apocryphal writings for a helpful understanding of Greek vocabulary in the inter-testamental period. "Abomination of desolation" is particularly interesting inasmuch as the writer of 1 Maccabees applied it to the erection of a heathen altar, perhaps to Zeus, in the Jerusalem temple at the leading of Antiochus Epiphanes in 164 B.C.

[27]See, e.g., John F. Walvoord, *Matthew: Thy Kingdom Come* (Chicago: Moody, 1974), pp. 180ff. D.A. Carson surveys a number of views in *The Expositor's Bible Commentary*, volume 8: *Matthew, Mark, Luke* (Grand Rapids: Zondervan, 1984), pp. 488ff. See especially his discussion of the dispensationalists, who see vv. 4-28 as referring to the Great Tribulation and vv. 36-40 to the secret "Rapture" of the church (p. 494), and Lagrange, Schlatter, Schniewind, etc., a very different group of scholars, who deny that "any part of the Olivet Discourse deals with the Fall of Jerusalem" but, rather, has to do with the Parousia (p. 492).

than from Matthew 24:4ff., especially when the latter is compared with its parallel account in Luke 21:20-24, an account whose interest singularly points to the Fall of Jerusalem.[28] Moreover, when Jesus says that "this generation[28] will not pass away until all these things take place" (verse 34), he plainly refers to an event which would take place within 40 years or so of this prophecy.

Granted, there is no possibility of satisfying all of the requirements of exegeting a demanding text like Matthew 24 in an elementary Greek textbook such as this.[29] But that is not what we are after. What you need to see is the pervasiveness of the Old Testament prophetic influence upon Jesus' own prophecy. It is easy to pick up an English Bible and read of famine, earthquake and the like, all in Matthew 24 par., and, listening to the evening news, come to the conclusion that the whole chapter refers exclusively to current events. What is not so easy is the concordance work which might lead us to conclude that Jesus was saying much the same thing as the prophets before him, and with specific reference to Jerusalem--again. Keep in mind that the New Testament

---

[28]BAGD's application of γενεά ("generation") as "the whole contemporaneous generation of Jews as a uniform mass confronting him (Jesus)," p. 154, is probably correct. Putting it differently, "this generation" refers to the very Jews who were eventually responsible for the crucifixion of Christ.

[29]It could be pointed out, for example, that this same prophetic terminology is sometimes used in the book of Revelation with reference to events other than the Fall of Jerusalem. It should be noted, however, that the context of Matthew 24 is quite specific. The disciples first asked about the fate of the historic city and only secondly about the sign of Christ's coming and the end of the age. Jesus seems (generally, at least) to answer the questions in turn.

quotes and alludes to the Old repeatedly. Never ignore, or even minimize, its possible influence on the vocabulary of the New Testament. How you interpret that influence may vary from text to text (not to mention, person to person), but you should always be aware of it.

**Maximizing the Use of the Lexicon.** Hypothetical questions regarding which tool we might use if no others were available are rather like asking a classical music buff to decide between Mozart and Beethoven. You might get an answer, but what would the world of music be without Mozart *or* Beethoven? Thankfully, we exegetes are not reduced to a concordance or a lexicon, but if put to that test BAGD would be our choice. This may sound contradictory since I have used the word "indispesable" in an earlier description of the concordance. But BAGD frequently contains every occurrence for a given word in the New Testament; actually, it does so far more often than not. What is more, BAGD regularly cites non-New Testament documents. As such, it is both a lexicon and a concordance, in a sense. In BAGD, a single asterisk (*) at the end of an article indicates that all the passages in which the word occurs in ancient Christian literature are given in the article; double asterisks (**) indicate that all New Testament passages are cited.

You may be wondering why the question is important in the first place. Simply put, full word studies take considerable time. To be sure, the more you do them the faster you will become, but they always take time. Therefore, it is important to know how to implement some shortcuts when you simply do not have adequate time for the full procedure. Learning which tool(s) to use and how to use them is critical in this abbreviated approach.

**Table 5.2:**
**A Quick Guide for Word Study.**

1. Once you have selected a word in a specific text, read and reread that text. Also become familiar with the context.
2. Consult BAGD.

    a.    Check the range of attestation.

    b.    Peruse the several major meanings, immediately asking which one best suits your text and context.

    c.    Be on the lookout for your passage in particular.

    d.    Make a decision regarding meaning. If you do not have enough information to do this:

        (1)    Look up several passages listed in BAGD, using the principle of immediacy.

        (2)    Check for significant contextual associations and possible meanings.

    e.    If you are still undecided, proceed to step 3.

3.    Determine which tool, beyond BAGD, you should use.

    a.    If you feel you simply have not seen enough of the New Testament, especially in the case of a frequent word, go to the concordance, again, using the principle of immediacy.

    b.    If you sense that the word needs further investigation in a non-New Testament document:

        (1)    Look it up in Hatch and Redpath for LXX occurrences.

        (2)    Study it in TDNT or NIDNTT otherwise.

    c.    If the term is concrete, e.g., house, boat, fish, or a proper name, study it in TDNT or NIDNTT.[30] These books are well suited for

---

[30]See Moises Silva, *Biblical Words and Their Meanings: An Introduction to Lexical Semantics* (Grand Rapids: Zondervan, 1983), pp. 101-108, for a more technically precise explanation of which words are most appropriate for study in TDNT. He does not use the word "concrete" at all, but speaks of words as either "fully, mostly, partly, or non-referential." To say that a word is "referential" is to say that it is associated with some "extra-linguistic reality." Proper names are highly referential since they refer to specific people. Hence, Silva sees "Plato" as highly referential. However, the adjective "beautiful" is non-referential. Summarizing,

such study.

d. If, on the other hand, the term does not fit into this category, be sure to look at LN and compare your word with other, similar words. See whether they help clarify the meaning of the word you are analyzing.

4. At this point you should be able to make a final decision.

## Practical Suggestions for the Preacher and Teacher.

What to do:

1. _Allow the word study to help write the sermon for you._ The beauty of word studies is that they flow right out of the text itself. They are not contrived, not filler, but the very stuff of which the sermon is made. Word studies are heavy on content, providing the audience with something to really chew on.

2. _Remember to conduct your studies from the Greek text._ Even the best preachers frequently rely upon English etymologies to explain the Biblical text. English etymologies are fine for studying the development of an English word, but they do not have much to do with Greek words as they were used and understood 2,000 years ago. Always allow the text and context to dictate what you will and will not say about a given word.

3. _Memorize the principles and procedures for selecting the right words to study_ in order to insure that you use your time efficiently. If a word is unclear to you, and therefore merits close study, it will likely be unclear to your audience. A thoughtful explanation is appropriate. If a word is theologically loaded, it will repay careful study in significant content in your presentation. If the word is re-

then, the clearer the referent the greater the benefit of TDNT.

peated, it merits consideration as well. Do not waste time with words whose meanings are obvious or marginally important.

4. *Present as much of the study as is needed to recreate the flavor of your word.* I vividly recall hearing a student preacher go on and on about the Classical, Septuagintal, and Rabbinic nuances of a Greek word in a sermon he preached some years ago. Unfortunately, he never attempted to make any connection between these meanings and his text. I do not remember what the word was, but I do recall how put off the audience was. Be as precise and to the point as possible. Strive for relevance.

5. *Study authors who know how to make the most of word studies.* There is an especially fine, succinct study of ἀγάπη in James Dunn's new commentary on Romans.[31] You should take a close look at it. Again, Leon Morris' new commentary on the same book is packed from cover to cover with relevant and helpful word studies.[32] There are numerous authors whose works are exemplary.[33] Always pay attention to the mechanics of their studies.

6. *Remember to study the entire phrase or clause in which your word appears.* Our word study of φρονέω, for example, involved careful analysis of the phrases "the same thing" and "in the Lord." In fact, these phrases played a major role in helping us understand

---

[31]The *Word Biblical Commentary*, vol. 38a, p. 739.

[32]Leon Morris, *The Epistle to the Romans* (Grand Rapids: Eerdmans, 1988).

[33]I am particularly impressed with the writings of D.A. Carson and I. Howard Marshall, whose commentaries on Matthew, in the Expositor's series, and Luke, in the New International Greek Commentary Series, respectively, are quite good.

precisely what and how Euodia and Syntyche were to think.

What Not to Do:

1. *Do not overdo a good thing*. Remember, word study is only one phase in the entire process of understanding the text. Generally speaking, it is not good to build an entire sermon outline on word studies. There may be exceptions, e.g., the lists of virtues and vices in Paul, but do not overdo it. This is an all-too-common mistake.

2. *Do not etymologize*.[34] That is, do not impose the etymological (or original) meaning, often the first one listed in the lexicon or the word study book, upon your word in every text where it occurs. Preachers who often talk about the "real" or "literal" meaning of a Greek word are usually etymologizing. It is as though the translation they use is incapable of making the Greek text understandable. Actually, what they are generally doing is translating what is already understandable and accurate into something which may well be understandable, but is miserably inaccurate. This whole procedure is wrong-headed and smacks against the principle of immediacy and the notion that words have meaning in specific contexts.

3. *Do not overload word meanings*. Had we concluded that φρονέω meant "have an attitude," "ponder," and "honor," all in Philippians 4:2, we would have concluded too much. Words have specific meanings in given contexts. A seminary professor once informed me of a student who prepared a word study on the 7 trumpets in Revelation 8-9. The student concluded that there were some 20 distinct nuances for σάλπιγξ in the Bible, all of which were present in that

---

[34] A word whose meaning is discussed at length, with numerous examples, in James Barr's *The Semantics of Biblical Language*, pp. 107ff.

passage, a remarkable conclusion! Avoid such generalizations. They are easy, and appear very preachable, but language simply does not work that way.

4.   On the other hand, *do not conclude that a single word always means the same thing.* This, too, is a fairly common fallacy. Back of it lies the linguistic presupposition that word meanings do not change. A quick glance at any major lexicon will quickly dispel such a notion.

5.   *Finally, remember not to get too technical.* What is obvious to you may not be so plain to your audience. Even words like "etymology" and "lexicon" may not make a bit of sense to them. Do not assume too much.

**Conclusion.**    Our approach to word study is heavily weighted toward understanding what a given word meant in New Testament times. It is what linguists call a *synchronic* approach, one which attempts to analyze a word as it was used during a specific period. I have not ignored *diachronic* analysis, that is, the attempt to understand what a word meant over a period of time, carefully tracing its shifts in meaning. But because this book is geared to basics, I have deliberately chosen to emphasize that part of word study which will most often make the greatest impact in your understanding of the message of the New Testament.

With time, you may wish to become more involved in diachronic word study. As we saw in the LXX analysis of the vocabulary of Matthew 24, it can be very important. Once again, TDNT and NIDNTT will be your best friends here. In fact, you will want to consult the unabridged, 10 volume "Kittel" (see bibliography below) in the study of some words.

For now, however, simply become increasingly familiar with the tools presented in this chapter, especially BAGD and the concordance. LN is new and has not yet been subjected to rigorous use and review in the scholarly journals.[35] But do not be afraid to use it; rather, use it in concert with the standard lexica and concordances. There is no other tool for New Testament studies quite like LN.

**Practice Studies.** These words and phrases should provide you with ample opportunity to test your skills at word study. Of course, you will have to spend some time reading and getting to know the texts and contexts in which they appear, but that too is a part of word study. Unless a particular approach is specified, you should follow either the full or quick word study guide. Try some words using each. As always, explain the results of your study as though you were preaching or teaching.

1. 1 John 2:28, μένετε.
2. Matthew 5:13, ἅλας.
3. Matthew 6:5, ὑποκριταί.
4. 1 John 2:15, κόσμον.
5. Matthew 5:48, τέλειοι.
6. Revelation 6:2, ἵππος λευκός. What does the "white horse" signify? Why?
7. Using LN and BAGD, compare the meanings of τῇ

---

[35]Do look at I. Howard Marshall's review in *The Evangelical Quarterly* 62 (2,1990):183-87. Marshall indicates that LN's approach is not altogether new. Walter Ripman's *A Handbook of the Latin Language* (1930) did much the same thing, though on a far smaller scale, for Latin. Marshall observes that LN is well written, simple, and interesting, but it is no replacement for BAGD. Further, he comments that lexica should do more than catalog meanings. BAGD's interest in specific "references" (similar to what we have called "contextual associations") is very helpful in performing word studies. These matters (and a few others) aside, Marshall was very pleased with LN. He concludes, "It will be clear that this reviewer is impressed by the positive virtues of LN but not so much by its rather sweeping criticisms of BAGD."

προσευχῇ, τῇ δεήσει, εὐχαριστίας, and τὰ αἰτήματα in Philippians 4:6. Does Paul intend to show clear distinctions in the meanings of these words or are they very similar, perhaps even synonyms?
8. Study ἀκολούθει με in John 21:22. Using the concordance, trace this and similar clauses throughout John's gospel, and, as you have time, the synoptics as well.
9. Compare the meanings of γινώσκω and οἶδα in 1 John. Does John apparently make a distinction in the meanings of these words or are they interchangeable?
10. 1 Corinthians 13:10, τέλειον. Plan to spend some time with this one.

**Bibliography.** The bibliography is divided into two sections, the first presenting tools about word study, and the second, tools actually used in performing word studies. The books by Barr, Cotterell & Turner, and Silva are advanced for beginners and require some understanding of linguistics. Black is pretty easy to follow. Those articles and books by Bock, Carson, Crouch, and Fee should be immediately helpful.

Barr, James. *The Semantics of Biblical Language.* Oxford: Oxford University Press, 1961.
Black, David Allan. *Linguistics for Students of New Testament Greek.* Grand Rapids: Baker, 1988.
Bock, Darrell L. "New Testament Word Analysis," in *Introducing New Testament Exegesis,* ed. Scot McKnight. Grand Rapids: Baker, 1988, pp. 97ff.
Carson, D.A. *Exegetical Fallacies.* Grand Rapids: Baker, 1984.
Cotterell, Peter, & Turner, Max. *Linguistics and Biblical Interpretation.* Downer's Grove: Intervarsity Press, 1989.
Crouch, Leon. "Greek Word Studies," in *Biblical Interpretation: Principles and Practice.* F. Furman Kearley, Edward P. Myers, and Timothy D. Hadley, eds. Grand Rapids: Baker, 1986.
Fee, Gordon D. *New Testament Exegesis.* Philadelphia: Westminster, 1983.

Silva, Moises. *Biblical Words and Their Meanings.* Grand Rapids: Zondervan, 1983.

I have repeatedly mentioned the following tools throughout this chapter. They are listed together here for your convenience.

Bachmann, H. and Slaby, H., eds. *Computer-Kondordanz zum Novum Testamentum Graece.* New York: W. de Gruyter, 1980.

Bauer, W. *A Greek-English Lexicon of the New Testament and Other Early Christian Literature.* Translated by W.F. Arndt and F.W. Gingrich. Revised ed. by F.W. Gingrich and F.W. Danker. Chicago: University of Chicago Press, 1979. (Abbreviated BAGD.)

Bromiley, Geoffrey. *Theological Dictionary of the New Testament.* One volume abridgment of TDNT, Gerhard Kittel and Gerhard Friedrich, eds. Grand Rapids: Eerdmans, 1985. (Abbreviated TDNT.)

Brown, Colin, ed. *The New International Dictionary of New Testament Theology.* 4 volumes. Grand Rapids: Zondervan, 1975. (Abbreviated NIDNTT.)

Hatch, E. and Redpath, H.A. *A Concordance to the Septuagint and the Other Greek Versions of the Old Testament.* 2 volumes. Graz: Akademische Druck-u. Verlagsanstalt, 1975; reprint, Grand Rapids: Baker, 1983.

Kittel, Gerhard, and Friedrich, Gerhard, eds. *Theological Dictionary of the New Testament.* 10 Volumes. Translated by Geoffrey Bromiley. Grand Rapids: Eerdmans, 1964.

Liddell, H. and Scott, R. *A Greek-English Lexicon: A New Edition Revised and Augmented Throughout with Supplement.* Revised by H.S. Jones and R. McKenzie. 9th ed. Oxford: Oxford University Press, 1924.

Louw, Johannes P., and Nida, Eugene A., eds. *Greek-English Lexicon of the New Testament Based on Semantic Domains.* 2 volumes. New York: United Bible Societies, 1988. (Abbreviated LN.)

Moulton, James Hope, and Milligan, George. *The Vocabulary of the Greek Testament, Illustrated from the Papyri and Other Non-Literary Sources.* 1930; reprint, Grand

Rapids: Eerdmans, 1976.   (Abbreviated M-M.)

Moulton, W.F., and Geden, A.S. *Concordance to the Greek Testament.* 5th ed. Edinburgh: T.&T. Clark, 1897.

Wigram, George. *The Englishman's Greek-English Concordance to the New Testament.*

## CHAPTER 6

## SYNTAX:
## ANALYZING MEANINGFUL UNITS OF THOUGHT

Some years ago I was given the unenviable assignment of teaching English to students who had grown up on double negatives, case and agreement problems, and improper (but unforgettable) colloquialisms. Reluctantly, I accepted. English was (and is) not my field, though I was at least a language teacher, but the experience eventually proved a good one. The students managed to acquire improved speech habits, and their teacher came upon a helpful approach to teaching English grammar to Bible students.

For a time we attempted a fairly traditional route, spending equal time with such matters as correct pronoun usage, case, and principal parts of difficult verbs. But when it became clear that this approach simply was not getting through, I decided to try a new tack alongside it. It is not that the approach was wrong--one does not learn a language without understanding how its parts relate to each other--but it was simply not enough. The students needed some other motive for learning grammar, one which went beyond being able to speak properly (though that should have been motive enough).

We began to read the New Testament, analyzing its parts of speech, studying phrases and clauses, focusing on categories like tense, voice, and number--all in the context of understanding Scripture. When students began to see how this approach enhanced their Bible study, they took grammar more seriously. Meanwhile, their spoken English gradually improved, largely due to this new-found motivation for learning grammar.

There were no miracles here. Some students refused to give up certain speech patterns. One went so far as to "bury" his English handbook in a nearby river when we had finished the course. He even prepared a eulogy and invited close friends (though he forgot to invite me). But all things considered, the class improved considerably when we adopted the new approach. Their attitude had improved, and attitude is everything in language studies.

If you are like many Greek students, you probably did not learn all of the parts of speech and categories of grammatical identification prior to taking your first semester of Greek. I frequently hear students comment, "I didn't know English until I took Greek." The statement is partly correct. Students do indeed know much English, even if they are not able to provide technically accurate descriptions of the bits and pieces of their native tongue. They have a good understanding of word order, a sizable vocabulary, and some understanding of grammar; else, they could not communicate, at least not at the college level.

But in order to understand another language, they will have to be able to describe the parts of their own and relate these to other, similar parts of speech in the second language. This is precisely why students solidify their understanding of English when they take a foreign language, and it is one among several reasons for paying careful attention to English grammatical descriptions. Many are the college students who, when they take Greek, wish they had paid better attention when they took English.

In studying Koine you have doubtless spent significant time with grammar. You have to. Hopefully, you have spent as much time (or will) seeing just how this understanding of grammar affects your knowledge of Scripture. It is when you get to this second level that grammar studies come to life. They help you see how the several parts of a passage relate to each other, provide precise explanations of what the text is actually saying, and even help organize your thoughts in sermon and lesson preparation. As such, the study of grammar becomes immensely practical, far more than this schoolboy ever dreamed.

**The Plan for This Chapter.** In this section we move from the analysis of individual words and certain phrases to *the ways in which words and phrases are combined to create meaningful units of thought*, and this we will call *syntax.*[1] This definition is intentionally broad in view of the fact that syntax involves every part of speech as well as how these parts relate to each other. Entire books are given over to the subject. You may be studying one even now. James A. Brooks and Carlton L. Winbery's *Syntax of New Testament Greek* is especially helpful in view of its numerous examples,[2] but there are other good intermediate and specialized grammars as well.[3] And then

---

[1]"Grammar" is broader yet. It includes both morphology and syntax. E.g., the ει ending on a third singular, present active verb represents a grammatical distinction though not a syntactical one. Remember, syntax involves the orderly arrangement of words and phrases, even clauses, but it does not include morphology.

[2](Lanham, MD: University Press of America, 1979).

[3]Esp. H.E. Dana and Julius R. Mantey, *A Manual Grammar of the Greek New Testament* (Toronto: The Macmillan Company, 1955), who survey the last several hundred years of Greek grammars admirably in the preface to their very successful work, which first appeared in 1927. See also Ernest DeWitt Burton, *Syntax of the Moods and Tenses in New Testament Greek* (Chicago: University of Chicago Press, 1900; reprint ed., Grand Rapids: Kregel, 1976), C.F.D. Moule, *An Idiom-Book of New Testament Greek*, 2d ed. (Cambridge: Cambridge University Press, 1959), H.P.V. Nunn, *A Short Syntax of New Testament Greek* (Cambridge: Cambridge University Press, 1912), and Maximilian Zerwick, S.J., *Biblical Greek, Illustrated by Examples*, adapted from Latin to English by Joseph Smith, S.J. (Rome: Scripta Pontificii Instituti Biblici, 1963). John

there are the heavyweights.[4]  With the advent of modern
computer software, new grammars will likely appear in
coming days.  But for our part the discussion of syntax
must be limited to summaries and carefully chosen examples.  You will need to consult one or several of these
grammars, especially Brooks and Winbery, for further
coverage.

Nor will we be able to cover every phase of syntax.
Whereas we will look at the noun, verb, article, and
adverbial participle, there remain such matters as conditional sentences and specific uses of the several moods
(e.g., subjunctives).  I have chosen the former because
elementary grammars do  not generally go into any depth
in their coverage, whereas the latter are most often
covered fairly well in beginning textbooks.

Finally, in order to distinguish between syntax and
discourse (next chapter), the discussion in this chapter
will stop at the sentence level.  If syntax is concerned
with the ways in which words are combined to create

Beekman and John Callow, *Translating the Word of God*
(Grand Rapids: Zondervan, 1974) do an especially fine and
modern analysis of the genitive case, pp. 249-266, while
James Allen Hewett, *New Testament Greek: A Beginning and
Intermediate Grammar* (Peabody, MD: Hendrickson Publishers, 1986), successfully combines elements of first and
second year Greek under a single cover.

[4]F. Blass and A. Debrunner, *A Greek Grammar of the New
Testament and Other Early Christian Literature*, translated and revised by Robert W. Funk (Chicago: University
of Chicago Press, 1961), represents the best of German
scholarship; James Hope Moulton, *A Grammar of New
Testament Greek*, vol. III, *Syntax*, by Nigel Turner (Edinburgh: T.& T. Clark, 1963), represents the best of
British scholarship; and A. T. Robertson, *A Grammar of
the Greek New Testament in the Light of Historical
Research* (Nashville: Broadman Press, 1934), represents
the best of American scholarship.

meaningful units of thought, discourse is more concerned with the ways in which clauses and sentences are combined to create meaningful paragraphs, chapters, and books.

**Why Study Syntax?** You probably have a pretty good idea, but here are a few matters to chew on:

1. *Differences in Greek and English word order.* The orderly arrangement of words in any language is important, but the particular significance of word order varies from language to language. Whereas English generally uses subject/verb/object word order in transitive sentences, Greek may employ a verb/subject/object sequence, or it may use an object/subject/verb order. It all depends upon the particular emphasis and/or style of the author. Generally speaking, the words nearest the beginning of the Greek sentence are being emphasized, though this is not always the case. Certain words, especially postpositives (e.g., δε and γάρ) and other conjunctions (e.g., καί) belong there. Nor is it unusual to see a nominative case near the beginning of a sentence. But pay special attention to accusatives and prepositional phrases at the beginning of sentences. The author is often drawing special attention to these by placing them there.

2. *Because it is not sufficient to translate a word at a time; people speak in whole sentences.* This is precisely why it is dangerous to use interlinear Greek texts without careful consideration of how the Greek words in them are connected to each other. Interlinears may give the impression that it is acceptable to translate one word at a time, but that simply is not the case. For instance, Greek infinitives are sometimes separated from the verbs which they complete by several words. Such is the case in Philippians 2:25, where the verb is separated from its infinitive by some 14 words. A word-for-word translation would read, "But I *considered* (it) advantageous Epaphroditus, my brother, fellow worker, and fellow soldier, and your apostle and servant to my need, *to send* to

you." Obviously, this translation will not do. In fact, this would be a glaring example of a split infinitive in English. If the Greek student is not careful to locate the infinitive soon after he translates the verb (which in this instance anticipates an infinitive) he might render the first part of the verse, "But I considered Epaphroditus advantageous...," when if fact it was the *sending* of Epaphroditus which Paul considered advantageous. Or he might translate, "I considered it advantageous, Epaphroditus,...," overlooking the accusative case of "Epaphroditus" altogether. Learning how to translate entire sentences, carefully noting how their several parts relate to one another, will allow you to avoid mistakes of this nature.

3. *Because a single grammatical construction may bear several possible meanings.* 1 John regularly employs the phrase ἐν τούτῳ to mean "by this (means)." John is especially prone to use this prepositional phrase when he wishes to suggests a test or means by which believers validate their Christian confession. Such is the case in 3:10 and 24, as well as 4:2 and 9. However, in chapter two the phrase has two distinct meanings. The correct translation of ἐν τούτῳ in 2:3 appears to be, "And *by this* we know that we have known Him," whereas 2:4 reads, "...and the truth is not *in this one*." The first use of the phrase suggests the *means* by which we know Christ, and the second, the *person* in whom the truth does not reside. One grammatical construction; two distinct meanings. The New Testament is filled with these flexible constructions. As with word studies, sensitivity to context is supremely important in determining the best sense.

4. *Because several grammatical constructions may convey the same meaning.* Here again the examples may be multiplied. Most verbs take accusatives as their objects, but some may take genitives (e.g., ἀκούω), and still others take datives (e.g., ἀκολουθέω). Hence, more cases than the accusative may serve as the object of a sentence. Again, both ἐν τῷ + the

infinitive and the present adverbial participle indicate action which occurs simultaneously with the action of the principal verb. And again, ἵνά and ὅπως with the subjunctive indicate purpose, but so does εἰς with the accusative, and so do certain adverbial participles, and a large number of infinitives. The "one construction, one meaning" notion (similar to the notion that every word has one meaning) is badly mistaken. Language is far too complex for such a simple approach.

5. *Because of the presence of idioms.* I am defining "idiom" here as a group of words which has a meaning other than the normal, literal meaning of the several words combined. (Those who "raise cane" in our culture do not actually grow plants with woody stems; they grow *angry*.) There are many idioms in the New Testament, and they cannot be translated a word at a time since they make no sense outside the special semantic relationships present when these words are combined. Some of these idioms were discussed (or at least mentioned) in the last chapter: "lamb of God," "Son of Man," and "righteousness of God." These may best be pursued through word and phrase study per the principles and procedures of chapter 4. But there are other idioms which are best approached through syntactical analysis: εἰ δὲ μὴ γε ("otherwise"), ἐφ ᾧ ("because"), etc. C.F.D. Moule's *Idiom-Book of New Testament Greek* is especially helpful for this kind of study.

6. *Because of its acceptance in the scholarly community, presence in theological writings, and role in exegesis.* The systematic study of syntax and its application to individual texts is well established as a necessary vehicle to proper interpretation. For centuries, especially the last three, it has proven helpful to countless students and scholars. Grammarians have labeled distinct categories of syntactical identification, which have in turn been incorporated in commentaries, theological wordbooks, journals, and other writings about Scripture. You

cannot hope to study the Greek text without some knowledge of syntax and syntactical categories.

__The Categories of Syntax.__ Already you have learned numerous tags for Greek forms, words like "aorist" and "dative." But unless you have read ahead, you may not have a feel for "datives of advantage" or "ingressive aorists." Such specialized descriptions are generally the stuff of which intermediate, not beginning, grammars are made. In this section you will be introduced to some of these more detailed categories with the help of limited discussions and tables which help summarize and clarify the meanings of the standard syntactical labels. The (modest) objective is to introduce you to these categories. Eventually, you will need to learn more of them in intermediate and advanced grammars. Simply get a feel for the categories and become familiar with the tables for now.

Although the categories are targeted at single words--present verbs, dative and accusative nouns, etc.--the function of these words can only properly be determined within the context of the entire sentence. In other words, the *syntactical* tasks of the parts of speech we will observe are determined by the orderly arrangement and relationship of all words present in the sentence, which is precisely why I have included this discussion in the chapter on syntax rather than the chapter on word studies. The focus is syntactical and not semantic.

The Indicative Verb. Although they do suggest *time*, indicative verbs focus upon the *kind of action* which takes place.[5] That is, they present action as either *linear* or *progressive* (chiefly in the present and imperfect), *punctiliar* or *undefined* (chiefly in the future and aorist), or *completed* (in the perfect and

[5]The future tense alone focuses upon the time element, though it is still appropriate to talk about the kind of action depicted by the future.

pluperfect). In keeping with the modern focus on authorial intent, recent studies have refined this understanding further by drawing attention to *aspect*, i.e., action viewed according to the author's intention.[6] If he chose an aorist tense to reflect future action, the writer may have done so to indicate that the action was as good as done; if a present for past action, he apparently wanted to present the thing accomplished as though it were actually happening in the present, perhaps for dramatic effect.

Following are New Testament examples of common uses of the six tenses, presented here by tense.[7] The syntactical categories (italicized) are pooled together from a variety of grammars, with special attention to the terminology in Brooks and Winbery and Dana and Mantey, the two most commonly used intermediate grammars. The explanations should prepare you for use with either.

The **present** tense is usually described as linear, progressive, continuous, or ongoing. The *descriptive* present highlights this kind of action, as in Philippians 1:3, "I (always) *give thanks* (εὐχαριστῶ) to God ...." 1 Corinthians 11:26 contains a clear *iterative* present (customary activity, often repeated at regular intervals), "As often as you eat this bread and drink this cup, you *proclaim* (καταγγέλλετε) the Lord's death," while the gospels contain numerous *historic* presents, used to →

---

[6]Scot McKnight, "New Testament Greek Grammatical Analysis," in *Introducing New Testament Interpretation*, pp. 84f.

[7]Examples throughout this chapter were selected from a variety of sources, including the grammars of Robertson, Turner, Brooks and Winbery, and Dana and Mantey. Many (probably most), however, were uncovered through personal research, at times with the aid of GRAMCORD. There are numerous examples from Philippians, The Sermon on the Mount, and First John (especially in the section on nouns) due to my research in these texts.

present a past event as though it were actually happening as the writer penned his book.[8] For example, Mark 1:40 reads, "And a leper *comes* (ἔρχεται) to him," when in fact the leper had *already* come (hence, *historic* present). The *aoristic* or *simple* present reminds us that not all present tense forms depict linear action, e.g., "Your sins *are* *forgiven* (ἀφίενται)" (Mark 2:5), while the *gnomic* present suggests a universal truth, e.g., "God *is* (ἐστιν) light" (1 John 1:5).

The **imperfect** tense, like the present, is linear. It depicts past action as ongoing. The *inceptive* imperfect views this progressive past action from the point of its origin, e.g., "He opened his mouth and *began to teach* (ἐδίδασκεν) them, saying, ..." (Matthew 5:1), or "Peter and the other disciple *began to go* (ἤρχοντο) to the tomb" (John 20:3), whereas the *descriptive* imperfect simply depicts the past action as linear, "And the two *were running* (ἔτρεχον), but the other disciple outran Peter" (John 20:4). The *voluntative* imperfect draws attention to a desired but impossible action, "I *could wish* (ηὐχόμην) that I were accursed for the sake of Israel" (Romans 9:3). *Customary* or *iterative* imperfects bespeak past action which took place on a regular basis, e.g., "They *used to release* (ἀπέλυεν) a prisoner according to custom" (Mark 15:6), whereas the *durative* imperfect is used of past action which continued for a time but ceased, e.g., "Why *were you seeking* (ἐζητεῖτέ) me?" (Luke 2:49).

The **future** tense is usually punctiliar, with greater emphasis upon the time element than either the present or imperfect. "I *will prepare* (ἐτοιμάσω) a place for you" (John 14:3) is *predictive* (and punctiliar), while "the one who began a good work in you *will continue to bring*

[8]Scott McKnight, "New Testament Greek Grammatical Analysis," p. 85, questions the category: "To explain these instances 'historically' confuses reality (how it happened) with depiction (how the author presents it)."

*it to completion* (ἐπιτελέσει)" (Philippians 1:6) is *progressive*. "You *will not murder* (φονεύσεις)" (Matthew 5:21) and "You *will not commit adultery* (μοιχεύσεις)" (Matthew 5:27) are both *commands*, but Romans 6:1, "What *shall we say* (ἐροῦμεν)?" is clearly a *deliberative* question.

Aorist tense indicatives usually indicate past action with no special emphasis at all. As a rule they are neither linear nor completed. Nor is the aorist the "once-for-all" tense, meaning that a specific action could not happen again.[9] The most prevalent aorist is the *constative*, i.e., that use of the aorist which has no reference to the beginning, progress, or completion of an action. Similar to the English past simple, the constative simply views past action as having happened, e.g., "I *planted* (ἐφύτευσα), Apollos *watered* (ἐπότισεν)..." (1 Corinthians 3:6). *Ingressive* aorists emphasize the beginning point of a past action, though with no emphasis on the continuation of that action, e.g., "(He) was dead and *came to life* (ἔζησεν)" (Revelation 2:8), while *culminative* aorists draw attention to the conclusion of a past action, e.g., "You *have heard* (ἠκούσατε) that it was said ..." (Matthew 5:21, 27, 33, et al.), overlapping significantly with the perfect tense form. The *gnomic* aorist bespeaks a generally accepted maxim, "The sun *rises* (ἀνέτειλεν)... and *withers* (ἐξήρανεν) the vegetation..." (James 1:11), but the *dramatic* aorist draws special attention to a current event, "This is my son in whom *I am pleased* (εὐδόκησα)" (Matthew 3:17). The *epistolary* aorist places the author in the same time framework as his readers by presenting as past what was actually present as he wrote, e.g., "I *considered* (ἡγησάμην) it necessary to send Epaphroditus to you" (Philippians 2:25).

[9]Of course, some actions depicted by the aorist may never occur again, but this is not so simply because the author chose an aorist to depict the action. You will need to look to other factors in making such a judgment.

Greek **perfects** draw attention to the effects of a past action. As such, the temporal focus is often more on the present than the past, though the perfect depicts action which is already completed. The *intensive* perfect makes much of present status and is quite similar in certain respects to the present tense, e.g., *"Have you been bound* (δέδεσαι) to a wife?" (meaning "Are you married?") and *"Have you been released* (λέλυσαι) from a wife?" (meaning "Are you unmarried, having formerly been married?"). Both questions appear in 1 Corinthians 7:27. The *consummative* perfect, on the other hand, views action as having happened and is similar to the aorist, though with some emphasis on the finished event, as in John 3:32, "That which he *has seen* (ἑώρακεν; perfect) and heard (ἤκουσεν; aorist), this he testifies." *Iterative* perfects suggest action repeated at various intervals, but, on the whole, completed, e.g., "That which *we have heard* (ἀκηκόαμεν) and *seen* (ἑωράκαμεν) with our eyes...." (1 John 1:1). (Note: The last example may also be viewed as consummative inasmuch as the focus seems to be upon the completion of the action, especially as these verbs are followed by the aorist ἐθεασάμεθα.)

The **pluperfect** tense, by far the least frequent of the six tenses, depicts a past state or lasting result which arose from some prior action. It is as though the perfect were being moved back a notch in time. As with the perfect tense, there is the *intensive* pluperfect, which emphasizes the results of a past act and is generally translated as past simple, e.g., "All the people *stood* (εἰστήκει) on the shore" (Matthew 13:2). The *consummative* pluperfect focuses attention on the completed action and generally employs the auxiliary *had* in translation. E.g., "Jews *had come* (ἐληλύθεισαν) to Mary and Martha to comfort them in the loss of their brother" (John 11:19).

You may have noticed that certain terms keep appearing among the explanations of the six tenses, words like "consummative," "gnomic," and "tendential." Table 6.1 summarizes these categories, complete with the name of the category, a brief explanation, the tense(s) in which it appears, and a simple translation of γράφω. [10] Of course, no tense will perform *every* function explained in each of these descriptions. Some, especially the pluperfect, are rather limited in what they can do. The table is presented here in the hope that it will simplify what may appear an enormous challenge to beginning exegetes. It should prove especially helpful in learning the names and significances of the syntactical categories.

## TABLE 6.1 THE INDICATIVE VERB[11]

| DESCRIPTIVE TERM | TENSES WHERE USED & TRANSLATION OF γράφω |
|---|---|
| Aoristic--simple action no particular emphasis | PRESENT ("I write") PERFECT ("I wrote") |
| Constative--action viewed in entirety; no special emphasis | AORIST ("I wrote") |
| Consummative--emphasis on completed action | PERFECT ("I have written") PLUPERFECT ("I had written") |
| Culminative--emphasis on the results of a completed action | AORIST ("I have written") |
| Customary--habitual action; similar to iterative | PRESENT ["I write (regularly)"] IMPERFECT ["I used to write (regularly)"] |
| Deliberative--questions of deliberation | FUTURE ("Shall I write?") |
| Descriptive--emphasis on the action itself, esp. w/a view to its progress | PRESENT ("I am writing") IMPERFECT ("I was writing") |

[10]Though for some verbs, esp. *gnomic* verbs, other Greek verbs are used.

[11]Many of these categories also apply to certain moods (or modes) of the verb, but you should focus on the indicative for the time being.

| | |
|---|---|
| Dramatic--action is heightened or emphasized | AORIST ("I *wrote*") PERFECT ("I have *just written*") |
| Durative--action which began in the past and continues to some undefined point | PRESENT ["I have been writing (until ?) ... "] |
| Epistolary--writer adopts time perspective of reader | AORIST ("I write") |
| Futuristic--action taking place in the future | PRESENT ("I am going to write") AORIST ("I wrote" for "I will write") |
| Gnomic--a universal truth | PRESENT ("Trees bear fruit") FUTURE ("People will work") AORIST ("The sun rises") |
| Historic--action which happened in the past, depicted as present | PRESENT ("I write" for "I wrote") |
| Imperative--a command | FUTURE ("You will write") |
| Inceptive--action viewed from its beginning | IMPERFECT ("I began to write") |
| Ingressive--action in its beginning | AORIST ("I began to write") |
| Intensive--emphasis on existing state | PERFECT (γέγραπται, "It is written") PLUPERFECT ("I *wrote*") |
| Iterative--action repeated at various intervals | PRESENT ["I write (regularly)"] IMPERFECT ["I wrote (regularly)"] PERFECT ("I have repeatedly written") |
| Predictive--predicted action | FUTURE ("I will write") |
| Progressive--ongoing action | FUTURE ("I will be writing") |
| Static--a perpetual condition | PRESENT ["People write (as they always have)"] |
| Tendential--contemplated action | PRESENT ("I *attempt* or *try* to write") |

|  | IMPERFECT ("I was *attempting* to write") |
|---|---|
| Voluntative--desired but impossible action | IMPERFECT ("I could *wish* I were able to write") |

The Verb and Exegesis. Thus far the discussion has centered on identifying the functions of the verb. Time now to put these to fuller use in exegesis with selected examples. But before doing this, you should review the basic sentence patterns in Greek. (You have probably already been acquainted with these in your beginning grammar.) They are:

1. Subject/verb.
2. Subject/verb/object.
3. Subject/verb/indirect object/object.
4. Subject/linking verb/complement.
   a. Subject/linking verb/noun.
   b. Subject/linking verb/adjective.
   c. Subject/linking verb/prepositional phrase.

Examples of the first three patterns:

| | Subject | Verb | Indirect Obj. | Object |
|---|---|---|---|---|
| 1. | ὁ Ἰωάννης<br>John | ἀπαγγέλλει.<br>is proclaiming. | | |
| 2. | ὁ Ἰωάννης<br>John | ἀπαγγέλλει<br>is proclaiming | | ζωήν.<br>life. |
| 3. | ὁ Ἰωάννης<br>John | ἀπαγγέλλει<br>is proclaiming | ἀνθρώπῳ<br>to a man | ζωήν.<br>life. |

Examples of pattern 4.:

| | Subject | Linking Verb | Complement |
|---|---|---|---|
| 4a. | ὁ θεὸς<br>God | ἐστιν<br>is | φῶς.<br>light (noun). |

**4b.** ὁ θεὸς     ἐστιν     ἅγιος.
     God        is       holy (adjective).

**4c.** ὁ θεὸς     ἐστιν     ἐν οὐρανῷ.
     God        is       in heaven
                                         (prep. phrase)

Some of these patterns will be important in analyzing the structure of the sentence. You will see why in the examples which follow.

The Verb. 1 Corinthians 3:6 contains three intransitive verbs (i.e., verbs which contain no object). Together with their subjects, they are (in English and Greek):

|   | Subject | Verb |
|---|---------|------|
| 1. | ἐγὼ | ἐφύτευσα |
|   | I | planted |
| 2. | ᾿Απολλῶς | ἐπότισεν |
|   | Apollos | watered |

**But** (ἀλλά)

|   | | |
|---|---|---|
| 3. | ὁ θεὸς | ηὔξανεν |
|   | God | was causing the growth |

Notice how the clauses are laid out. The sentence pattern (1) is established in bold print, with the subjects and verbs in their appropriate columns. These are lined up in order to show that the clauses are *coordinate*, that is, that they each contain the same elements and stand in a series. The adversative ἀλλά is brought to the left-hand column because it marks a significant contrast between the subjects and verbs of the first two clauses and the subject and verb of the third.

What is significant here is the shift of tense from aorist (in clauses 1 and 2) to imperfect (in clause 3).

Whereas Paul and Apollos simply planted and watered (both constative aorists), God *was causing the growth.* Whether He was doing so with a view to the origin of this action (inceptive imperfect) or on a regular basis (customary imperfect) or with some other special emphasis will have to be determined on the basis of the contextual considerations.

1 Corinthians 3 must be seen against chapter 1, where Paul remarks that some of the Corinthians are following him, others Apollos, others Peter, and still others Christ. 3:4 resumes this discussion, with particular emphasis upon Paul and Apollos, adding that these are nothing more than mere men, servants of God. He follows verse six drawing attention to the joint venture and oneness of the workers (v. 8). The duration of the chapter is concerned with building well against the day of Christ's return.

In view of the emphasis upon the equally valid service of Paul and Apollos, it seems that the apostle is drawing attention to the fact that God was working both through the actions of Paul and of Apollos in his use of the aorist and imperfect tenses in this text. To get the significance of this, consider this diagram.

AORIST Paul planted,                    Apollos watered,

but

IMPERF. God was bringing the growth all along the way.

Whereas the two aorists represent past action as having happened during the stays of Paul and Apollos in Corinth, the imperfect speaks of God's continued working throughout the period of planting and watering the seed. Were we to view the imperfect as inceptive, the emphasis would lie solely on the work of Paul; if voluntative, upon something only contemplated, but never achieved. But neither fits this context. The verb is *descriptive* of what went on for some period of time, specifically, the entire period of time during which Paul and Apollos worked, as well as the interval between them. The fact that God was at work in both of their ministries calls attention to the irrelevance and inappropriateness of Corinthian cliques which followed (or claimed to follow) a single person's leadership. Moreover, it draws attention to the one whom they should follow in the first place--God.

1 John 1:1 and 3 presents an interesting and exegetically significant use of Greek verbs. (Verse two appears to be parenthetical. We will look at it in a moment.) Perfects, aorists, and presents stand in juxta-position with the result that we can clearly see how the several tenses appear to relate to each other.

| Object | Subject | Verb | Ind. Obj. |
|--------|---------|------|-----------|
| What | we | *have heard* (iterative perf.) | |
| What | we | *have seen* (iterative perf.) | |
| What and | we | *beheld* (culminative aor.) | |
| | Our hands | *handled* (culminative aor.) | |
| What and | we | *have seen* (iterative perf.) | |
| (What) | we | *have heard* (iterative perf.) | |
| | we | *are proclaiming* (descriptive present) | |
| | | | to you. |

The sentence pattern is subject/verb/indirect object/ object (pattern 3). But in this case we have retained the Greek word order (object/subject/verb) in the diagram in order to preserve the Johannine emphasis on the rela-tive pronoun (ὅ), "That which" or "What."

Notice:

1. That John begins with the perfect tense, used to describe what appears to have happened at repeated

intervals in the past but with some lasting impression on the author. Hence, the *iterative* perfect.

2. That the two iterative perfects are followed by two aorists, which, like the perfects, have to do with sensory perception. Because these aorists are preceded and followed by iterative perfects, they are likely *culminative* aorists, emphasizing to a degree the results of the beholding and touching, with much the same force as the perfect tense form.

3. That the last indicative verb in this sentence (ἀπαγγέλλομεν) is present tense, likely *descriptive*, perhaps *iterative* (in keeping with the earlier perfects). In either case, the action continues.

John's clear progression flows from past to present with his carefully chosen verb tenses. What he regularly sensed in the past drove home a lasting impression which, in turn, led to equally regular proclamation. The impact of the Gospel on him was not without significant effect.

The same progression is seen in verse 2, where the text says:

| | Subject | Verb | Ind. Obj. | Object |
|---|---|---|---|---|
| | The life | *was revealed* | | |
| and | We | *have beheld* | | |
| and | | *are witnessing* | | |
| and | | *are announcing* | to you | eternal life. |

Here, as before, what was revealed (*constative* aorist, focusing only on the fact that life was revealed, viewed in summary fashion), John had beheld (on more than one occasion; hence, *iterative* perfect), which led to regular testimony (*descriptive* or *iterative* presents).

The Noun. Because modern grammarians are not agreed on the number of cases present in Koine Greek--some see five,[12] others eight[13]--I have attempted to be sensitive to both, while adopting the five case approach. Both approaches have merit, but what matters most is that you understand how Greek noun forms function, not what they are called. (Of course, you will have to adopt some regular approach to the noun system, and knowing both the five and eight case approaches will be helpful, especially in your reading of commentaries and related literature.) These five case forms, together with brief descriptions, are:

Nominative--generally indicates the subject or predicate nominative of the sentence; may also overlap with the Vocative (described below).

Genitive--the case of description, or the "noun of noun" case; shares the same form as the Ablative (eight case system), the case of separation.

Dative--the case of personal interest, often the indirect object; shares a single form with the Locative (eight case system), which shows location, and the Instrumental (also eight case), which shows means or agency.

[12]J. Gresham Machen, *New Testament Greek for Beginners* (New York: The Macmillan Company, 1952), p. 25, Eugene Van Ness Goetchius, *The Language of the New Testament* (New York: Scribner's, 1965), pp. 302ff., James Allen Hewett, *New Testament Greek* (Peabody, Mass.: Hendrickson Publishers, 1986), pp. 18f., and most recently James M. Efird, *A Grammar for New Testament Greek*, pp. 17f., observe five cases. Hewett appeals to Blass, *A Greek Grammar*, pp. 79-109, in support of his position.

[13]William Hersey Davis, *Beginner's Grammar of the Greek New Testament* (Nashville: Broadman, 1923), pp. 29f., Ray Summers, *Essentials of New Testament Greek* (Nashville: Broadman, 1950), pp. 16f., and more recently Huber Drumwright, Jr., *An Introduction to New Testament Greek* (Nashville, Broadman: 1980), pp. 24-25, all present eight cases. The approach is based upon the earlier work of A.T. Robertson, *Grammar of the Greek New Testament*, pp. 446ff.

Accusative--generally indicates the object of the verb; often the object of a preposition.
Vocative--the case of address.

Following are more precise descriptions of the functions of these cases, along with New Testament examples. Please note that: (1) not all categories of noun syntax presented in the intermediate grammars are presented here, and (2) many of the nouns which follow often appear with prepositions which further clarify their use in the sentence. I have attempted to include examples which do not utilize prepositions. However, this has not always been possible, and for those examples where prepositions do precede the noun, I have indicated this. For an excellent treatment of prepositions with the several cases consult Brooks and Winbery, *Syntax*, pp. 65-70.

The **nominative** case designates the subject of the Greek verb. Since the verb will itself indicate the person and number of the subject, the nominative only clarifies further what the verb has already indicated. This is especially true of third person verbs, whose subjects are not completely clear from verbal inflection alone. The *subject* nominative indicates who or what performed the action or was acted upon, e.g., "The *life* (ζωή) was revealed" (1 John 1:2) and "*We* (ἡμεῖς) are writing these things" (1 John 1:4), while the *predicate* nominative is the object or complement of equative (copulative) verbs like γίνομαι and εἰμί. For example, "And this is the *message* (ἀγγελία) which we have heard" (1 John 1:5) and "God is *light* (φῶς)" (1 John 1:5).

Names frequently appear in nominative case, at times irrespective of their function in the sentence. When a nominative case name is used where we might expect a genitive, dative, or accusative, it is a nominative of *appelation*, e.g., "He will be called a *Nazarite* (Ναζαραῖος)" (Matthew 2:23), where we might have expected the accusative Ναζαραῖον. The nominative of *apposition* generally renames the subject, supplying additional information about same, e.g., "Paul, an *apostle* (ἀπόστολος), not from men, nor through a man, but through Jesus Christ and God the Father" (Galatians 1:1). Some nominatives seem to have no regular syntactical relationship with other elements in the sentence and do not fit neatly into any of the categories we have covered. These are known as *independent* or *absolute* nominatives and fall into one of several groups (change of grammatical construction, nominatives in salutations to letters, etc.), too many for discussion in a summary of this sort. Brooks and Winbery cover them nicely.[14]

By far the most complex of the several cases, the **genitive** gives definition to the substantive it attends. It may limit, describe, or tell what kind, to mention only some of the possibilities. A frequent case,[15] it is often very significant exegetically. We have already hinted at this in the discussion of the meaning of "faith of Jesus" in chapter 3. You should work diligently to understand and apply precisely the meanings which the genitive suggests. No other case will require so much of your energy.

In the presentation which follows, those categories which are considered genitive by both five and eight case grammarians are covered first. A second section presents the genitives of source, separation, etc., or, as these are termed in the eight case system, the ablative.

Prominence of place goes to the genitive of *description*, that use of the case which grammarians see in nearly all genitives, but which is more prominent in some than in others, e.g., "(Christ) will transform our body *of humiliation* (ταπεινώσεως)" (Philippians 3:21) = "(Christ) will transform our *humble* body." Genitives of

[14]See pp. 5-7.

[15]Beekman and Callow, *Translating the Word of God*, remark, "the translator is likely to encounter a genitive phrase ... about twice in every three verses, if not more often" p. 249.

*possession* appear with some frequency in the New Testament. You should think of possession as referring to ownership of material items, e.g., "Go into home *your* (σου)" (Mark 2:11) and "(A woman) touched the edge of *his* (αὐτοῦ) garment" (Matthew 9:20), though Brooks and Winbery broaden the notion considerably.[16] The genitive of *relationship* is used to suggest kinship (father, mother, son, daughter, etc.) and social ties (slave, master, etc.).[17] In Philippians 1:2 the text reads, "Grace and peace to you from God *our* (ἡμῶν) Father," where ἡμῶν suggests not ownership, but relationship or spiritual kinship.

Genitives frequently appear with nouns of action, or nouns which depict events, words like hope (ἐλπίς) and love (ἀγάπη). Because it is often difficult to see just how the genitive relates to the action noun which precedes it, students sometimes have difficulty mastering these genitives. Pay careful heed to the following explanations and examples.

When you determine that the noun preceding the genitive is an action noun, *restate the entire phrase as though it were a proposition.* In order to do this you will need to determine whether the word in genitive case is doing the acting or is the recipient of the action. It will help, initially at least, if you label the two nouns *A.* and *B.* Consider this example from Philippians 3:14:

---

[16]*Syntax*, pp. 8-9. Included are such examples as 2 Corinthians 1:1, "apostle *of Christ Jesus* (Χριστοῦ Ἰησοῦ)" and John 1:12, "children *of God* (θεοῦ)," both of which could be considered genitives of relationship, esp. the latter.

[17]Beekman and Callow, *Translating the Word of God*, distinguish further between "relationship" and "role," placing words not strictly involving kinship in the latter category (e.g., "servant" and "Lord").

                                    *A.*        *B.*
διώκω εἰς τὸ βραβεῖον τῆς ἄνω κλήσεως τοῦ θεοῦ

                                       *A.*      *B.*
"I am pursuing the prize of the upward call of God."

Noun *A.* is always the action noun, in this instance, "call." Noun *B.* is the genitive whose function we are trying to ascertain, here, "God." In order to see what options lie before us, we must change noun *A.* into a verb and try noun *B.* first as its subject and then as its object. Does "call of God" mean:

    *B.*  *A.*
1. "God calls (Paul)," where *B.* is the *subject* of *A.*, or

    *A.*  *B.*
2. "(Paul) calls God," where *B.* is the *object* of *A.*?

In the first instance, the genitive ("God") is considered *subjective*; in the second, *objective*. The "call *of God*" in Philippians 3:14 appears to be a subjective genitive, i.e., God calls Paul. This conclusion is based on the fact that Paul regularly uses κλῆσις ("call") with passive forms of the cognate verb (καλέω), e.g., "the calling with which you were called" (Ephesians 4:1), indicating that God calls believers to fellowship with Him. (Cf. 1 Corinthians 7:20 and Ephesians 4:4.) Moreover, the context is clearly concerned with Paul's heavenward calling.

Because of their complexities, it is best to solidify your understanding of subjective and objective genitives by way of multiple examples. Table 6.2 (next page) should be helpful in distinguishing between the two. Study it.

You may have noticed that it is necessary to supply a subject or object in order to restate these phrases in table 6.2 as propositions. (I have indicated these supplied words with parentheses.) This is necessary and usually easy to do. The context nearly always provides such subjects and objects. Hopefully, these examples have reinforced the value of clarifying the relationship of words within phrases through reordering them as statements in English. You should practice the approach in your study of genitives until you are thoroughly familiar with their many uses.

### Table 6.2: Subjective and Objective Genitives

**SUBJECTIVE GENITIVES:**

| GENITIVE PHRASE | RESTATEMENT |
|---|---|
| "the love *of God*" | God loves (us). |
| "the baptism *of John*" | John baptized (people). |
| "the judgment *of God*" | God will judge (people). |
| "the faith *of you*" | You believe/trust. |
| "the witness *of us*" | We bear witness. |

**OBJECTIVE GENITIVE:**

| GENITIVE PHRASE | RESTATMENT |
|---|---|
| "the love *of God*" | (We) love God. |
| "the gift *of the Spirit*" | (God) gives the Spirit. |
| "the breaking *of bread*" | (Someone) breaks bread. |
| "blasphemy *of God*" | (Someone) blasphemes God. |
| "the hope *of Christ*" | (Someone) hopes in Christ. |

Certain genitives indicate *time*, e.g., "Pray that your flight does not come *of* (or *during*) winter (χειμῶνος)" (Matthew 24:20); others *measure*, "You were bought *at a price* (τιμῆς)" (1 Corinthians 6:20), indicating the length to which God went in order to save the Corinthians; and still others, *place* or *location*, e.g., "so that he might dip the tip of his finger *in water* (ὕδατος)" (Luke 16:24). None of these uses is highly frequent in the New Testament, but you will encounter each if you do much reading in the text.

The genitive of *apposition*, on the other hand, is fairly common. Like the nominative of apposition, it renames and in some way clarifies the identity of the noun which precedes it. E.g., "the fruit *of right-eousness* (δικαιοωύνης)" may mean "the fruit which is righteousness" in Philippians 1:11. Similarly, the "prize *of the call* (κλήσεως) of God" (Philippians 3:14) may be "the prize which is the call of God." *Reference* is yet another function of the genitive, as in James 1:13, where "God is not capable *of evil things* (κακῶν)." The phrase could as easily and correctly be rendered, *"with respect to evil things."*

Some genitives describe, whereas others distinguish. Some answer the question "What kind?" while others tell "From whom or what?" Thus far, we have studied genitives of the first variety. The genitives of the second ("ablatives" in the eight case system) suggest a severing or separation of some kind. There is no formal clue which distinguishes them from genitives which merely describe--and this is precisely why some grammars do not recognize the ablative case in Koine--but by New Testament times the genitives of *separation*, *means*, *source*, and several others were frequently preceded by ἀπό, ἐκ, and ὑπό, prepositions which clearly suggest these meanings.

The genitive/ablative of *separation* is used to indicate distinct groups, often with an emphasis upon their great dissimilarity. Ephesians 2:12 illustrates this function of the case nicely, "At that time you were without Christ, cut off *from the citizenship* (τῆς ἐπαγγελίας) of Israel, and strangers *from the covenants* (τῶν διαθηκῶν) of promise." Other genitives/ablatives, often introduced by ἐκ or ἀπό, indicate the *source* from whom or which someone receives something, as in Matthew 5:37, "Anything more than these is *from the evil one* (ἐκ τοῦ πονηροῦ)." Some genitives/ablatives, together with prepositions such as διά, ἐκ, and ὑπό, suggest *means* (impersonal), and still others, with the help of ἀπό, διά, παρά, and ὑπό, *agency* (personal). Means is illustrated in Philippians 1:19, "I know that this will lead to my deliverance *through* your *prayer* (διὰ τῆς δεήσεως) and the *supply* (ἐπιχορηγίας) of the Spirit of

Jesus Christ," while agency is just as clear in 1:28, "not being frightened *by* (your) *opponents* (ὑπὸ τῶν ἀντικειμένων) ...."

Some genitives/ablatives are used in *comparisons* where the word preceding the genitive/ablative will be a comparative adjective, often with a τερος ending). Such is the case in Matthew 5:37, where the text reads, "Anything greater *than these* (τούτων) is from the evil one," and 6:26, "Are you not far more valuable *than they* (αὐτῶν)?"

Finally, the *partitive* genitive/ablative suggests a part/whole relationship, indicating either a *constituent* relationship, where the genitive forms the whole of which the noun preceding it is a part, e.g., "the right hand *of you* (σου)" (Matthew 5:30), or a *quantitative* relationship, where the genitive forms the sum of which the noun preceding represents only a fraction, e.g., "a third *of the land* (τῆς γῆς)" and "a third *of the trees* (δένδρων)" (Revelation 8:7).

Time now to consider the **dative** case, or the case of personal interest. As with the genitive/ablative discussion, those categories which are considered dative by both five and eight case grammarians are covered first. Additional paragraphs detail the instrumental and locative of the eight case system.

The *indirect object* will appear in dative case, as in 1 John 1:3, "We are proclaiming *to you* (ὑμῖν) that which we have seen and heard." So will persons for whose *advantage* the activity of the verb has taken place, e.g., "You shine like lights in the world, holding forth the word of life, so that (you are) a boast *for me* (μοι) in the Day of Christ" (Philippians 2:16). *Disadvantage* is equally a function of the dative, as in Philippians 1:28, "Stand in one Spirit ... not being frightened by your adversaries, which is a sign of destruction *against them* (αὐτοῖς)."

At times the dative, like the genitive, indicates possession. See, e.g., Mark 5:9, where the question is asked, "What is the name *to you* (σοι)?" or "What is *your* name?" Other datives, like certain genitives and accusatives, are used of *reference* or *respect*. For instance, Matthew 6:25 reads, "Stop worrying *as regards* your *life* (ψυχῇ)" and Philippians 1:30, "You are hearing *with reference to me* (ἐμοί)," where the preposition ἐν works with the dative to suggest this meaning.

The dative of *location* (or "locative" in the eight case system) is prominent in New Testament Greek and is often introduced by ἐν. Paul, for example, writes "to the saints *in Philippi* (ἐν φιλίπποις)" using a dative/locative of *place* (Philippians 1:1), while the dative/locative may also be used to indicate a specific *time*, for instance, Acts 21:26, "*On* the next *day* (ἡμέρᾳ) Paul took the men and was purified with them." Datives/locatives of *sphere*, which depict a realm in neither space nor time, appear as well, as in Matthew 5:3, "Blessed are the poor *in spirit*" and Philippians 1:7, "I have you *in* my *heart* (καρδίᾳ)."

The dative of *means* (or "instrument of means" in the eight case system) is fairly frequent, again, often appearing with a preposition: "If the salt loses its savor, *by what means* (ἐν τίνι) will it be restored?" (Matthew 5:13), and "But I say to you not to swear at all, neither *by means of heaven* (ἐν τῷ οὐρανῷ) ... nor *by means of earth* (ἐν τῇ γῇ)" (Matthew 5:34f.). There is also the dative/instrumental of *manner*, "Christ will be magnified *boldly* (ἐν ... παρρησίᾳ) now as always" (Philippians 1:20), and *cause*, "The rest of the brothers in the Lord have become confident *because of* my *chains* (δεσμοῖς)" (Philippians 1:14). Finally, the dative/instrument of *association* makes its way into the pages of the New Testament on a regular basis: "I rejoice and will continue to rejoice *with all of you* (πᾶσιν ὑμῖν)" (Philippians 2:17).

Grammarians treat the **accusative** as the case of extension. "The accusative indicates how and to what the action of the verb is extended."[18]   The accusative of *direct object* is probably the use with which you have the greatest familiarity, e.g., "He gave him *the name* (τὸ ὄνομα) which is above every name" (Philippians 2:9) and "Complete my *joy* (τὴν χάραν)" (Philippians 2:4).

But there are other, lesser known uses of the accusative.   As in English, Greek has a *double* accusative, for example.   Philippians 3:17 is illustrative, "You have *us* (ἡμᾶς) as a *type* (τύπον)."   The *cognate* accusative, an accusative whose root is the same as that of the verb preceding it, appears infrequently, as in Luke 2:9, "They feared (ἐφοβήθησαν) a great *fear* (φόβον)" and Matthew 6:19, "Stop storing up (θησαυρίζετε) for yourselves *treasures* (θησαυροὺς)."   The accusative of *reference* is more common than either double or cognate accusatives and has much the same meaning as the genitive and dative of reference: "We should grow up into him *in respect to all things* (πάντα)" or, better, "*in every respect*" (Ephesians 4:15).

As with verb tenses, some of the syntactical categories of the noun are shared by several cases.   For example, both the nominative and the genitive may indicate apposition, and both genitive and dative may be used to indicate possession.   Table 6.3 has been prepared with this overlap in mind.   It is an important summary of information presented throughout the section on noun syntax.   You should become thoroughly familiar with the categories summarized in it, along with those forms which may represent them.   Please note that there are more categories in the left-hand column than are covered in this chapter (e.g., genitive of advantage, dative/ instrument of agency, and accusative of measure).   You may need to consult more advanced grammars for full explanations of these, though most are virtually self explanatory.

[18]Brooks and Winbery, *Syntax*, p. 45.

Table 6.3:
Categories of Noun Usage Summarized

| Category and Form(s) in Which Used | Word(s) Used in Translation |
|---|---|
| 1. Advantage--GCF, DCF[19] | "for" |
| 2. Agency--GCF (*ABCF*), DCF (*ICF*)[20] | "through, by" |
| 3. Appelation (proper names in NCF)--NCF | -- |
| 4. Apposition (renaming)--NCF, GCF | "that is, namely" |
| 5. Association--GCF, DCF (*ICF*) | "with" |
| 6. Attendant Circumstance--GCF | "with" |
| 7. Cause--GCF (*ABCF*), DCF (*ICF*) ACF | "because (of)" |
| 8. Cognate Accusative--ACF | -- |
| 9. Comparison--GCF (*ABCF*) | "... than" |
| 10. Description--GCF | -- |
| 11. Direct Object--GCF,DCF,ACF | -- |
| 12. Disadvantage--DCF | "against" |
| 13. Double ACF--ACF | -- |
| 14. Indirect Object--DCF | "to ..." |
| 15. Manner--DCF (*ICF*),ACF | "...ly" and others |
| 16. Means--GCF(*ABCF*), DCF(*ICF*) | "by, with, through" |
| 17. Measure--GCF, DCF(*ICF*),ACF | various |

[19] Abbreviations used are: NCF (nominative case form); GCF (genitive case form); ABCF (ablative case form); DCF (dative case form); LCF (locative case form); ICF (instrumental case form); ACF (accusative case form); VCF (vocative case form); ART (article).

[20] When a form is considered genitive in the five case system, but ablative in the eight case system, the five case name appears first, with the eight case name following in parentheses and italicized. The same principle holds for dative, which shares the same form with the locative and instrumental in the eight case system.

| | |
|---|---|
| 18. Oaths--GCF,ACF | "by" |
| 19. Object--GCF | -- |
| 20. Opposition--GCF (*ABCF*) | "against" |
| 21. Partitive--GCF (*ABCF*) | "one of, a third of, etc." |
| 22. Place--GCF, DCF (*LCF*) | "in, at" |
| 23. Possession--GCF,DCF | possessive pronouns |
| 24. Purpose--GCF (*ABCF*),ACF | "in order to, to, so that" |
| 25. Rank--GCF (*ABCF*) | "above all" |
| 26. Reference--GCF,DCF,ACF | "as regards, with ref. to" |
| 27. Relational--GCF,ACF | uses terms of kinship |
| 28. Respect--GCF,DCF,ACF | "as regards, with ref. to" |
| 29. Result--ACF | "so that" |
| 30. Separation--GCF (*ABCF*) | "from, away from" |
| 31. Source--GCF (*ABCF*) | "from" |
| 32. Subject--GCF | -- |
| 33. Time--GCF,DCF (*LCF*) | "while, during, after, before" |

The <u>Noun</u> and <u>Exegesis</u>: <u>A</u> <u>Few</u> <u>Examples</u>. Philippians 1:3, a verse whose meaning seems obvious, may not be so simple to translate after all. The verse reads, "I give thanks to my God on every remembrance of you." The key question centers in the meaning of the genitive "of you" (ὑμῶν). Is it *subjective* ("You remember me") or *objective* ("I remember you"). Either is possible. Once more, the context will provide answers for this syntactical problem, but the answers are not all that simple. In the first place, we should remember that the Philippians had indeed remembered Paul when others had not. Philippians 4:15 is clear on this, "You know ... that when I left Macedonia not one church shared in the matter of giving and receiving except you alone...." This relatively remote context would seem to call for a subjective genitive in 1:3. However, as with word and phrase study, the more immediate the context the more relevant. When in 1:4 Paul continues, "Always in my every prayer for all of you ...," it seems that the genitive is objective, i.e., "I remember you." Either reading is possible, but the latter seems preferable.

Other significant case/function identifications in Philippians 1 include: (1) 1:2, where grace and peace come jointly *from God* and *the Lord Jesus Christ* (an ablative of *source*), (2) 1:4, "always *by means of* my *prayer* (dative/instrument of *means*) *for* all *of you* (genitive of *advantage*) *with joy* (genitive of *manner?* = "joyously") making intercession, and (3) 1:11, "filled *with respect to the fruit* (accusative of *reference*) *of righteousness* (genitive of *apposition*, i.e., the fruit which *is* righteousness) *through Jesus Christ* (genitive/ ablative of *agency*) *for* the *glory* and *praise* (accusative of *purpose*) *of God* (*objective* genitive). It is not difficult to see how such identifications may be helpful both in exegesis and exposition with the cases answering such questions as *how, why,* and *with respect to whom or what.* (Table 6.4 summarizes these English interrogatives, together with Greek cases, words, moods, tenses, etc. which may answer them, below.) Remember, some nouns are preceded by prepositions (as is the case with several of these examples). Their functions and meanings are determined both with the grammar[21] and the lexicon.

The Article. The development of the Greek article has been designated "one of the most interesting things in human speech."[22] Whether such a remark is completely accurate is debatable in this age of modern linguistics, but whatever the outcome of such a debate, the Greek article is a versatile and complex part of Koine, one which deserves its own treatment.

There is concensus among grammarians that the article's chief function is to identify, point out, draw attention to, at times with an emphasis upon distinguishing one item (or a group of items) from another (or others). Quite generally, the presence of the article is

---

[21]Esp. Brooks and Winbery, *Syntax*, pp. 65-67.

[22]A.T. Robertson, *A Grammar*, p. 754.

akin to the presence of "the" in English, while the absence of the article is often like having "a" or "an." However, there are times when *anarthrous* words, words not preceded by an article, are considered definite. For example, nouns followed by possessive pronouns and/or certain adjectives do not need articles to indicate their degree of specificity. Hence, ἡ δεξίος χεὶρ αὐτοῦ means "his right hand" and οἰκία αὐτῶν, "their house," where χεὶρ and οἰκία are definite not because they have an article (neither does), but because their attending pronouns/adjectives are contextually specific.

The article used to *specify* or *distinguish* one item from another is everywhere present in the New Testament. See, e.g., Philippians 1:27, where Paul urges the believers to "continue to live worthily of the Gospel (τοῦ εὐαγγελίου) of Christ." In this instance the presence of the article and the qualifying genitive τοῦ Χριστοῦ ("of Christ") combine to make εὐαγγελίου unambiguous. It is not *any* good news for which they are to live worthily, but specifically the Good News that Christ has died for the sins of the world. The same kind of thing happens with substantives which indicate a class or group, as in Luke 10:7, where "The worker (ὁ ἐργάτης) is worthy of his wages."

*Abstract nouns* are frequently attended by the article in order to provide a "determined concrete application."[23] So it is that Paul indicates that the Christian's salvation is τῇ χάριτι ("by grace") in Ephesians 2:8. It is not *any* grace which saves the believer, but the specific grace which comes only by faith to those who are in Christ.[24]

*Proper names* and their equivalents frequently appear

---

[23]Zerwick, *Biblical Greek*, p. 57, #131.

[24]The use of εὐαγγελίου in the previous paragraph also illustrates the point since εὐαγγελίου, like χάρις, is an abstract noun.

with the article in the New Testament, perhaps for emphasis,[25] at times for clarity. ὁ κύριος, for example, though not technically a proper name, generally refers to Christ, while κύριος refers to God in Pauline literature.[26] And while θεός, like κύριος, is not actually a proper name, it certainly approximates a name, frequently with the article, as in Philippians 1:3, "I constantly thank my *God* (τῷ θεῷ)," where the article may also be used to denote *previous reference*. That is, Paul has already said that "grace and peace come from *God* (θεοῦ)" in verse 2. In order to show that the God to whom he offers his thanks in verse 3 is the same God whom he mentioned in verse 2, he precedes θεῷ with the article.

Nouns *connected by* καί come under special consideration when they are preceded by the article. Thus, when two or more nouns are connected by καί and only the first has an article, the several nouns are to be understood *as a group*. However, when each noun is preceded by an article then the nouns clearly refer to different entities. In Philippians 1:7, Paul pictures his "defense and confirmation (τῇ ἀπολογίᾳ καὶ βεβαιώσει) of the Gospel" as a unified action. The same happens in Philippians 1:20, where he speaks of his "eager expectation and hope (τὴν ἀποκαραδοκίαν καὶ ἐλπίδα)", and in 4:20, where he speaks of "God (who is) also our Father (τῷ θεῷ καὶ πατρί)," in this case, a single person. But separate entities are just as clearly in view in 4:6, where Paul speaks of "each prayer and every petition (παντὶ τῇ προσευχῇ καὶ τῇ δεήσει)" of the Philippians, and in 3:19, where he calls attention to "the god ... and the glory (ὁ θεὸς ... καὶ ἡ δόξα)."

At times, the article appears with the predicate nominative in sentences which contain a linking verb. Its function is to distinguish the subject nominative

---

[25]Brooks and Winbery, *Syntax*, p. 69.

[26]Zerwick, *Biblical Greek*, p. 54; Moulton, *A Grammar*, p. 174.

from the predicate nominative, which will not have the article. This is why the article appears with λόγος in the well-known statement, "The Word was God (θεὸς ἦν ὁ λόγος)," in John 1:1. It simply distinguishes the subject (λόγος) from its complement (θεός). It was never intended to suggest that the Word was simply "a" god. To the contrary. The emphatic position of θεος argues the reverse, "The Word was *God!*"

The article may be used *in place of* other parts of speech from time to time. Hence, its use as a *pronoun* in Philippians 1:7, where Paul says, "I have you in *my* heart (ἐν τῇ καρδίᾳ)," and in 2:30, "risking *his* life (παραβολευσάμενος τῇ ψυχῇ)." If the article sometimes replaces a pronoun it may also replace a noun, as in Galatians 5:24, where the text speaks of "*the people* of Christ Jesus (οἱ τοῦ Χριστοῦ Ἰησοῦ)," and Philippians 3:13, "forgetting the *matters* behind me (τὰ ... ὀπίσω ἐπιλανθανόμενος)."

<u>A Word About Adverbial Participles.</u> You probably already know that a word like "while" is frequently supplied when translating the present tense adverbial participle; "after" with the aorist. Such information appears in first year grammars. But you may not be aware that there are other ways to translate adverbial participles. For example, some seem to express *cause.* Such is the case in Philippians 1:6, "I give thanks to my God ... *because I am confident* (πεποιθώς) of this very thing," and 1:14, "And the rest of the brothers in the Lord *on account of their confidence* (πεποιθότας) as a result of my imprisonment have dared to speak more boldly ...." Others seem to suggest the *means* or *instrument* by which something is accomplished. Hence, Philippians 2:2 and 4, "Complete my joy *by having* (ἔχοντες) the same love ... (and) *by* not *noticing* the things of others." Philippians 2:6 may well contain a *concessive* participle, "*Although* he *was* (ὑπάρχων) in the form of God, he did not consider equality with God something to be grasped,"[27]

---

[27]This could, however, be causal, i.e., "(Precisely)

while ἐκλυόμενοι in Galatians 6:9 is clearly *conditional*, "Do not stop doing good, for we shall reap in due time *if we do not waver.*" Still other adverbial participles may suggest *purpose* (e.g., Acts 3:26) or the *manner* in which a thing is accomplished. Some even appear to have the force of an *imperative*. (See, e.g., Romans 12:9-19.) You should be aware of these possibilities since they do at times make a significant difference in how we read a text. The intermediate grammars cover adverbials in some detail.

Of course, adverbial participles appear in dependent clauses and must be related back to a verb, usually an indicative or an imperative. At times, there will be more than one such participle. When this is the case, it is helpful to coordinate these participles under the verb or imperative in the following manner:

Verb (Include the entire independent clause here).
    Participle a.
    Participle b.   (Subordinate all dependent clauses.)
    Participle c.

In this way you can see clearly what the key supporting clauses are. Consider the following New Testament examples of the imperative with adverbial participles.

**Ephesians 5:18:**

"Be <u>filled</u> with the Spirit"
πληροῦσθε ἐν πνεύματι
    a.   <u>Speaking</u> to each other in psalms and hymns ...
       λαλοῦντες ...
    b.   <u>Singing</u> praises in your heart to the Lord
       ᾄδοντες καὶ ψάλλοντες ...[28]

*because* he was in the form of God he did not consider equality with God something to be grasped."
    [28]The meanings of these participles are quite similar; hence, the single English verb, "Singing...."

   c.  Giving Thanks always ...
      εὐχαριστοῦντες ...
   d.  Subjecting Yourselves to one another ....
      ὑποτασσόμενοι ....

## Matthew 28:19-20:

"Make disciples of all nations"
μαθητεύσατε     πάντα τὰ ἔθνη
   a.  Baptizing them...
      βαπτίζοντες...
   b.  Teaching them...
      διδάσκοντες...

In both examples, it seems that the supporting clauses tell us *how* to fulfill the content of the imperatives. These are participles of *means* or *instrumental* participles. Sermonic structure cannot be far away. A sermon from Ephesians 5:18ff., for example, might proceed as follows:

Thesis: You must continually be filled with the Spirit.
Question:  How is this done?
   a.  By speaking to each other...
   b.  By singing to one another...
   c.  By giving thanks...
   d.  By subjecting yourselves to one another....

Sometimes, several adverbial participles will follow an indicative verb, as in Philippians 1:1ff.:

"I Give Thanks to my God on my every remembrance of you"
εὐχαριστῶ    τῷ θεῷ μου ἐπὶ πάσῃ   τῇ μνείᾳ  ὑμῶν
   a.  Making intercession always...
      ποιούμενος τὴν δέησιν...
   b.  Being Confident of this very thing....
      πεποιθὼς       αὐτὸ τοῦτο....

Whereas participle a. (ποιούμενος) appears to answer the "when" question relative to thanksgiving, participle b. (πεποιθώς) is more concerned with the "why" of Paul's thanksgiving. The former is merely *temporal*, while the latter is *causal*.  In other words, the participles answer *different* questions, whereas the participles following the imperatives (in the two examples above) answered the *same* question ("How?") in different ways.

Be on the lookout for multiple adverbial participles attached to a single verb or imperative.  These often provide significant help in understanding the structure of a text.

A Practical Approach.  A critical step in the exegetical process is the asking and answering of the basic interrogatives of a text, much as we have attempted to do with these participles (though adverbial participles by no means answer all of the interrogatives).  Who was involved? What was he/she doing? Why? When? Where? For whom? With what/whom? By what means? What were the results?  How did it happen?  One of the tremendous benefits of this approach is its almost immediate impact upon exposition.  At times these kinds of questions, systematically asked of a text, may even help provide the structure of a sermon or lesson, again, as we have seen with adverbial participles.

The syntactical categories presented throughout this chapter consistently help address the kinds of questions asked here.  For example, the category of agency answers the question, "By whom?"  Means answers "How?"  Cause provides a reason, telling us "why" a thing happens, while location shows us "where" it happens.  In order for you to become familiar with Greek syntactical features which regularly give answer to these and other questions, you should become familiar with Table 6.4, "The Interrogatives: What to Look For" (next page).

### Table 6.4
### The Interrogative: What to Look For

| The Question | Words and Forms Which May[29] Suggest An Answer |
|---|---|
| WHO? | Substantives of all kinds (nouns, adjectives, adjectival participles, pronouns, etc.) |
| WHICH? | Substantives of all kinds |
| WHAT?[30] (general) | Indicative Verbs Imperatives Subjunctives Optatives Participles Infinitives Substantives of all kinds |
| WHAT? (what resulted?) | Many Verbs in Various Moods Clauses begun with ὥστε and occasionally ἵνα |
| WHAT? (what kind?) | Genitive Case Form (basic function of the case) |
| WHERE? | Genitives of Place Datives/Locatives of Place and Sphere, including those begun with prepositional phrases, esp. ἐν |

[29]By all means remember that a single grammatical form may perform several distinct functions. E.g., genitives may suggest time, subject, object, advantage, etc. But no genitive is capable of all of these in a single text.

[30]A very general question with equally general indicators.

| WHEN? | Certain Adverbs, e.g., πάντοτε ("always") |
|---|---|
| | Some Durative Verbs |
| | Historic and Futuristic Verbs |
| | Some Customary or Iterative Verbs |
| | Certain Progressive Verbs |
| | Genitives of Time |
| | Datives/Locatives of Time |

| WHY? (what cause?) | Causal Participles |
|---|---|
| | Causal Infinitives (διὰ τὸ + inf.) |
| | Certain Genitives/Ablatives, Datives/Instrumentals, and Accusative Case Forms, often preceded by prepositions |

| WHY? (what purpose?) | Purposive Adverbial Participles |
|---|---|
| | Purposive Infinitives (εἰς τὸ + inf.; τοῦ + inf.; πρὸς τὸ + inf.; etc.) |
| | Purposive Subjunctives (ἵνα, ὅπως, πρίν) |
| | Certain Genitives/Ablatives and Accusatives, often preceded by prepositions |

| HOW? (what manner?) | Most verbs, esp. those which are descriptive, dramatic, durative, inceptive, ingressive, progressive, tendential and voluntative. |
|---|---|
| | Nouns of Agency in Genitive/Ablative and Dative/Instrumental Case Forms, often with prepositions |
| | Nouns of Manner in Dative/Instrumental and Accusative Case Forms, often with prepositions |
| | Nouns of Means in Genitive/Ablative and Dative/Instrumental Case Forms, again, often with prepositions |

| HOW? (what means?) | Nouns of Agency in Genitive/Ablative and Dative/Instrumental Case Forms, often with prepositions |
|---|---|
| | Nouns of Means in Genitive/Ablative and Dative/Instrumental Case Forms, often with prepositions |

| HOW OFTEN? (what frequency?) | Verbs that are customary or iterative, and certain descriptive and progressive verbs |
|---|---|

**Putting It All Together.** Philippians 1:9-11 forms a single sentence in the Greek text. It follows the subject/verb/object pattern, though the object (τοῦτο) is expanded with several additional clauses which tell us precisely what τοῦτο ("this thing") refers to. The diagram below should help you to see just how the object is fully developed.

The key principles used in this diagram are the principles of *coordination* and *subordination*. The following basic observations may be helpful in learning to tell whether the elements of the sentence should be aligned (coordinate) or indented (subordinate).

1. Line up all clauses, phrases, and words connected by a coordinating conjunction (e.g., καί, δέ, ἀλλά, οὖν, διό, and ἤ).

2. Indent all clauses, phrases, and words connected by a subordinating conjunction (e.g., ἵνα, ὅτι, ὥστε, ὅπως, and ὡς).

3. Indent most prepositional phrases.[31]

The basic sentence reads:

| Subject | Verb | Object |
|---|---|---|
| I | am praying | this .... |
| -- | προσεύχομαι | τοῦτο . . . . |

---

[31]See Walter Liefeld, *New Testament Exposition* (Grand Rapids: Baker, 1984), p. 52 and esp. Gordon Fee, *New Testament Exegesis* (Philadelphia: Westminster, 1983) pp. 61-66, for further help.

But the content of Paul's prayer, as previously noted, is made plain only in his rather elaborate expansion of the object (τοῦτο). Here is that expansion, complete with the syntactical functions of important clauses and phrases in capital letters (in parentheses) on the left side of the page.

(CONTENT)[32] that your love may continue to abound
        ἵνα ἡ ἀγάπη ὑμῶν ἔτι περισσεύῃ
(MEASURE)[33]                 more and more
                     μᾶλλον καὶ μᾶλλον

(DCF/LCF of              in full knowledge
  SPHERE a.)            ἐν ἐπιγνώσει
                       and
                       καὶ
(DCF/LCF of              all understanding
  SPHERE b.)            πάσῃ αἰσθήσει

(PURPOSE 1) in order for you to approve the best things
        εἰς τὸ δοκιμάζειν ὑμᾶς τὰ διαφέροντα

(PURPOSE 2)[34] so that you may be
        ἵνα ... ἦτε

[32]Certain clauses which begin with ἵνα introduce the content of a preceding statement. In other words, when Paul says, "I pray *this*," the ἵνα clause is used to tell us just what *this* is. On this, see C.F.D. Moule, *Idiom Book of New Testament Greek* (Cambridge: Cambridge University Press, 1960), pp. 145-146.

[33]Certain adverbs, like some nouns, are used to indicate the measure or length to which the action of the verb extends, in this case, "more and more."

[34]This is the intended RESULT of purpose 1. There is little difference between the two. In fact, a purpose *is* an intended result. The important thing is that you understand that purpose 2 flows out of and depends upon the successful completion of purpose 1. (This is reflected in the outline below.)

| | |
|---|---|
| (ADJECTIVAL COMPLEMENT) | blameless and pure |
| | εἰλικρινεῖς καὶ ἀπρόσκοποι |
| (DCF/LCF OF TIME) | in the Day |
| | εἰς ἡμέραν Χριστοῦ |
| (GCF OF DESCRIPTION) | of Christ |
| | Χριστοῦ |
| (INTENSIVE PERF. PARTICIPLE)[35] | filled with the fruit |
| | πεπληρωμένοι καρπὸν |
| (GCF OF APPOS.) | of righteousness |
| | δικαιοσύνης |
| (GCF/ABCFAGENCY) | through Jesus Christ |
| | διὰ Ἰησοῦ Χριστοῦ |
| (ACF OF PURPOSE) | for the glory and praise |
| | εἰς δόξαν καὶ ἔπαινον |
| (OBJECTIVE GCF) | of God. |
| | Θεοῦ. |

Using Table 6.4 and a healthy dose of common sense, we may now apply the appropriate interrogatives to the text using the same scheme. This time, I have replaced the syntactical categories with these interrogatives. The expanded object now appears as follows:

| | |
|---|---|
| (WHAT?) | that your love may continue to abound |
| | ἵνα ἡ ἀγάπη ὑμῶν ἔτι ... περισσεύῃ |
| (HOW MUCH?) | more and more |
| | μᾶλλον καὶ μᾶλλον |
| (WHERE? IN WHAT REALM a.) | in full knowledge |
| | ἐν ἐπιγνώσει |
| | and |
| | καὶ |
| (WHERE? IN WHAT REALM b.) | all understanding |
| | πάσῃ αἰσθήσει |

[35]The emphasis is upon the character of believers at the point of Christ's return, the *state* in which they find themselves when He comes back.

(WHY? a.)      in order for you to approve the best things
εἰς τὸ δοκιμάζειν ὑμᾶς τὰ διαφέροντα

(WHY? b.)      so that you may be
ἵνα ... ἦτε

(WHAT? a.)                     blameless and pure
εἰλικρινεῖς καὶ ἀπρόσκοποι

(WHEN?)                        in the Day
εἰς ἡμέραν Χριστοῦ

(WHAT KIND?)                 of Christ
Χριστοῦ

(WHAT? b.)            filled with the fruit
πεπληρωμένοι καρπὸν

(WHICH IS?)[36]                of righteousness
δικαιοσύνης

(THROUGH WHOM?)       through Jesus Christ
διὰ Ἰησοῦ Χριστοῦ

(FOR WHAT PURPOSE?)    for the glory and praise
εἰς δόξαν καὶ ἔπαινον

(WHOM?)                         of God.
Θεοῦ.

The next step is to put this information in some usable form. I suggest the following outline. Notice that it is not slavishly built upon questions (though some do show up), much less syntactical labels. The goal here is not to reproduce the fine points of previous endeavors, but to use these details to help prepare an outline which is geared toward clearly communicating the meaning of this text to your audience without distracting discussions about kinds of clauses, phrases, and the like.

Proposition: Paul prays for the Philippians.

I.   WHAT he prays: that their love may continue to abound.
    A.  To what extent? More and more.

---

[36]That is, "filled with the fruit which is righteousness."

    B.  In what areas?
        1.  Complete knowledge
        2.  Full understanding
II.  WHY he prays this:
    A.  For the moment, so that they may be able to approve the best things.
    B.  For the future (to the extent that they are now able to approve the best things) that they will be:
        1.  Blameless and pure on the Day of Christ.
        2.  Filled with the fruit which is righteousness.
           a.  This happens through the agency of Jesus Christ.
           b.  It is intended for the glory and praise of God.

Not every text is equally given to this approach to diagraming. It is especially difficult to examine much of the gospels and Acts in this way. We will explore other fruitful and complimentary avenues of seeing how clauses, even whole sentences and paragraphs, are related to each other in the coming chapter on discourse. Meanwhile, there are several helpful texts which introduce procedures of diagraming.[37] You should take a careful look at some of these.

**Some Syntactical Suggestions for the Exegete.** Most of these tips are aimed at exegesis more than exposition. Grammatical and syntactical discussions do not often go well from the pulpit, though you may fare better in the classroom on such matters. If you have done your analysis well, you will not have to leap into weighty excurses on grammar and syntax.

[37]I have already mentioned Fee, *New Testament Exegesis*, pp. 60ff., and Liefeld, *New Testament Exposition*, pp. 45-56. But you should also consider Walter C. Kaiser, Jr., *Toward an Exegetical Theology* (Grand Rapids: Baker, 1981), pp. 174ff.

In any case, always:

1.  *Weigh the options* before deciding on the function of a noun, verb, etc.   What appears clear to you may not be so clear to the next person.   Consult grammars and commentaries,[38] especially some of the newer commentaries which print the Greek text and offer technical discussions of syntax.   You will learn much by reading these if they are well researched and written objectively.   On the other hand, do not quit thinking for yourself.   Continue to work at your own identifications.

2.   Be especially sensitive the syntactical *setting* of your text.   Note such matters as *characteristic* tenses, case functions, sentence patterns, and the like.[39] Learn something about the *style* of your author. Carefully note *shifts* (verb tense, sentence pattern, etc.), especially unexpected ones, as you are translating.

3.   *Become thoroughly familiar with an intermediate grammar.*   This brief introduction to selected features of Greek syntax simply is not enough.   You need to purchase and put to good use a more extensive grammar, such as Brooks and Winbery's *Syntax of the New Testament*.   Since the effectiveness of syntactical analysis is directly related to whether you know what to look for,   solid familiarity with such a grammar is

[38]See also Wesley J. Perschbacher's *Refresh Your Greek* (Chicago: Moody Press, 1989).   Perschbacher systematically covers the entire New Testament, with helpful syntactical identifications of the sort covered in this chapter.

[39]C.F.D. Moule, *An Idiom-Book of New Testament Greek* (Cambridge: Cambridge University Press, 1975) and James Hope Moulton, ed., *A Grammar of New Testament Greek* (Edinburgh: T.& T. Clark, 1976), volume 4: *Style*, by Nigel Turner, are especially helpful.

required for careful exegetes. Granted, syntax is not easy. Grammar studies are, on the whole, in decline. It is important that you help reverse this trend, not least because these studies are so vital to good hermeneutics.

4. Perhaps most important of all, *when you are in doubt about the function of a noun or verb, return to the BASIC function of the case or tense.* For example, whether the genitive is subjective or objective, it is still in some sense *descriptive.* Carefully commit to memory the single most important function of every part of speech, tense, case, and the like. Explain words accordingly when there appear several equally valid but more technically precise explanations for Greek forms and phrases.

But do not:

1. *Think of Syntax as Irrelevant.* The multiplication of syntactical categories is often bewildering to students. There are, for example, some 27 or more genitives/ablatives. Students sometimes question the legitimacy of such proliferation. They question whether Paul or John or Matthew would have thought of a genitive as "subjective" or a present as "historic," and, admittedly, these authors probably would not have. However, they grew up *speaking* Greek, enjoying such plusses as voice inflection, bodily gesturing, and other sensory devices vital to spoken communication. Above all, they *heard* their (now dead) language during most of their waking hours and knew almost *intuitively* what was and was not acceptable. We, on the other hand, enjoy none of these benefits as we sit in the study with only the text before us. Moreover, the approach we have taken in this chapter is no different from explaining to a foreigner that "*by* the road" is locative or spatial, "*by* noon" is temporal or time oriented, and "*by* the help of a friend" is instrumental or means oriented. Learning a second language generally requires such a procedure.

2. *Force a form into a syntactical category in order to support a pet doctrine.* There is a tendency, once we have learned the several categories, to want to put them to work for our pet systems of theology. Such technical descriptions sound authoritative and appear to give credibility to our explanations of the text. But in the final analysis, we must be honest with the text and sensitive to such matters as style, context, and setting. Remember, the more immediate the syntactical context, the more relevant. Do not waste your study by fitting the categories of syntax to your system. If you do, you are at best no better for having spent time with the language, and, at worst, not entirely honest.

3. *Multiply the categories of syntax if at all possible.* Though it is just possible that the grammars, especially the intermediate grammars, have left certain legitimate syntactical categories out of their discussions, it is best to introduce new categories cautiously and only in the clear presence of multiple examples for a given usage.

**Practice Problems.** Try your hand at analyzing as many nouns, verbs, articles, and adverbial participles as seem significant to the exegesis of the texts listed below. Then analyze some of these sentences as I have done here at the end of the chapter. Begin by analyzing the sentence pattern, and proceed using the principles of coordination and subordination, as you are able. You may find it helpful to consult Fee's *New Testament Exegesis* and/or Liefeld's *New Testament Exposition* for further help on matters of coordination and subordination.

1. John 1:14, 17.
2. 1 John 1:5.
3. 1 John 2:28.
4. Matthew 6:5.
5. Philippians 2:9-11. Be sure to comment upon the possible significance of the subjunctives in vv. 10-11.
6. 1 Thessalonians 1:2-6. A real challenge. Be sure to look for adverbial participles.

**Bibliography.** Most of these titles have been introduced throughout the pages of this chapter. Once again, I have limited the size of this bibliography in the hope that you will put these books to work in the study.

Brooks, James and Winbery, Carlton. *Syntax of New Testament Greek.* New York: University Press of America, 1979.

Beekman, John and Callow, John. *Translating the Word of God.* Grand Rapids: Zondervan, 1974. Take a close look at chapter 16, "The Genitive Construction," and Appendix E., "A Propositional Display of Philemon."

Dana, H.E. and Mantey, Julius R. *A Manual Grammar of the Greek New Testament.* New York: Macmillan, 1955.

Fee, Gordon D. *New Testament Exegesis.* Philadelphia: The Westminster Press, 1983. See esp. pp. 60ff.

Hanna, Robert. *A Grammatical Aid to the Greek New Testament.* Grand Rapids: Baker, 1983. A verse-by-verse analysis of significant grammatical points covered in other major grammars. Very helpful format.

Harris, Murray J. *Colossians & Philemon: Exegetical Guides to the Greek New Testament.* Grand Rapids: Eerdmans, 1991. A new series which includes theology, exegesis, structural analysis of Greek sentences, and homiletical ideas. Looks to be extremely helpful for the preacher and teacher.

Huey, F.B. and Corley, Bruce. *A Student's Dictionary for Biblical and Theological Studies.* Grand Rapids: Zondervan, 1983. Very helpful in providing the meaning of technical grammatical vocabulary.

Liefeld, Walter. *New Testament Exposition.* Grand Rapids: Zondervan, 1984.

Moule, C.F.D. *An Idiom-Book of New Testament Greek.* Cambridge: Cambridge University Press, 1975.

Moulton, James Hope, gen. ed. *A Grammar of New Testament Greek.* 4 vols. Edinburgh: T.& T. Clark, 1963. Vol. 3: *Syntax*, by Nigel Turner.

Perschbacher, Wesley J. *Refresh Your Greek.* Chicago: Moody Press, 1989.

## CHAPTER 7

## DISCOURSE:
## LOOKING AT THE WHOLE

Beginning Greek grammars regularly include a section on "direct" and "indirect" discourse, where the former provides the exact words of the speaker (e.g., Jesus said, "I am the light of the world"), while the latter indicates an indirect quote (e.g., Jesus said that He is the light of the world).[1] Unfortunately, this discussion of features of quotation is generally the only setting in which the word *discourse* appears among these grammars, but the notion of discourse, as defined by modern linguists, goes much farther than a simple discussion of the features which may indicate the presence of a quote.

**A Definition.** When applied to the analysis of texts, "discourse" refers to "any coherent stretch of language."[2] A discourse may tell a story, offer a report, or prescribe specific instructions, all with the use of well chosen and carefully ordered words. An entire letter is a discourse. So is a novel. Matthew is a discourse, as is 1 Corinthians. What makes a discourse intelligible, indeed, what makes a discourse a discourse,

---

[1]Notice that the two are distinguished in English by the presence of quotation marks for a direct quote and the word "that" for an indirect quote. In Greek εἶπεν ("He said") often indicates a direct quote, while ὅτι ("that") regularly suggests an indirect quote.

[2]Peter Cotterell & Max Turner, *Linguistics & Biblical Interpretation* (Downers Grove, Illinois: InterVarsity Press, 1989), p. 230.

is the careful structuring of its many thoughts through various means, a few of which will be discussed in this chapter.

Whereas we stopped at the sentence level in the previous chapter, here we will attempt to see how selected Greek words and phrases, as well as grammatical components like time shifts and person/ number combinations, serve to provide structure and signal meaning for groups of sentences within a book. We will be working largely at the paragraph level, and mainly with grammatical and linguistic forms (as opposed to literary genre and analysis of themes, etc.). Remember, this is by no means a comprehensive introduction to discourse analysis. Such a study goes well beyond the boundaries of what this book seeks to accomplish. If you wish to pursue the relationship of discourse analysis to Bible study more comprehensively, especially as it relates to the analysis of an entire book of the New Testament, there are several texts which you may find helpful.[3]

**Tools to Consider.** Since discourse analysis involves such large blocks of text, this part of the inquiry into the relevance of Greek for preaching and teaching may seem formidable, too formidable for serious pursuit among

---

[3]Among those designed for Bible students are John Beekman and John Callow, *Translating the Word of God* (Grand Rapids: Zondervan, 1974), and Kathleen Callow, *Discourse Considerations in Translating the Word of God* (Grand Rapids: Zondervan, 1974). These books are especially geared to the Bible translator and, like Louw and Nida's lexicon, offer regular and detailed comments on the idiosyncrasies of numerous languages. Directly related to the interpretation of texts are E. A. Nida, J. P. Louw, A. H. Synan, and J. v W. Cronje, *Style and Discourse, with Special Reference to the Text of the Greek New Testament* (Cape Town: the Bible Society, 1983), and, more recently, Peter Cotterell & Max Turner, *Linguistics & Biblical Interpretation* (Downer's Grove, Illinois: InterVarsity Press, 1989). Both books are helpful, but you should read Cotterell & Turner first.

beginning students.     After all, why worry about translating a chapter (much less, a book) when you are having
trouble with a paragraph, even   a sentence. For this reason you may wish to employ an interlinear[4] (with your
instructor's approval) as you peruse larger sections of
Greek text.   If you do, please observe the following:

1.     *The interlinear is no substitute for* UBS3.
Interlinear texts do not as a rule contain a textual
apparatus, punctuation apparatus, or lists of Old
Testament quotations as in UBS3.   Their choppy arrangement of Greek and English (the latter underneath
the former) makes for difficult, even fragmented,
reading, and may result in *reduced*, not heightened,
comprehension of the text if not used with extreme
care.

2.     *The interlinear approach to translation is flawed.*
That is to say, when translated a word at a time,
sentences do not make sense. For example, John 1:1
would  read, "In beginning it was the Word and the
Word it was with the God and God it was the Word."
This  word-for-word  translation  leaves  much  to  be
desired.    Among  its  problems  are  the  following:  (1)
the prepositional phrase ἐν ἀρχῇ appears to mean "In
(a) beginning" here, when in fact anarthrous nouns
(i.e., those without the article) directly preceded by
a preposition are often definite, (2) we cannot tell
that the subject of the verb ἦν ("it was") is ὁ λόγος
("the Word") from the English alone since the two are
not connected in any syntactical relationship in the
translation, and (3) although the Greek word order is
preserved, it does not correspond to good English word
order, thus creating the possibility of a misunder-
standing on the part of the English reader. In view of
problems like these, you should continue to pursue
translation and parsing skills without the interlinear.   Do not make it your regular text.

[4]A book which contains both the Greek text and one or
more English translations.

3.  *On the other hand, interlinears do allow for quick overview of large sections of Scripture,* and it is precisely here that you may find them helpful. Repeated or shifting moods, tenses, person/number combinations, voice, and vocabulary may be detected quickly with the benefit of an interlinear, despite its problems. Connecting and transition words become especially clear, and their significance stands out all the more since they have come under close individual inspection. Recent translations often obscure such words (or leave them out altogether) and though their reasons for omitting these connectors are often legitimate,[5] English readers sometimes lose critical connections in the text.

But please remember that the interlinear is only as helpful as your knowledge of the Greek it contains. Again, it is no substitute for the better critical texts, and may become a hindrance if you are not careful to use it sparingly and only in the analysis of large blocks of text. It is extremely easy to become overconfident and make numerous misidentifications if you rely solely on the English translation to help you "parse" Greek words. As a rule of thumb, *never do with the interlinear what you could have accomplished with* UBS3 *or* NA26.

A remarkable new software product, GRAMCORD (see preface), is particularly helpful in the analysis of large blocks of text. Its capability of analyzing shifts

---

[5]Domain 91 in Louw and Nida, *Greek-English Lexicon*, consists of "discourse markers," words which may signal a new sentence or a transition of some sort. These are among the words often left untranslated in modern English versions. If γάρ, for example, functions much as a capital letter at the beginning of the first word in an English sentence, then why should it be translated at all? Its "translation" would seem to appear in the capitalized English letter. However, the English reader would have no way of knowing that it was present in the first place and would be in no position to make a judgment about assigning some other meaning to γάρ.

of mood and tense or person and number (and countless other grammatical combinations) allows you to see at a glance the "flow" of a lengthy passage, even a book. GRAMCORD is available at affordable rates, especially to member institutions. Ask your instructor if your institution has a sight license with the GRAMCORD Institute. If it does, be sure to secure computer time with someone who can demonstrate the use of this product.

A third tool, Louw and Nida's *Greek-English Lexicon* (LN), will be discussed at various points in this chapter. Its format allows for convenient grouping of words which play a major role in discourse analysis.

**Markers.** Linguists often use words like "grouping" and "cohesion" when describing the elements of discourse,[6] words which generally point to their concern to know just how a text (or oral presentation) fits together. There is tremendous emphasis upon detecting how characters and progressions combine to make the whole, complete with its unity of theme and diversity of characters and events. Concern for determining the "high point" of the story or letter, together with what precedes and follows it, is also important.

In all of this, the linguist looks for what we will call "markers," indicators which suggest this unity and diversity and which, in the final analysis, contribute to understanding the whole. These may take one of several forms, including markers which suggest time, location, and who the participants in the discourse are. In fact, examples of shifts of tense, significance of voice, and function of case forms, all from previous chapters, serve to "mark" meaning in texts. In other words, we have been involved in *elements* of discourse analysis, up to and including the sentence level, in nearly every chapter of this book. But because discourse analysis involves the consideration of a single text, not simply the individual grammatical or semantic components of several, we have

---

[6]See, e.g., Nida et al., *Style and Discourse*, p. 15, and Kathleen Callow, *Discourse Considerations*, 19ff.

not actually performed such an analysis. Following is a discussion of three kinds of markers, together with illustrations of each.

**Markers of Transition.** The New Testament writers at times used a word or group of words to signal a transition from one *topic* (or *subtopic*) to the next. Three examples will help you to see how this works.

Matthew 5:21-48 stands as a unit, in part, by reason of the repetition of certain catch words at regular intervals. After 5:17-20 spells out the abiding significance of the Old Testament, and especially the importance of practicing righteousness in a measure far exceeding the righteousness of the Scribes and Pharisees, verses 21ff. suggest just how this is to be accomplished. In these verses Jesus provides six examples, 5 of which begin with Ἠκούσατε ὅτι ἐρρέθη ["You (have) heard that it was said"]. These examples appear in verses 21, 27, 33, 38, and 43. A sixth verse (31) simply has Ἐρρέθη δὲ ("And it was said"), though it too introduces a fresh example.[7]

Significantly, each instance of Ἠκούσατε is followed in the next verse by ἐγὼ δὲ λέγω ("But *I* say"), providing further structure for this part of the discourse and suggesting the cohesiveness of the entire unit (5:21-48). Jesus is repeatedly challenging current assumptions (signaled by Ἠκούσατε) with His own authoritative teaching (introduced by ἐγὼ δὲ λέγω). Although the whole section is held together by the regular use of these markers, it is also clear that they continually introduce *new* examples, and thus serve to shift from one (sub)topic to the next within the larger passage.

Chapter six employs a similar device, though not as extensively. In this instance, Ὅταν ("Whenever") regularly marks a transition from one example to the next.

[7]Perhaps Ἠκούσατε is left out in this instance since the third example (divorce) is so closely tied to the second (adultery).

The general subject is a continuation of the theme of righteousness (δικαιοσύνην), which first appears in the Beattitudes (5:6 and 10), and again in 5:20. Jesus calls attention to this theme once more in 6:1, where He instructs His hearers not to practice their righteousness in front of people in order to be seen by them. Three distinct areas of personal righteousness are then singled out, each introduced by ῞Οταν. They are almsgiving (6:2), praying (6:5), and fasting (6:16).

Summarizing, in both Matthew 5 and 6 these markers (῞Ηκούσατε, ἐγὼ δὲ λέγω, and ῞Οταν) are used to suggest diversity and continuity. On the one hand, they stand in series and thus link thematically related portions of entire chapters together. On the other, they signal movement from one example to the next within these larger sections. Such seems to be their two-dimensional function in the discourse. This understanding should help you to mark the limits of passages you will preach and teach accurately.

Paul employs a similar marker in multiple settings. Περὶ δέ ("And now about ...") appears 5 times in the last part of 1 Corinthians (7:1, 7:25, 8:1, 12:1, and 16:1). In every one of these instances, the apostle is moving from one subject to the next, probably in answer to questions the Corinthians had posed for him (7:1). In 7:1 he proceeds with a discussion about marriage and divorce; in 7:25 he shifts the discussion to focus on the unmarried; in 8:1 the topic is entirely new as Paul remarks on food offered to idols; in 12:1 he moves on to "spiritual matters"; and in 16:1, to the collection for the Judean saints. What is of interest here is the fact that Paul uses a regular marker of transition over the course of *ten chapters.* There are seemingly other sections not introduced with Περὶ δέ within these ten chapters, especially in chapter 11 (e.g., proper appearance in worship, vv. 2-15), but even these may fit into the larger questions initially signaled by περὶ δέ, and may therefore be considered subsections.[8]

[8]Consider, for example, the entire section from

Here again, the analysis may help you determine what sections belong together for purposes of expository preaching and teaching. It is better to go with Paul's divisions than arbitrary ones, far better to view his thematic connections than to impose yours artificially. Further, such analysis may help you understand other texts which contain the Περὶ δέ marker (or one like it), passages like 1 Thessalonians 4:9ff.[9]     In this instance

8:1--11:34. It begins Περὶ δε τῶν εἰδωλοθύτων ("And now about meat offered to idols"), and proceeds with a discussion of the exercise of personal freedom in choosing what Christians should and should not eat. Paul concludes that he personally will not eat anything, including meat sacrificed to idols, which might cause a brother to stumble, implying that the Corinthians should do same (8:13). But in chapter 9 he launches into seemingly unrelated waters, describing as he does the "rights of an apostle." Closer inspection reveals, however, that this chapter is a part of his agenda to keep Christians from exercising their own "rights" in a manner inconsistent with the needs of others. (See especially 9:22-23.) The warnings from Israel's spiritual mismanagement (10:1-13) further underscore the need for personal discipline, while in 10:14--11:1 he returns directly to the issue first raised in 8:1, imbibing in food and drink offered to idols. Chapter 11, also seemingly unrelated, does however conclude with a discussion of the Lord's Supper and its proper exercise, probably viewed as the Christian alternative to food offered to idols. By announcing a major topic and weaving several related and supporting threads throughout chapters 8-11, Paul has plainly shown the grand distinction between the idol's feast and the Lord's table, and has in so doing shown that Christians no longer have anything to do with food offered to idols.

[9]Though you will not be preaching it, the *Didache*, an early Christian writing (c. A.D. 120), also employs περὶ δὲ in sections VII.1 ("Now concerning baptism"), IX.1 ("Now concering the Eucharist"), and XI.3 ("Now con-

Paul introduces the subjects of "brotherly love" (4:9) and "times and seasons" (5:1) with the use of Περὶ δέ, perhaps here, as elsewhere, in answer to questions posed to him. This is evidenced by his statement in 4:9, "And now about brotherly love, you do not have a need for me to *write to you*." One wonders why he would feel the need to mention writing to them if they had not asked him to do so in the first place. Thus, it seems that Περὶ δέ not only signals a new topic, but answers a specific question raised by those being addressed. You will be asked to test this conclusion when you examine yet another passage which contains περὶ δέ, Matthew 24:36, listed with the other practice problems at the end of this chapter.

If certain markers signal a transition from one topic to the next, others signal a transition from one *event* to another. Such is the case with Matthew's frequent use of the genitive absolute. Though he does not always describe a new event with this construction, the following examples from chapters 2 and 8 demonstrate that it is at least a regular feature in the first gospel (genitive absolutes in italics):

1. 2:1, "*After Jesus was born* in Bethlehem of Judea ... wise men came ...."
2. 2:13, "*After they left*, an angel ... appeared."
3. 2:19, "And *when Herod died*, ... an angel of the Lord appeared ...."
4. 8:1, "And *when He went down* from the mountain, many crowds followed Him."
5. 8:5, "And *when He went* into Capernaum, a Centurion went to Him ...."
6. 8:28, "And *when He went* into ... the country of the Garadenes ... two demon-possessed men met Him ...."

In each case, there is a change in the focus of the text as some new event is introduced. Wise men come; an angel directs Joseph to go to Egypt; another directs his

cerning the apostles and prophets").

return; Jesus leaves the scene of the Sermon on the Mount; a Centurion comes for his servant's healing; two demon-possessed men come from the tombs to meet Him. New characters. Sudden announcements. Regular requests. Especially is there an emphasis upon going places with verbs like ἐγείρω, εἰσέρχομαι, and καταβαίνω. The genitive absolute frequently signals *movement.*[10]

Actually, this construction is just right for changing events and introducing new characters since the subject of the genitive absolute is never the same as the subject of the main clause in a Greek sentence. Therefore, there must be at least two participants (usually people) involved in any sentence containing a genitive absolute. It is a case where grammatical structure is well-suited to linguistic function.

**Personal and Relational Markers.** Every discourse depicts relationships which exist among its several elements (personal and impersonal). Such relationships contribute to the cohesion of the whole by showing precisely how its parts are linked together. There are many ways to trace important connections; among them, the use of pronouns (personal and relative) and person/number combinations in the verb (especially in the absence of pronouns). Three examples, all of them from Paul, demonstrate the significance of some of these markers.

Some time ago, a student came to me with a question about the subject of Colossians 1:28, which reads, "*We* are proclaiming Him, instructing every person and teaching every person in all wisdom." His question centered in the persons to whom the "We" of this verse refers. It certainly includes Paul, but who else? To find an answer we traced the personal pronouns and person/number combinations in the verbs of Colossians 1. The following pattern emerged:

---

[10]Of course, other markers of a similar nature are used by Matthew, especially present and aorist participles. See, e.g., 8:14 and 18, and 9:1 and 9.

1. In 1:1-14, the subject is generally first plural, probably referring to Paul and Timothy (1:1).
2. In 1:15-20, the subject shifts to third person singular with regular reference to Christ.
3. In 1:21-23, the subject shifts again, this time to the Colossians themselves (second person plural).
4. In 1:24-26, the subject is Paul (first singular), while in verse 27 it is God (third singular).
5. Finally, in 1:28 Paul shifts back to first plural, the same combination he used in 1:1-14.

In summary, Paul's subjects in chapter 1 range from "We" to "He" to "You," and back to "We" in 1:28. Since he used the first plural in reference to himself and Timothy early in chapter 1, it is likely that the "We" of 1:28 resumes the discussion begun in 1:1-14. For the sake of clarity it is probably best, therefore, to render the verse, "We (that is, Paul and Timothy) proclaim Him ...."

Or consider 1 Thessalonians 2:13-17, a text I was assigned to preach recently. In chapters 1 and 2 there is a fascinating correlation between the appearance of alternate meanings of γίνομαι (to "be" and "become") and regular shifts from first person plural ("We") to second person plural ("You"). These shifts of meaning and grammar appear as follows:

A   1:5 "You know what *We* were (ἐγενήθημεν) "
B   1:6 "*You* became (ἐγενήθητε) imitators"

A   2:5 "*We* were (ἐγενήθημεν) not flattering"
A   2:7 "*We* were (ἐγενήθημεν) babes in your midst"
B   2:8 "*You* became (ἐγενήθητε) dear friends"

A   2:10 "*We* were (ἐγενήθημεν) blameless"
B   2:14 "*You* became (ἐγενήθητε) our imitators"

This careful play on the meanings of γίνομαι, together with the shifts in person, shows precisely how the two principal participants in chapters one and two (Paul and company on the one hand, and the Thessalonians on the other) relate to each other. In essence, *what the one was the other became.* (A sermon title cannot be far away!) The appearance of words like "type" (1:7) and "imitators" (1:6; 2:14) further underscores the notion that the Thessalonian believers had begun to live the Christian life as Paul had presented it to them.

Galatians 3:15-29 presents several relational markers which help us to see just how Paul's argument unfolds. The most important features are (1) a general shift from third singular ("it") to first plural ("we") to second plural ("you"), and (2) the regular and careful use of various conjunctions (especially δέ, ἵνα, and γάρ) which help distinguish the several concerns of the passage. Figure 7.1 helps sort all this' out for verses 21-29. Take a close look at it.

## Figure 7.1

| Verse/conj/person | | Statement |
|---|---|---|
| 21 | οὖν 3 | Therefore, is the law against the promises? ... Certainly not! |
| | εἰ γάρ 3 | For if a law capable of giving life were given |
| | 3 | then righteousness would have come from law. |
| 22 | ἀλλά 3 | But Scripture has hemmed in all things under sin. |
| | ἵνα 3 | So that the promise ... may be given to those who believe through the faith of Jesus Christ. |
| 23 | δέ 1 | But before faith came we were confined by law ... |
| 24 | ὥστε 1 | so that the law has become our custodian ... |
| | ἵνα 1 | so that we might be justified by faith. |
| 25 | δέ 1 | But now that faith has come, we are no longer under a custodian. |

| 26 | γάρ | 2 | For all of you are sons of God through faith in Christ Jesus. |
| 27 | γάρ | 2 | For as many of you as were baptized into Christ put Him on. |
| 28 | (none) | 3 | There is neither Jew nor Greek, slave nor free, male nor female, |
| | γάρ | 2 | For you are all one in Christ Jesus. |
| 29 | εἰ δέ | 2 | And if you are of Christ, |
| | ἄρα | 2 | Then you are the descendents of Abraham, heirs .... |

Did you notice that Paul speaks quite impersonally of the relationship of the law to the Promise in verses 21-22, never involving himself directly (first person), much less the Galatians (second person). However, he becomes more intimate in verses 23-24, remarking that "*we* were shut up by law ... (which) has become *our* custodian ... so that *we* may be justified." And in verses 25-29, he is very direct as he informs the Galatians, "*You* are sons of God ... *You* are one in Christ ... *You* are the seed of Abraham." The significance of the pattern probably lies in a heightened emphasis on the content of verses 26-30. Paul is making a very direct application to the Galatians, an application which lies at the heart of the message of the entire book. No fewer than four times in as many verses he mentions Christ. What's more, he focuses on the Galatians' *participation* in Christ. They are sons through faith *in Christ Jesus* (ἐν Χριστῷ Ἰησοῦ); they were baptized *into Christ* (εἰς Χριστὸν); they are one *in Christ Jesus* (ἐν Χριστῷ Ἰησοῦ); and they are *of Christ* (Χριστοῦ). What better medicine for people who tended to rely all too heavily on the law, not clearly perceiving the source of their salvation?

Now notice the conjunctions in the column to the left. There is a regular pattern of markers of contrast (ἀλλά and δέ), followed by main clauses, which are in turn followed by subordinate clauses that provide purposes and reasons for the assertions introduced by ἀλλά and δέ. Interestingly, each time ἀλλά or δέ appears in verses 22-25, it introduces a factual statement about the believer's relationship to the law:

1. But (ἀλλά) Scripture  has hemmed in all  things under sin (22).
2. But (δέ) before faith came, we were hemmed in by law (23).
3. But (δέ) now that faith has come, we are no longer under a custodian (25).

All  other  clauses  are  subordinate.   The  significance? The  key  focus  is  the  believer's  relationship  to  the  law, especially  in  verses  23-25,  both  of  which  appear  in  first person  plural.   That  there  is  a  time  shift  from  verse  23 to  verse  25  is  also  significant.   The  former  describes the  believer's  relationship  to  the  law  prior  to  Christ's coming,  while  the  latter  shows  how  that  relationship  has changed since His coming.

Still  another  significant  point  remains  to  be  made from  this  analysis.   Did  you  notice  that  there  is  a  con-junction  of  some  sort  introducing  nearly  every  clause  in the  section?   Why,  then,  is  there  no  conjunction  intro-ducing  the  statement  in  verse  28  ("There  is  neither  Jew nor  Greek,  slave  nor  free,  male  nor  female")?   And,  along with  this,  why  has  Paul  shifted  from  second  plural  to third  singular  here,  right  in  the  heart  of  his  direct application?  That  he  is  in  some  way  calling  attention  to the  remark  is  undoubtedly  true  by  reason  of  its placement.   Then  too,  it  may  have  seemed  that  to  present such  a  universal  concept  as  the  oneness  in  Christ  of  Jew and  Greek,  slave  and  free,  and  male  and  female  in  second person  would  have  been  out  of  place.  Whatever  your conclusions  on  the  matter,  the  absence  of  a  conjuction preceding  this   very  compact[11]  and  apparently  parenthe-tical  remark  seems  important  in  view  of  the  fact  that  all other  clauses  in  this  section  are  introduced  by  conjunc-tions.

There  are  so  many   ways   to  express  relationships.  At

_____

[11]On  the  significance  of  compactness  in  discourse,  see Nida et al., *Style and Discourse*, pp. 44-45.

the microlevel (a term applied to the smallest levels of discourse), conjunctions and prepositions are particularly given to showing how events relate to persons and things. Domain 89, "Relations," in the Louw/Nida lexicon (volume 1, pp. 777ff.) is particularly helpful in sorting these out, as is the appendix on prepositions in Brooks and Winbery, *Syntax of the New Testament* (pp. 65ff.). Domain 90, "Case," explores "the relation of participants to events or states,"[12] while domain 91 covers "Discourse Markers" (a rather narrow use of the term "markers" to describe several words which have lost much of their usual meaning). Domain 92, "Discourse Referentials," summarizes pronouns commonly used to refer attention to a person or thing in the discourse. You should peruse all of these domains in order to get a feel for the sort of words which may trigger relationships among persons, things, and events.

**Repetition.** Cohesion is frequently brought about through repetition. We have already seen something of this in chapters 2 (morphemes) and 3 (words), but it is equally true that repeated *grammatical* components bring unity to a text. For example, in Acts 17:16-21 Luke consistently uses the imperfect tense to depict events which were going on on a daily basis. Here, Paul was constantly vexed by what he continued to behold (idols), and spoke of Christ regularly in the synagogue and in the market place. The Epicureans and Stoics kept on calling him a babbler because he continued to preach Jesus and the resurrection. However, when the scene shifts from his regular daily activities to a specific address on the Areopagus, so do the tenses. In verses 22ff., we find a mix of presents, aorists, and perfects, all summoned to account for the past and present actions of God. In part, it is Luke's use of imperfects in the earlier section that provides Paul a sort of "platform" from which to speak to the philosophers. Take your cue from him; in your sermon or lesson on this text, set the stage with verses 16-21, and play it out with verses 22-27.

---

[12]Louw and Nida, *Greek-English Lexicon*, vol. 1, p. 796.

Or consider John's careful use of questions in the seventh chapter of his gospel. You are likely aware of the fact that Greek questions begun with οὐ (οὐκ, οὐχ) anticipate a positive response (e.g., "You *did* go to the store, didn't you?"), while those begun with μή call for a "no" answer (e.g., "*You* didn't go to the store, *did* you?"). There are ten such questions in the dialogue of John 7. Two begin with οὐχ, seven with μή, and one with μήποτε.

These questions serve to hold the passage together as a series of brief, related paragraphs, but they do more. They highlight *assumptions*, the varied assumptions of the people and Pharisees regarding the identity of Jesus (vv. 25, 26, 31), assumptions about the origin of the Christ (vv. 41-42), and assumptions about how people should respond to Jesus (vv. 47-48). One query, raised by Nicodemus, called into question the negative predispositions of the chief priests and Pharisees toward Jesus' actions. Since the law allowed for a hearing, Jesus surely deserved one (v. 52). But the Pharisees only retorted, "You aren't from Galilee too, are you?" (v. 52). Whatever else you do with this text, be sure to analyze these assumptions carefully. There is more than ample room for application in view of modern assumptions about the origin and person of Jesus.

**Suggestions.** The following tips may prove helpful.

1. *Use the right tools.* If you need an interlinear use one, but remember the cautions cited earlier in this chapter. You will also find Louw and Nida's lexicon particularly helpful in locating selected elements of discourse. Be sure to consult it regularly.

2. As always, *there is usually no need to go into detail about how you arrived at your paragraph divisions, etc. in the sermon.* Simply use these elements of discourse analysis as a tool to help structure the exposition.

3. However, if your analysis leads you to see paragraph divisions in a way that is obviously at variance

with the pew Bibles, and if the division is not otherwise obvious in English, you should consider saying something about it, *especially if it makes a radical difference in your understanding of the text.*

4. When you have finished parsing the various forms in your passage, *make careful comparisons noting such matters as repetition, patterns, and transition words.* Explore every possible connection.

5. At the same time, *be careful not to overdo it.* If you carry this too far it is quite possible to see *too many* connections, that is, connections which do not in reality exist.

6. *Be sure to balance the discourse concerns of this chapter with others, especially matters of content.* Discourse analysis is heavy on content analysis. In order to get the complete picture, you should carefully trace and analyze themes, story lines, tone, and the like. (See bibliography items below for further help in this.)

7. Above all, remember to *think "big picture."* Parsing words and identifying case functions are important, but these are rather like reading a digital watch. You see the numbers minute by minute, but you do not see them in the same way as you see the hands on the face of a clock. There is no sense of perspective, no "background" against which to place the naked numbers. So it is with Greek. Putting correctly parsed forms, morphological analyses, word studies, and syntactical identifications into the larger framework of discourse is all-important if you hope to gain a sense of proper proportion in your exegesis, and your preaching for that matter.

**Conclusion.** There are other kinds of markers not covered in this chapter, especially markers of time. Domain 67 in Louw and Nida will provide help in locating these (volume 1, pp. 628ff.). Many of them are quite obvious. Phrases such as "The next day" and "After this" are fairly frequent in Scripture, especially in the gos-

pels and Acts.    In particular, ἐγένετο ("And it happened") seems to signal a progression of time in certain
texts (e.g., Matthew 13:53), though not in others (e.g.,
Luke 2:1).    Be ever aware of the fact that events do not
always follow one after the other in Scripture, even when
they appear to.    Cotterell & Turner's reconstruction of
Mark 6:14ff. is illustrative of this fact.[13]

I have attempted to give you only a *feel* for elements
of discourse in this final chapter.    If, for example, you
are more sensitive to transitional markers, indicators of
paragraph structure, relationships which exist between
events and people/things, and grammatical repetition as
an aid to cohesion--and all of these within the larger
framework of the book you are studying--then I have been
successful.    Careful attention to such seemingly small
matters as tense, voice, case, gender, and number at the
*paragraph* level is what is important here.    If you can
rise above simple parsing and see the interrelatedness of
factors such as these, you are on the productive road to
discourse analysis.

**Practice Problems.**    At least two of these arise from
studies conducted elsewhere in this chapter.    You may
need to review these in order to come to a satisfactory
conclusion.

1.    Using a concordance, study πάλιν in John's gospel.
In what way(s) does it appear to be used in the
discourse?    You may wish to consult both BAGD and LN.

2.    Take a careful look at Matthew's use of περὶ δέ in
24:36.    Does Matthew use this marker as Paul did?    What
about the parallel in Mark 13:32?    Be sensitive to the
presence or absence of questions.

3.    Trace the person/number combinations in Galatians
4:1-7.    How do these compare with those we examined in
3:21-29?    What does this "flow" suggest, if anything?

[13]*Linguistics & Biblical Interpretation*, p. 235.

4. The presence of ἀκολούθει μοι in John 21:19 and 22 seems significant. (ἀκολουθοῦντα appears in verse 20.) But these verses belong to completely different paragraphs in certain translations. Should they? Are there other markers which may indicate otherwise?

5. Using a concordance, study the occurrences of μὴ γένοιτο in Romans. Does this optative, together with other regular features (you have to find them) appear to be significant in the structure of the book?

6. Take a look at ἀγαπητοί and τεκνία in 1 John using a concordance. Any significance as markers?

**Bibliography.** All of these titles appear throughout the chapter. They need no special introduction. Many works on discourse deal almost exclusively with the *spoken* word. I have not included these for obvious reasons.

Beekman, John, and Callow, John. *Translating the Word of God.* Grand Rapids: Zondervan, 1974.
Callow, Kathleen. *Discourse Considerations in Translating the Word of God.* Grand Rapids: Zondervan, 1974.
Cotterell, Peter, & Turner, Max. *Linguistics & Biblical Interpretation.* Downer's Grove, Ill.: Intervarsity Press, 1989.
Nida, E.A., and Louw, J.P. *Greek-English Lexicon of the New Testament Based on Semantic Domains.* 2 Volumes. New York: United Bible Societies, 1988.
Nida, E.A., Louw, J.P., Snyman, A.H., and Cronje, J. v W. *Style and Discourse: With Special Reference to the Text of the Greek New Testament.* Cape Town: Bible Society, 1983.

# APPENDIX A:
# CHIEF MSS, VERSIONS, AND FATHERS

This appendix lists important mss, versions, and fathers (especially those cited frequently in UBS3 and NA26) by text-type, date, and contents. Manuscript dates are provided on the lefthand side of the page. The manuscripts themselves are listed in the appropriate text-type column (Alexandrian, Western, etc.). Standard abreviations[1] for manuscript contents (e = Gospels; a = Acts; p = Paul; c = General Epistles; r = Revelation) appear at appropriate places within the columns.

Consult these charts frequently in the practice of textual criticism. They are designed to give you a feel for the relative importance of given mss, versions, and fathers at a glance. They are not designed to replace the fuller analyses of these mss in books mentioned throughout chapters two and three, but only as handy reference helps.

There is some debate about the text-type of several mss listed here (I, for example). This is so because there is simply no foolproof method of reconstructing families of texts. However, a large measure of agreement exists for the text-type identification of most of the mss, versions, and fathers included in this appendix.[2]

[1]See UBS3, p. xi.

[2]I have consulted and compared Metzger, *Text of the New Testament*, pp. 36-92, *A Textual Commentary on the New Testament* (also by Metzger), pp. xxix-xxx, Greenlee, *New*

As noted in chapter 2, the Caesarean text is highly dubious. Some recent literature does not even acknowledge it. If anything, it consists of a group of mss, roughly related, though with significant variety. The second column in this chart consists of these mss, which are probably best labeled "mixed," though of some importance in determining the text of the New Testament. It is perhaps best not to think of them as a distinct text-type.[3]

### THE TEXT-TYPES

| Alexandrian Mss | Mixed Mss | Western Mss | Byzantine Mss |
|---|---|---|---|
| II | | | Irenaeus(e) Diatessaron(e) | |
| II/III | $p^{66}$(e) $p^{46}$(p) Clement-Alex. | | | |
| III | $p^{75}$(e) $p^{45}$(a) $p^{47}$(r) Origen (part) | $p^{45}$(e)[4] Origen (part) | $p^{29}$(a) $p^{48}$(a) Tertullian (e) | |

*Testament Textual Criticism*, esp. pp. 117-118, Aland and Aland, *The Text of the New Testament*, pp. 96-159, Michael W. Holmes, "*New Testament Textual Criticism*," pp. 59-60, and the introduction to UBS3, pp. xiiiff., in the preparation of this chart. Of course, not all of these authors agree on every identification offered here.

[3]See esp. Holmes, "New Testament Textual Criticism," who lists many of these (and other mss) as "Other Important MSS," pp. 59-60.

[4]Though perhaps not in Matthew.

|      | Alexandrian Mss | Mixed Mss | Western Mss | Byzantine Mss |
|------|-----------------|-----------|-------------|---------------|
| III/ |                 |           | $p^{38}$(a) 0171(e) |       |
| IV   | Coptic$^{sah}$(eapc) <br> Coptic$^{boh}$(eapc) |  |            |               |
| IV   | ℵ (eapcr) <br> B (eapc) |         |             |               |
|      |                 | Armenian (e) | Latin Versions | Gothic (eapcr) |
|      | Athanasius (eac) <br> Cyril-Alex. (eac) | Eusebius (e) <br> Cyril-Jerus. (e) |  |  |
| V    | A(apcr) <br> C (eapcr) <br> T(e) I(p) <br> 048(apc) | | D(eac) | A(e) |
|      | W(Lk 1-8:12, Jn) | W(Mk 5-16) | W(Mk 1-5) | W(Mt,Lk 8-24) |
|      |                 | Georgian (e) <br> Pal Syriac (e) | Latin Versions (epc) |  |
| VI   | Z(e) H(p)       |           | D(p) E(a) <br> Syriac$^{s,c}$ (portions) | P(e)[5] |
| VII  | $p^{74}$        |           |             |               |
| VIII | L(e) <br> Ψ(eapc) | $p^{41}$(a) |           | E(e) |

[5]Ms number = (024); contrast ninth century P(a).

|       | Alexandrian<br>Mss | Mixed<br>Mss | Western<br>Mss | Byzantine<br>Mss |
|-------|--------------------|--------------|----------------|------------------|
| IX    | 33(eapc)<br>892(e) (Mk) | $\Theta$(e)<br>1(e)<br>(in $f^1$) |  | F(e) G(e)<br>H(ea)<br>L(apc)<br>M(e) |
| IX    |  |  |  | P(a)[6]<br>V(e) $\Lambda$(e)<br>$\Pi$(e) $\Omega$(e) |
| X     | 1739(pc) | 1582(e) | 1739(a) | S(e) $\Gamma$(e)<br>046(r) |
| XI    | 2344(r)<br>81(apc)<br>104(apc)<br>1006(r)<br>1854(r)<br>1175(apcr) | 28(e)<br>700(e)<br>788(e) |  |  MANY |
| XII   | 1611(r)<br>1241(ec)<br>326(apc) | 1071(e)<br>(many mss<br>from $f^{13}$) |  | LATE<br><br>MINUSC. |
| XIII  | 2053(r) | 13(e) (from<br>$f^{13}$) |  |  |

[6]Ms number = (025); contrast sixth century ms P(e).

## APPENDIX B: DATES AND LOCATIONS
## OF THE EARLY VERSIONS

Discovering the origins and influence of New Testament versions is a demanding study in itself.  Since versions were created to reach and edify peoples in the lands surrounding Palestine, each version has a unique story.[1] Some of these early translations (e.g., the Latin Vulgate) are more famous than others, and some are more helpful than others in studying textual problems.  In particular, you should pay careful attention to the Old Latin versions, Coptic (Sahidic and Bohairic), and the Syriac versions.

As with Greek mss, versions have their own ms histories.  Some 8,000 mss of the Latin Vulgate are known today, their dates ranging from the fifth to the fifteenth centuries.[2] This difficulty aside, certain versions are useful to textual critics since their locales are fairly secure and their dates are often quite early. When early versions from a wide variety of geographical locales support a given reading, it is worthy of careful consideration.

[1]Please see *The Early Versions of the New Testament: Their Origin, Transmission, and Limitations*, by Bruce M. Metzger (Oxford: Clarendon Press, 1977), an excellent introduction to the versions and their significance for textual criticism.

[2]Greenlee, *Scribes, Scrolls, and Scripture*, p. 31. Metzger, *Versions*, indicates that there may be more than 10,000 mss of the Vulgate, p. 334.

The specific areas pinpointed on this map are those where the versions were clearly used, but there were other areas where these languages were spoken and where the versions may also have been used. Gothic was likely read throughout much of Europe, Syriac to the east in Mesopotamia, and Latin in North Africa.[3]

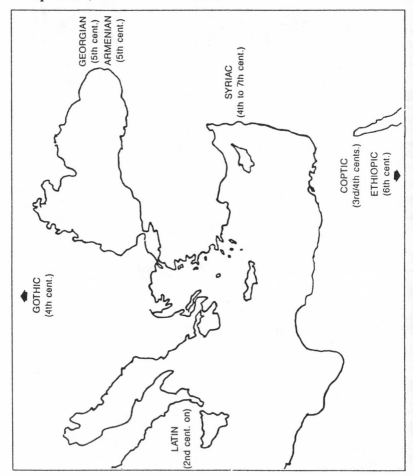

[3]See Metzger, *Versions*, pp. 3, 288f., and 377.

# APPENDIX C: DATES AND LOCATIONS
## OF THE CHURCH FATHERS

Although the church fathers do not play an over-whelmingly critical role in determining the text of the New Testament, it would be wrong to overlook them completely. The UBS3 apparatus certainly does not. It regularly lists multiple fathers for its readings. This chart should help you get a feel for some of these men, their locations, and when they lived.

You should be aware that certain fathers traveled extensively, may have lived in multiple locations (e.g., Origen, who lived first in Alexandria, later in Jerusalem, and again in Alexandria; and Jerome, who spent some time in Rome and later in Bethlehem), often quoted from memory, and may have had multiple textual traditions or families at their disposal. In other words, there was a significant level of "cross-pollination" among their copies of the New Testament.

Still, it is helpful to know some of their primary locations in order to help assess the geographical distribution for a given reading. This, then, is the chief value of this map of the fathers.

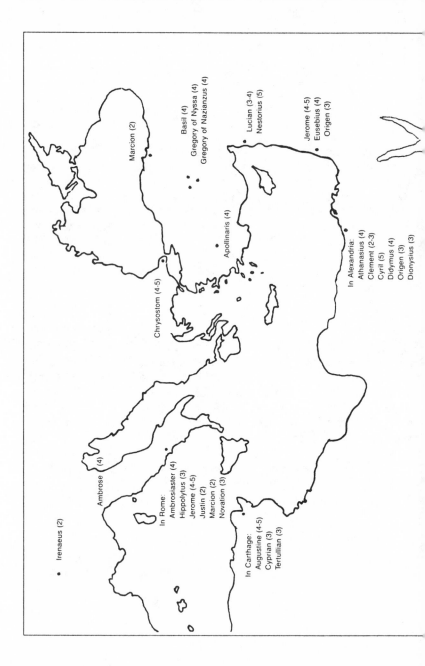

# APPENDIX D:
## SOME COMMON ROOT MORPHEMES

These roots have been chosen on the basis of frequency and possible exegetical significance.[1] The list is not exhaustive. The meanings given with these roots are only the roughest attempts at supplying some central idea for each root and should not be used to draw weighty lexical conclusions.

Several observations will help you use this chart effectively. 1. Those morphemes (and morpheme combinations) preceded with an asterisk (*) are not generally listed as distinct roots in the lists of Metzger and Greenlee, but do appear as given here with some frequency in the New Testament. 2. Additional forms/endings of selected roots show up in parentheses following the root. These are included in order to assist you in locating these roots in the text. 3. Certain roots which once contained digamma (ϝ), a letter which does not appear in the New Testament, are spelled as they appear in Scripture, without digamma.

---

[1] I have consulted Barclay M. Newman, Jr., *A Concise Greek-English Dictionary of the New Testament* (London: United Bible Societies, 1971), and compared the lists in Thomas Rogers, *Greek Word Roots*, and Bruce Metzger, *Lexical Aids for Students of New Testament Greek*, in drawing up this list.

1. ἀγ--go, lead
2. ἁγ--holy
3. ἀγγελ--message
4. ἀκο(υ)--hear
5. ἀρχ--beginning, chief
6. βα--go
7. βαλ (βλη)--toss, throw
8. βαφ(π)--dip, plunge
9. γεν--be, beget
9. γνο(ω)--know
10. γραφ--write
11. δεικ--show
12. δεχ--take
*13. διακ--serve
*14. διδασκ(χ)--teach
15. δικ--show
16. δο--give
17. δοκ(ξ)--think, seem, glory
*18. δουλ--slave
*19. δυν--able, powerful
20. ἐρχ--go
21. ἐχ--have
22. ἐργ--work
23. θαν--die
24. θε--put
*25. ἰσχυ--strong
26. καθ--clean
27. καλ (κλη)--call
28. κει--lie
*29. κοιν--common
30. κοπ--cut, chop
31. κρι(ν)--distinguish, separate
32. κυρ--supreme, lord
33. λαβ--take, receive
34. λεγ--say, speak
35. λυ--loose, free
36. μεν--remain
37. μακ--large
38. μεγ--large
39. μερ--part
40. νο(υ)--know
*41. οἰκ--dwelling
42. ὁμ--like, as
43. ὀπ--see
*44. παι(δ)--young person[2]
*45. παντ(ς)--every, all
*46. πορ--go
*47. πορν--unlawful inter-course
*48. πιπ(τ)--fall
*49. πισ, πειθ--bind, trust
50. πλα (πλη)--fill
*51. σωτ (σωζ)--safe
52. σκα(η)--covering
53. στα (ιστη)--stand
54. στελ--send, set
55. στρεφ--turn
*56. τασσ--arrange, order
57. τελ--end, complete
58. τι(μ)--honor
59. φαν (φαιν)--show
60. φερ--carry
*61. φρον--think
62. χαρ (χαιρ)--rejoice
*63. ψευδ--lie
64. ψυχ--life

[2]Often associated with teaching.

# APPENDIX E:
## IMPORANT AFFIXES AND THEIR MEANINGS

This appendix consists of two parts. The first provides prepositional prefixes along with their rough meanings, and the second, noun suffixes and their meanings.

Prepositional Prefixes. Alternate spellings appear in parentheses. Please note that the meanings given with these prepositions are appropriate for many, though not all, of the compounds in which the prepositions appear. These are not necessarily the lexical meanings of the prepositions themselves.

1. ἀνά (ἀν)--up
2. ἀντί (ἀντ, ἀνθ)--oppose, against
3. ἀπό (ἀπ)--from
4. διά (δι)--(does not appear to have a central meaning in its compounds)
5. εἰς--into
6. ἐκ (ἐξ)--out, from
7. ἐν (ἐμ, ἐγ, ἐλ)--in
8. ἐπί (ἐπ, ἐφ)--on, upon
9. κατά (κατ, καθ)--against
10. μετά (μετ, μεθ)--alter, change
11. παρά (παρ)--alongside
12. περί--about, around
13. πρό--before, first
14. πρός--toward, with, facing
15. σύν--with, together
16. ὑπέρ--high, above, beyond
17. ὑπό--under

**Noun Suffixes.** This list includes some suffixes which were not covered in chapter four, together with others which were covered.

1. Class or agent--της, ευς
2. Process--σις, μος, εια
3. Result (or a thing itself)--μα
4. Quality--συνη
5. Abstraction--η, α (first declension nouns)
6. Concrete--ος, ον, η (2nd and 1st declension nouns)
7. Diminutive--ιον

## APPENDIX F:
## WRITERS AND WRITINGS
## FREQUENTLY CITED IN BAGD
## AND OTHER LEXICA

Lexica can be difficult to use simply because students do not know much about the authors who are cited in them. The problem does not lie with the lexicon, which generally contains an extensive list of names, works, and dates (though this information is often filled with difficult abbreviations), but with haphazardous readers, who hurriedly skip over these enigmatic names in search of meanings. Spend some time with pp. xxiv-xxxvi in BAGD. Familiarize yourself with some of the major authors and works regularly cited throughout the lexicon. As you have time, learn something about the lives and times of these writers, and about their relationship to the Christian faith, if there was one.[1]

This appendix is designed to familiarize you with some of the major authors and works referenced in BAGD. Though it is by no means comprehensive, it does provide data on the authors and writings most frequently cited at or near the beginning of most articles. Those authors

[1]You can do this in a number of ways. Perhaps the simplest is to use a general encyclopedia such as *Encyclopedia Britannica*. For ancient authors and books in some way associated with the church, *The New International Dictionary of the Christian Church*, J.D. Douglas, gen. ed., rev. ed. (Grand Rapids: Zondervan, 1974) is especially good.

and titles prefaced with an asterisk are especially prominent.

**Aeschyl.**--Aeschylus, fifth cent. B.C. Greek poet.
**Ant.**--*The Antiquities of the Jews.* See Josephus.
**Appian.**--Appianus, second cent. A.D. Roman historian.
**Aristoph.**--Aristophanes, fifth to fourth cent. B.C. Athenian poet and dramatist.
**Aristot.**--Aristotle, fourth cent. B.C. Greek philosopher.
**B.**--*The Epistle of Barnabas*, traditional second century Apostolic Father.
**Bell.**--*The Wars of the Jews.* See Josephus.
**1 Cl.**--*First Clement*, second cent. Apostolic Father.
**Dio Chrys.**--Dio Chrysostom, first to second cent. A.D. Greek sophist and rhetorician.
**Diod.**--Diodorus, first cent. B.C. Greek historian.
**Dit. Or.**--published collection of inscriptions.
**Dit. Syll.**--published collection of inscriptions.
***En.**--*Enoch*, or *Ethiopic Enoch*, is a lengthy and important pseudepigraphal product of the second and first centuries B.C., written by a Jew.
**Epict.**--Epictetus, first cent. Greek philosopher.
***Ep. Arist.**--*The Epistle of Aristeas*, 2d cent. B.C. A pseudonymous letter written by an Alexandrian Jew. It purports to explain the origin of the LXX.
**Eur.**--Euripides, fifth cent. B.C. Greek tragedy writer and playwright.
**H.**--Hermas, traditional second cent. Apostolic Father who wrote *The Shepherd*.
**Hes.**--Hesiod, seventh cent. B.C. Greek poet.
**Hippocr.**--Hippocrates, fifth to fourth cent. Greek physician.
**Hm.**--Hermas, *Mandates*, in *The Shepherd*. See Hermas.
**Hs.**--Hermas, *Similitudes*, in *The Shepherd*. See Hermas.
**Hv.**--Hermas, *Visions*, in *The Shepherd*. See Hermas.
**Hdt.**--Herodotus, fifth cent. B.C. Greek historian.
***Hom.**--Homer, perhaps as early as the eighth century B.C., was an epic Greek poet and the author of the *Iliad* and *Odyssey*. BAGD frequently lists Homer first among its references. "Hom+ " suggests that a word was

first used in a literary sense in Homer and was used in later literature, etc. as well.

*inscr.--Inscriptions. Usually refers to inscribed artifacts such as tombstones and other large monuments roughly contemporary with the New Testament.

*Jos.--Flavius Josephus, a first century Pharisaic Jew who authored the famous *Antiquities of the Jews* and *Wars of the Jews*. He had significant ties with Rome and even became a Roman citizen. Very important in illustrating the meaning of New Testament vocabulary.

Lucian--second cent. A.D. teacher and martyr.

*LXX--The *Septuagint* (Latin "seventy" = LXX), the earliest translation from Hebrew into Greek, dating from the second and third centuries B.C. Frequently quoted in the New Testament, the LXX was the Bible of Hellenistic Jews. Numerous recensions (later editions) of the LXX arose in time.

1-4 Maccs.--*Maccabees*, apocryphal writings dating from the second and first centuries B.C.

*pap.--The papyri. Documents of all kinds (not just New Testament) discovered in Upper Egypt, beginning in the 19th century. The pap. evidence the use of Biblical Greek in everyday life, document what that life was like, and provide literary documents as well.

PGM--A collection of Greek magical papyri.

*Philo--Philo of Alexandria (first century A.D.) was a Jew who combined monotheism with Greek philosophy. He wrote extensively on the Old Testament and used allegory as a vehicle for the marriage of the Old Testament and Greek thought.

Pind.--Pindar, fifth cent. B.C. Greek poet.

Pla.--Plato, fourth cent. B.C. Greek philosopher.

Plut.--Plutarch, first and second cent. A.D. Greek biographer.

Polyb.--Polybius, second cent. B.C. Greek historian.

POxy.--The Oxyrhynchus Papyri, apocryphal collections of the sayings of Jesus.

Sext.Emp.--*Sextus Empericus*, second cent. A.D. collection of Greek religious teachings.

Sib. Or.--The *Sibylline Oracles*, a collection of Jewish and Christian writings from the early Christian centuries, with a clear disdain for heathen peoples and their practices.

**Sir.**--Sirach, an apocryphal book.

**Soph.**--Sophocles, fifth cent. B.C. Greek poet.

**Strabo**--first century B.C./A.D. Greek geographer.

*****Test. 12 Patr.**--*The Testaments of the Twelve Patriarchs.* A pseudepigraphal product of the intertestamental period, written at the end of the 2nd cent. B.C. (perhaps with some later editions). Contains the "final remarks" of the twelve sons of Jacob.

**Thu.**--Thucydides, fifth cent. B.C. Athenian historian.

# AUTHOR INDEX

# SUBJECT INDEX

## SCRIPTURE INDEX